PROJECT MANAGEMENT ANALYTICS

A Data-Driven Approach to Making Rational and Effective Project Decisions

Harjit Singh, MBA, PMP, CSM
Data Processing Manager III, State of California

Publisher: Paul Boger
Editor-in-Chief: Amy Neidlinger
Executive Editor: Jeanne Glasser Levine
Development Editor: Natasha Wollmers
Cover Designer: Chuti Prasertsith
Managing Editor: Kristy Hart
Project Editor: Elaine Wiley
Copy Editor: Paula Lowell
Proofreader: Chuck Hutchinson
Indexer: MoJo's Indexing and Editorial Services
Compositor: Nonie Ratcliff
Manufacturing Buyer: Dan Uhrig

© 2016 by Harjit Singh
Published by Pearson Education, Inc.
Old Tappan, New Jersey 07675

For information about buying this title in bulk quantities, or for special sales opportunities (which may include electronic versions; custom cover designs; and content particular to your business, training goals, marketing focus, or branding interests), please contact our corporate sales department at corpsales@pearsoned.com or (800) 382-3419.

For government sales inquiries, please contact governmentsales@pearsoned.com.

For questions about sales outside the U.S., please contact international@pearsoned.com.

Company and product names mentioned herein are the trademarks or registered trademarks of their respective owners.

Printed in the United States of America

First Printing November 2015

ISBN-10: 0-13-418994-9
ISBN-13: 978-0-13-418994-9

Pearson Education LTD.
Pearson Education Australia PTY, Limited
Pearson Education Singapore, Pte. Ltd.
Pearson Education Asia, Ltd.
Pearson Education Canada, Ltd.
Pearson Educación de Mexico, S.A. de C.V.
Pearson Education—Japan
Pearson Education Malaysia, Pte. Ltd.

Library of Congress Control Number: 2015949108

To my father, Sardar Puran Singh,

from whom I learned hard work, honesty, and work ethics,

and

to my wife Harjinder and daughters Kavleen and Amanroop
for their patience, unconditional love, and constant inspiration
throughout this project!

Table of Contents

Part 2 Project Management Fundamentals

Part 3 Introduction to Analytics Concepts, Tools, and Techniques

Acknowledgments

I would like to acknowledge the contributions of my friends, past and present colleagues, supervisors, and students who helped me bring this book to life with their valuable feedback, inspiration, moral support, and encouragement. In particular, I extend my sincere thanks to Amy Cox-O'Farrell (Chief Information Officer, *Department of Consumer Affairs*, State of California), Mary Cole (President, *DeVry University*, Folsom, California), Mark Stackpole, MA (Academic Affairs Specialist, *DeVry University*, Folsom, California), Staff (*Sigma PM Consulting*, Rocklin, California), Jaswant Saini (President, *Saini Immigration*, Fresno, California and Chandigarh, India), Surinder Singh (President, *Singh Construction*, Corona, California), JP Singh (President, *Omega Machine & Tool*, W. Sacramento, California), Jaspreet Singh (President, *Wesco Enterprises*, Rancho Cordova, California), Ric Albani (President, *RMA Consulting Group*, Sacramento, California), and Laura Lorenzo (former President, *Project Management Institute*, Sacramento Valley Chapter).

My special thanks go to Randal Wilson, MBA, PMP (author, Operations and Project Manager at *Parker Hose and Fittings*, and Visiting Professor at *Keller Graduate School of Management, DeVry University*, Folsom, California), Dr. Bob Biswas (author and Associate Professor of Accounting at *Keller Graduate School of Management, DeVry University*, Folsom, California), Gopal Kapur (founder of the *Center for Project Management* and *Family Green Survival*, Roseville, California), and Jorge Avila (Project Director, *Office of Technology*, State of California) for their expert guidance and encouragement to me throughout this project.

I sincerely appreciate Jeanne Glasser Levine (Project Executive Editor at Pearson), Elaine Wiley (Project Editor at Pearson), Natasha Lee (Development Editor for Pearson) and Paula Lowell (Copy Editor for Pearson) for their thorough reviews, critique of the manuscript, valuable suggestions, and support to keep me motivated. In addition, many thanks to Paul Boger and his production crew at Pearson for their hard work in making this project a reality.

Last but not least, I am indebted to my wife Harjinder and my daughters Kavleen and Amanroop for their understanding, encouragement, and steadfast support during this journey.

Harjit Singh
Rocklin, California

About the Author

Harjit Singh earned his MBA from University of Texas and his master's degree in Computer Engineering from California State University, Sacramento. He is a Certified Scrum Master, Lean Six Sigma professional, and holds PMP (Project Management Professional) credentials. He has more than 25 years of experience in the private and public sector as an information technology engineer, project manager, and educator. Currently, he is working as a data processing manager III at the State of California. In addition, he is also a visiting professor/adjunct faculty at Keller Graduate School of Management, DeVry University and Brandman University, where he teaches project management, business management, and information technology courses. Prior to this, he worked at Hewlett-Packard for 15 years as a systems software engineer and technical project manager. He is also a former member of the Board of Directors for the Sacramento Valley Chapter of the Project Management Institute (PMI) where he served in the capacity of CIO and vice president of relations and marketing.

1

Project Management Analytics

Learning Objectives

After reading this chapter, you should be familiar with the

- Definition of analytics
- Difference between analytics and analysis
- Purpose of using analytics in project management
- Applications of analytics in project management
- Statistical approach to project management analytics
- Lean Six Sigma approach to project management analytics
- Analytic Hierarchy Process approach to project management analytics

> "Information is a source of learning. But unless it is organized, processed, and available to the right people in a format for decision making, it is a burden, not a benefit."
> —*William Pollard (1828–1893), English Clergyman*

Effective project management entails operative management of uncertainty on the project. This requires the project managers today to use analytical techniques to monitor and control the uncertainty as well as to estimate project schedule and cost more accurately with analytics-driven prediction. Bharat Gera, Line Manager at IBM agrees, "Today, project managers need to report the project metrics in terms of 'analytical certainty.'" Analytics-based project metrics can essentially enable the project managers to measure, observe, and analyze project performance objectively and make rational project decisions with analytical certainty rather than making vague decisions with subjective uncertainty. This chapter presents you an overview of the analytics-driven approach to project management.

What Is Analytics?

Analytics (or *data analytics*) can be defined as the systematic quantitative analysis of data or statistics to obtain meaningful information for better decision-making. It involves the collective use of various analytical methodologies, including but not limited to statistical and operational research methodologies, Lean Six Sigma, and software programming. The computational complexity of analytics may vary from low to very high (for example, big data). The highly complex applications usually utilize sophisticated algorithms based on statistical, mathematical, and computer science knowledge.

Analytics versus Analysis

Analysis and analytics are similar-sounding terms, but they are not the same thing. They do have some differences.

Both are important to project managers. They (project managers) can use analysis to understand the status quo that may reflect the result of their efforts to achieve certain objectives. They can use analytics to identify specific trends or patterns in the data under analysis so that they can predict or forecast the future outcomes or behaviors based on the past trends.

Table 1.1 outlines the key differences between analytics and analysis.

Table 1.1 Analytics vs. Analysis

Criterion	Analytics	Analysis
Working Definition	Analytics can be defined as a method to use the results of analysis to better predict customer or stakeholder behaviors.	Analysis can be defined as the process of dissecting past gathered data into pieces so that the current (prevailing) situation can be understood.
Dictionary Definition	Per *Merriam-Webster* dictionary, *analytics* is the method of logical analysis.	Per *Merriam-Webster* dictionary, *analysis* is the separation of a whole into its component parts to learn about those parts.
Time Period	Analytics look forward to project the future or predict an outcome based on the past performance as of the time of analysis.	Analysis presents a historical view of the project performance as of the time of analysis.

Criterion	Analytics	Analysis
Examples	Use analytics to predict which functional areas are more likely to show adequate participation in future surveys so that a strategy can be developed to improve the future participation.	Use analysis to determine how many employees from each functional area of the organization participated in a voice of the workforce survey.
Types of Analysis	Prediction of future audience behaviors based on their past behaviors	Target audience segmentation Target audience grouping based on multiple past behaviors
Tools	Statistical, mathematical, computer science, and Lean Six Sigma tools, and techniques-based algorithms with advanced logic Sophisticated predictive analytics software tools	Business intelligence tools Structured query language (SQL)
Typical Activities	Identify specific data patterns Derive meaningful inferences from data patterns Use inferences to develop regressive/predictive models Use predictive models for rational and effective decision-making Develop a SharePoint list to track key performance indicators Run SQL queries on a data warehouse to extract relevant data for reporting Run simulations to investigate different scenarios Use statistical methods to predict future sales based on past sales data	Develop a business case Elicit requirements Document requirements Conduct risk assessment Model business processes Develop business architecture

Why Is Analytics Important in Project Management?

Although switching to the data-driven approach and utilizing the available analytical tools makes perfect sense, most project managers either are not aware of the analytical approach or they do not feel comfortable moving away from their largely subjective legacy approach to project management decision-making. Their hesitation is related to lack of training in the analytical tools, technologies, and processes. Most project management books only mention these tools, technologies, and processes in passing and do not discuss them adequately and in an easily adaptable format. Even the *Project Management Body of Knowledge Guide* (*PMBOK*), which is considered the global standard for project management processes, does not provide adequate details on an analytics-focused approach.

The high availability of analytical technology today can enable project managers to use the analytics paradigm to break down the processes and systems in complex projects to predict their behavior and outcomes. Project managers can use this predictive information to make better decisions and keep projects on schedule and on budget. Analytics does more than simply enable project managers to capture data and mark the tasks done when completed. It enables them to analyze the captured data to understand certain patterns or trends. They can then use that understanding to determine how projects or project portfolios are performing, and what strategic decisions they need to make to improve the success rate if the measured/observed project/portfolio performance is not in line with the overall objectives.

How Can Project Managers Use Analytics in Project Management?

Analytics finds its use in multiple areas throughout the project and project management life cycles. The key applications of analytics in this context include, but are not limited to, the following:

Assessing feasibility: Analytics can be used to assess the feasibility of various alternatives so that a project manager can pick the best option.

Managing data overload: Due to the contemporary Internet age, data overload has crippled project managers' capability to capture meaningful information from mountains of data. Analytics can help project managers overcome this issue.

Enhancing data visibility and control via focused dashboards: An analytics dashboard can provide a project manager a single view to look at the big picture and determine both how each project and its project team members are doing. This information comes in handy for prioritizing project tasks and/or moving project team members around to maximize productivity.

Analyzing project portfolios for project selection and prioritization: Project portfolio analysis is a useful application of analytics. This involves evaluating a large number of project proposals (or ideas) and selecting and prioritizing the most viable ones within the constraints of organizational resources and other relevant factors.

Across all project organizations in general, but in a matrix organization in particular, multiple projects compete for finite resources. Organizations must select projects carefully after complete assessment of each candidate project's feasibility based on the organization's project selection criteria, which might include, but not be limited to, the following factors:

- Technical, economic, legal, political, capacity, and capability constraints
- Cost-benefits analysis resulting in scoring based on various financial models such as:
  - Net present value (NPV)[1]
  - Return on investment (ROI)[2]
  - Payback period[3]
  - Breakeven analysis[4]
- Resource requirements
  - Internal resources (only functional department resources, cross-functional resources, cross-organizational resources, or any combination of the preceding)
  - External resources
  - Both internal and external resources
- Project complexity
- Project risks
- Training requirements

---

[1] NPV is used to compare today's investment with the present value of the future cash flows after those cash flows are discounted by a certain rate of return.

[2] ROI = Net Profit / Total Investment

[3] Payback period is the time required to recoup the initial investment in terms of savings or profits.

[4] Breakeven analysis determines the amount of revenue needed to offset the costs incurred to earn that revenue.

Analytics can help organizations with selecting projects and prioritizing shortlisted projects for optimal allocation of any scarce and finite resources.

Improve project stakeholder management: Analytics can help improve project stakeholder management by enabling a project manager to predict stakeholder responses to various project decisions. Project stakeholder management is both art and science—art because it depends partly on the individual skillset, approach, and personality of the individual project manager, and science because it is a highly data-driven process. Project managers can use analytics to predict the outcomes of the execution of their strategic plans for stakeholder engagement management and to guide their decisions for appropriate corrective actions if they find any discrepancy (variance) between the planned and the actual results of their efforts.

Project stakeholder management is much like customer relationship management (CRM[5]) in marketing because customers are essentially among the top-level project stakeholders and project success depends on their satisfaction and acceptance of the project outcome (product or service). Demographic studies, customer segmentation, conjoint analysis, and other techniques allow marketers to use large amounts of consumer purchase, survey, and panel data to understand and communicate marketing strategy. In his paper "CRM and Stakeholder Management," Dr. Ramakrishnan (2009) discusses how CRM can help with effective stakeholder management. According to him, there are seven Cs of stakeholder management:

1. Concern
2. Communicate
3. Contribute
4. Connect
5. Compound
6. Co-Create
7. Complete

Figure 1.1 illustrates the seven Cs of stakeholder management.

The seven Cs constitute seven elements of the project stakeholder management criteria, which can be evaluated for their relative importance or strength with respect to the goal

---

[5] *CRM* refers to a process or methodology used to understand the needs and behaviors of customers so that relationships with them can be improved and strengthened.

of achieving effective stakeholder management by utilizing the multi-criteria evaluation capability of the *Analytic Hierarchy Process* (AHP).[6]

Figure 1.1 Seven Cs of Project Stakeholder Management

Web analytics can also help managers analyze and interpret data related to the online interactions with the project stakeholders. The source data for web analytics may include personal identification information, search keywords, IP address, preferences, and various other stakeholder activities. The information from web analytics can help project managers use the adaptive approach[7] to understand the stakeholders better, which in turn can further help them customize their communications according to the target stakeholders.

Predict project schedule delays and cost overruns: Analytics can tell a project manager whether the project is on schedule and whether it's under or over budget. Also, analytics can enable a project manager to predict the impact of various completion dates on the bottom line (project cost). For example, Earned Value Analytics (covered in Chapter 8, "Statistical Applications in Project Management") helps project managers avoid surprises by helping them proactively discover trends in project schedule and cost performance.

Manage project risks: Another area in a project's life cycle where analytics can be extremely helpful is the project risk management area. Project risk identification, ranking, and prioritization depend upon multiple factors, including at least the following:

- Size and complexity of the project
- Organization's risk tolerance
- Risk probability, impact, and horizon
- Competency of the project or risk manager

---

[6] Read Chapter 6, "Analytical Hierarchy Process," to learn about AHP.

[7] The process of gaining knowledge by adapting to the new learning for better decision-making.

Predictive analytics models can be used to analyze those multiple factors for making rational decisions to manage the risks effectively.

Improve project processes: Project management involves the execution of a multitude of project processes. Thus, continuous process improvement is essential for eliminating waste and improving the quality of the processes and the product of the project. Improvement projects typically involve four steps:

1. Understand the current situation.
2. Determine the desired (target) future situation.
3. Perform gap analysis (find the delta between the target and the current situations).
4. Make improvement decisions to address the gap.

Analytics can help project managers through all four process improvement steps by enabling the use of a "Project Management —Lean Six Sigma" blended or hybrid methodology for managing the projects with embedded continuous improvement.

Project Management Analytics Approach

The project management analytics approach can vary from organization to organization and even from project to project. It depends on multiple factors including, but not limited to, organizational culture; policies and procedures; project environment; project complexity; project size; available resources; available tools and technologies; and the skills, knowledge, and experience of the project manager or project/business analysts. This book covers the following approaches to project management analytics:

- Statistical
- Lean Six Sigma
- Analytic Hierarchy Process

You will look at the application of each of these approaches and the possible combination of two or more of these approaches, depending upon the project characteristics.

Statistical Approach

"Lies, damned lies, and statistics!
Nothing in progression can rest on its original plan."
—*Thomas S. Monson (American religious leader and author)*

Throughout the project life cycle, project managers must deal with a large number of uncertainties. For instance, project risks are uncertainties that can derail the project if they are not addressed in a timely and effective way. Similarly, all project baselines (plans) are developed to deal with the uncertain future of the project. That's why the project plans are called *living documents* because they are subject to change based on future changes. Because picturing the future precisely is hard, best estimates are used to develop the project plans.

Statistical approach comes in handy when dealing with project uncertainties because it includes tools and techniques that managers can deploy to interpret specific patterns in the data pertaining to the project management processes to predict the future more accurately.

Quantitative measure of a process, when that process is performed over and over, is likely to follow a certain frequency pattern of occurrence. In other words, there is a likelihood or probability of recurrence of the same quantitative measure in the long run. This likelihood or probability represents the uncertainty of recurrence of a certain quantitative value of the process. Statistical analysis can help predict certain behaviors of the processes or systems in the environment of uncertainty, which is fundamental to data-driven decision-making.

We use the following analytical probability distributions to illustrate how a statistical approach can help in effective decision-making in project management:

- Normal distribution
- Poisson distribution
- Uniform distribution
- Triangular distribution
- Beta distribution

Normal Distribution

Depicted in Figure 1.2, the normal distribution is the most common form of the probability density function. Due to its shape, it is also referred to as the *bell curve*. In this distribution, all data values are symmetrically distributed around the mean of the probability. The normal distribution method constitutes a significant portion of the statistical content that this book covers because the project management processes involve a number of normal events.[8]

---

[8] For example, project selection criteria scores, stakeholders' opinions, labor wages, project activity duration, project risk probability, and so on.

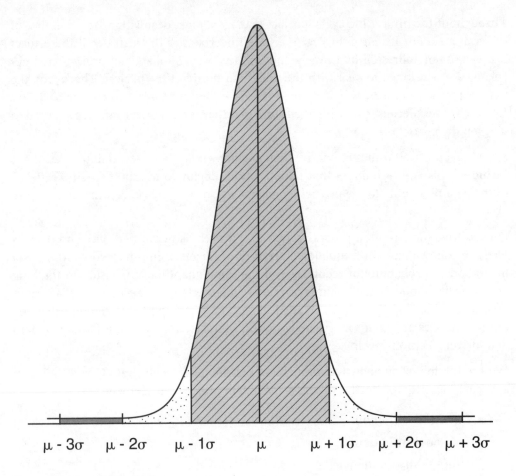

Figure 1.2 Normal Distribution

Normal distribution is the result of the process of accumulation. Usually, the sum or average of the outcomes of various uncertainties constitutes an outcome whose probability distribution is a normal distribution.

For data with a normal distribution, the standard deviation has the following characteristics:[9]

- **68.27%** of the data values lie within one standard deviation of the mean.
- **95.45%** of the data values lie within two standard deviations of the mean.
- **99.73%** of the data values lie within three standard deviations of the mean.

---

[9] This is also known as the *empirical rule*.

Poisson Distribution

Poisson distribution is the result of the process of counting. Figure 1.3 depicts the shape of a typical Poisson distribution curve.

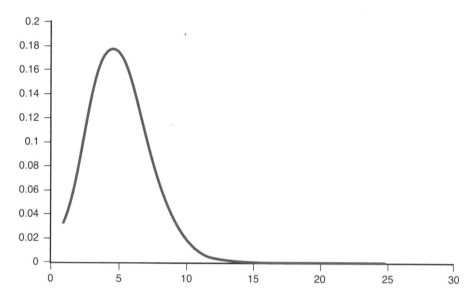

Figure 1.3 Poisson Distribution

This distribution can be used to count the number of successes or opportunities as a result of multiple tries within a certain time period. For example, it can be used to count

- The number of projects human resources acquired in a period of two months
- The number of project milestones completed in a month
- The number of project tasks completed in a given week
- The number of project change requests processed in a given month

Chapter 4, "Statistical Fundamentals I," covers the Poisson distribution in more depth and examines how this distribution can be used in project management to count discrete,[10] countable, independent events.

---

[10] *Discrete random variables* are small in number and can be counted easily. For example, if a random variable represents the output of tossing a coin, then it is a discrete random variable because there are just two possible outcomes—heads or tails.

Uniform Distribution

Illustrated in Figure 1.4, a uniform distribution is also referred to as a rectangular distribution with constant probability.

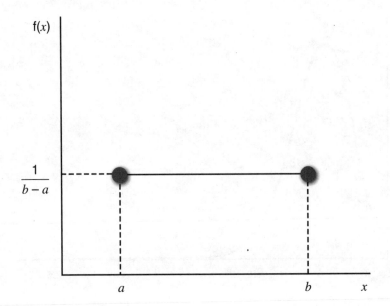

Figure 1.4 Uniform Distribution

The area of the rectangle is equal to the product of its length and its width.

Thus, the area of the rectangle equals $(b - a) * 1/ (b - a) = 1$.

What does this mean? This means that for a continuous[11] random variable, the area under the curve is equal to 1. This is true in the case of a discrete random variable as well provided the values of the discrete random variable are close enough to appear almost continuous.

The unit area under the curve in Figure 1.4 illustrates that relative frequencies or probabilities of occurrence of all values of the random variable, when integrated, are equal to 1. That is:

---

[11] When there are too many possible values for a random variable to count, such a random variable is called a *continuous random variable.* The spacing between the adjacent values of the random variable is so small that it is hard to distinguish one value from the other and the pattern of those values appears to be continuous.

$$\int_{b-a} \text{all } f(X)\, dX = 1$$

In this equation, dX is an increment along the x-axis and $f(X)$ is a value on the y-axis.

Uniform distribution arbitrarily determines a two-point estimate of the highest and lowest values (endpoints of a range) of a random variable. This simplest estimation method allows project managers to transform subjective data into probability distributions for better decision-making especially in risk management.

Triangular Distribution

Unlike uniform distribution, the triangular distribution illustrates that the probability of all values of a random variable are not uniform. Figure 1.5 shows the shape of a triangular distribution.

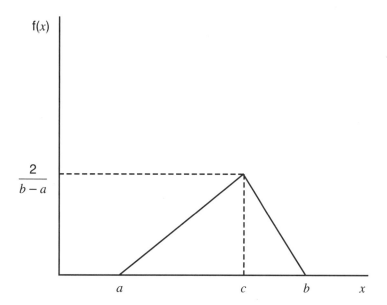

Figure 1.5 Triangular Distribution

A triangular distribution is called so because of its triangular shape. It is based on three underlying values: *a* (minimum value), *b* (maximum value), and *c* (peak value) and can be used estimate the minimum, maximum, and most likely values of the outcome. It is also called *three-point estimation*, which is ideal to estimate the cost and duration associated with the project activities more accurately by considering the optimistic, pessimistic, and realistic values of the random variable (cost or duration). The skewed nature of this distribution represents the imbalance in the optimistic and pessimistic values in an event. Like all probability density functions, triangular distribution also has the property that the area under the curve is 1.

Beta Distribution

The beta distribution depends on two parameters—α and β where α determines the center or steepness of the hump of the curve and β determines the shape and fatness of the tail of the curve. Figure 1.6 shows the shape of a beta distribution.

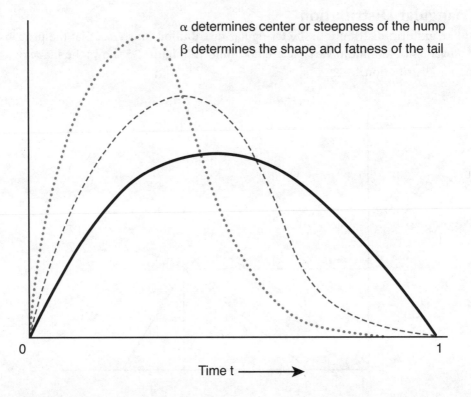

Figure 1.6 Beta Distribution

Like triangular distribution, beta distribution is also useful in project management to model the events that occur within an interval bounded by maximum and minimum end values. You will learn how to use this distribution in PERT (Program Evaluation and Review Technique) and CPM (Critical Path Method) for three-point estimation in Chapter 8.

Lean Six Sigma Approach

The *Lean*[12] *Six Sigma*[13] approach encompasses reduction in waste and reduction in variation (inaccuracy). For decisions to be rational and effective, they should be based on an approach that promotes these things. That is the rationale behind the use of the Lean Six Sigma approach in project management analytics.

NOTE

"Lean-Six Sigma is a fact-based, data-driven philosophy of improvement that values defect prevention over defect detection. It drives customer satisfaction and bottom-line results by reducing variation, waste, and cycle time, while promoting the use of work standardization and flow, thereby creating a competitive advantage. It applies anywhere variation and waste exist, and every employee should be involved."

Source: American Society of Quality (ASQ). http://asq.org/learn-about-quality/six-sigma/lean.html

---

The goal of every project organization in terms of project outcome is SUCCESS, which stands for

$\underline{S}$MART[14] Goals Established and Achieved

$\underline{U}$nder Budget Delivered Outcome

$\underline{C}$ommunications Effectiveness Realized

$\underline{C}$ore Values Practiced

$\underline{E}$xcellence in Project Management Achieved

$\underline{S}$chedule Optimized to Shorten Time to Delivery

$\underline{S}$cope Delivered as Committed

The projects are typically undertaken to improve the status quo of a certain prevailing condition, which might include an altogether missing functionality or broken functionality. This improvement effort involves defining the current (existing) and the target conditions, performing gap analysis (delta between the target and the current condition),

---

[12] The *Lean* concept, originated in Toyota Production System, Japan, focuses on reduction in waste.

[13] The *Six Sigma* concept, originated in Motorola, USA, focuses on reduction in variation.

[14] $\underline{S}$pecific, $\underline{M}$easurable, $\underline{A}$chievable, $\underline{R}$ealistic, and $\underline{T}$imely

and understanding what needs to be done to improve the status quo. The change from the current condition to the target condition needs to be managed through effective change management. Change management is an integral part of project management and the Lean Six Sigma approach is an excellent vehicle to implement changes successfully.

The DMAIC Cycle

Like the project management life cycle, Lean Six Sigma also has its own life cycle called the *DMAIC cycle*. DMAIC stands for the following stages of the Lean Six Sigma life cycle:

Define

Measure

Analyze

Improve

Control

The DMAIC is a data-driven process improvement, optimization, and stabilization cycle. All stages of the DMAIC cycle are mandatory and must be performed in the order from "define" to "control." Figure 1.7 depicts a typical DMAIC cycle.

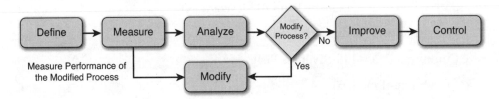

Figure 1.7 DMAIC Cycle

The various stages of the DMAIC cycle are briefly described here (refer to Chapter 7, "Lean Six Sigma," for detailed discussion on the DMAIC cycle):

- **Define:** Define the problem and customer requirements.
- **Measure:** Measure the current performance of the process (establish baseline), determine the future desired performance of the process (determine target), and perform gap analysis (target minus baseline).
- **Analyze:** Analyze observed and/or measured data and find root cause(s). Modify the process if necessary but re-baseline the performance post-modification.

- **Improve:** Address the root cause(s) to improve the process.
- **Control:** Control the future performance variations.

The PDSA Cycle

Project quality is an integral part of project management. The knowledge of Lean Six Sigma tools and processes arms a project manager with the complementary and essential skills for effective project management. The core of Lean Six Sigma methodology is the iterative PDSA (**P**lan, **D**o, **S**tudy, **A**ct) cycle, which is a very structured approach to eliminating or minimizing defects and waste from any process.

Figure 1.8 shows the PDSA cycle. We discuss this cycle as part of our discussion on the applications of the Lean Six Sigma approach in project management.

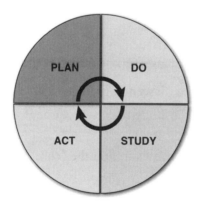

Figure 1.8 PDSA Cycle

Brief explanations of the building blocks of the PDSA cycle follow (refer to Chapter 7 for detailed discussion on the PDSA cycle):

- **Plan:** The development of the plan to carry out the cycle
- **Do:** The execution of the plan and documentation of the observations
- **Study:** The analysis of the observed and collected data during the execution of the PDSA plan
- **Act:** The next steps based on the analysis results obtained during study

Lean Six Sigma Tools

The Lean Six Sigma processes involve a lot of data collection and analysis. The various tools used for this purpose include the following:

- **Brainstorming:** To collect mass ideas on potential root causes
- **Surveys:** To collect views of the individuals who are large in number and/or outside personal reach
- **Five whys:** A method that asks five probing questions to identify the root cause
- **Value stream mapping:** Process map analysis to identify wasteful process steps
- **Cause and effect or fishbone or Ishikawa diagram:** A tool to help with brainstorming on the possible root causes
- **Control charts:** To identify "common" and "special" causes in the stream of data observed over a period of time
- **Correlation:** To study the correlation between two variables
- **Cost-benefits analysis:** To estimate the cost of implementing an improvement plan and the benefits realized
- **Design of experiments:** To identify the recipe for the best possible solution
- **Histograms:** Unordered frequency (of defects) map
- **Pareto charts:** Ordered (descending) frequency (of defects) map
- **Regression analysis:** To study the effect of one variable with all other variables held constant
- **Root cause analysis:** Analysis to find the "cure" for a problem rather than just "symptoms treatment"
- **Run charts:** Observed data over a period of time
- **SIPOC[15] chart:** Process analysis to identify input and output interfaces to the process

These tools are discussed in more detail in Chapter 7.

The Goal of Lean Six Sigma–Driven Project Management

Executing only those activities that are value adding, when they are needed, utilizing minimum possible resources, without adversely impacting the quality, scope, cost, and delivery time of the project.

---

[15] SIPOC (**S**upplier, **I**nput, **P**rocess, **O**utput, **C**ustomer) is a process analysis tool.

How Can You Use the Lean Six Sigma Approach in Project Management?

We will examine a hybrid approach by blending the DMAIC cycle with the project management life cycle, which project managers can use to find the root cause(s) of the following project path holes and recommend the appropriate corrective actions to fix them.

- Schedule delays
- Project scope creep
- Cost overruns
- Poor quality deliverables
- Process variation
- Stakeholder dissatisfaction

Analytic Hierarchy Process (AHP) Approach

Proposed by Thomas L. Saaty in 1980, the AHP is a popular and effective approach to multi-criteria-driven decision-making. According to Saaty, both tangible and intangible factors should be considered while making decisions. "Decisions involve many intangibles that need to be traded off. To do that, they have to be measured alongside tangibles whose measurements must also be evaluated as to how well they serve the objectives of the decision maker," says Saaty.

You can use the AHP approach in any scenario that includes multiple factors in decision-making. For example:

- Deciding which major to select after high school
- Deciding which university to select after high school
- Deciding which car to select for buying
- Deciding which projects to select for inclusion in the portfolio

Often in decision-making, the intangible factors are either overlooked or the decisions are just made based on subjective or intuitional criteria alone. The AHP approach is a 360° approach, which includes both subjective and objective criteria in decision-making. The key characteristic of this approach is that it uses pairwise comparisons[16] of all the possible factors of the complex problem at hand and evaluates their relative importance to the decision-making process. For example, project management decision-making

---

[16] Pairwise comparisons include comparison of each factor in the decision-making criteria against every other factor in the criteria.

criteria may include three factors: schedule flexibility, budget flexibility, and scope flexibility. To make a decision, the project manager must consider the relative importance of each of the three factors against every other factor in the criteria. Schedule, budget, and scope are the triple constraints of project management and a tradeoff often has to be made to find the right balance among them based on the business need and/or the project environment. For instance, less flexibility in scope requires schedule, budget, or both to be relatively more flexible.

Chapter 6 covers the AHP approach in more detail. This book makes extensive use of this approach in recommending data-driven methodology for making the most effective and rational project management decisions, including the following:

- Project selection and prioritization
- Project risk identification and assessment
- Selection of project risk response strategy
- Vendor selection
- Project resource allocation optimization
- Project procurement management
- Project quality evaluation

Summary

The mind map in Figure 1.9 summarizes the project management analytics approach.

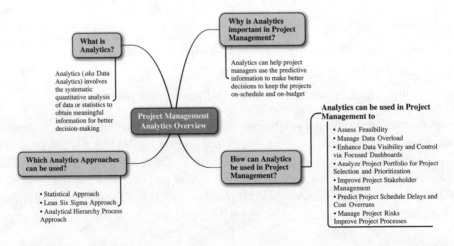

Figure 1.9 Project Management Analytics Approach Summary

Key Terms

Analytic Hierarchy Process (AHP)

Analytics

Beta Distribution

Breakeven Analysis

Continuous Random Variable

Cost-Benefit Analysis

Critical Path Method (CPM)

Customer Relationship Management (CRM)

Discrete Random Variable

DMAIC Cycle

Earned Value Analysis

Empirical Rule

Lean Six Sigma

Net Present Value (NPV)

Normal Distribution

NORMDIST

Payback Period

PDSA Cycle

Poisson Distribution

Program Evaluation and Review Technique (PERT)

Return on Investment (ROI)

SIPOC

Three-Point Estimating

Triangular Distribution

Uniform Distribution

Value Stream Mapping

Case Study: City of Medville Uses Statistical Approach to Estimate Costs for Its Pilot Project

To encourage sports and fitness among students from kindergarten to 12th grade, the education department of the city of Medville, Pennsylvania, conceived a 12-month pilot project to provide special free training, nutrition, and sports gear to the students of a select 10 schools. The goal of this project was to cover 70% of the student population under the new program. The initial challenge was to figure out the funds required to run this project and also the plan to carry out the project work.

For scope management, the project management committee divided the student population in different age groups and estimated the cost for students in each age group. Table 1.2 depicts the various student age groups and the cost estimates.

Table 1.2 Estimated Project Cost for Various Student Age Groups

Student Age Group	Estimated Cost Per Student
Less than 10 years old	$2,000
10 to 15 years old	$5,000
More than 15 years old	$3,000

The project assumed that the total population of students (2,000 students) was normally distributed with a mean age of 12 and a standard deviation of 3. The following statistical calculations for normal distribution were used to make decisions.

Determine Target Age Group for Initial Project Pilot

For normal distribution,

- 1 σ covers roughly 68% of the population, which implies 68% of the total 2,000 students fall in the age group 9 to 15 (12 +/– 3).

- 2 σ covers roughly 95% of the population, which implies 95% of the total 2,000 students fall in the age group 6 to 18 (12 +/– 6).

Because the goal of the pilot project was to cover 70% of the student population, students in age group 6 to 18 were selected for the initial pilot.

Estimate Project Costs for the Target Age Group

The target age group contained student population from all three population bands listed in Table 1.2. Thus, cost estimates pertaining to those population bands or age groups had to be considered for calculating costs for the target age group (6 to 18 years old). The project figured it out using the Excel NORMDIST[17] function as follows:

> Percentage of target students belonging to age group under 10 years (6 to 10 years old) = NORMDIST (10, 12, 3, 1) – NORMDIST (6, 12, 3, 1) = 22.97%

> Cost Allocation for 6- to 10-year old students = (2000 * 22.97% * 2000) = $918,970

> Percentage of target students belonging to age group 10 to 15 years (10 to 15 years old) = NORMDIST (15, 12, 3, 1) – NORMDIST (10, 12, 3, 1) = 58.89%

---

[17] **NORMDIST(x, μ, σ, 1)**, where x = random variable (upper or lower end of the age-group range), μ = mean age in the age-group, σ = standard deviation, and 1 stands for cumulative.

Cost Allocation for 10- to 15-years-old students = (5000 * 58.89% * 2000)
= $5,888,522

Percentage of target students belonging to age group over 15 years = 1 –
(22.97% + 58.89%) = 18.14%

Cost Allocation for over 15-year-old students = (3000 * 18.14% * 2000)
= $1,088,432

**Total Estimated Cost for All Target Students for the Initial Pilot = $918,970 +
$5,888,522 + $1,088,432 = $7,895,924**

Case Study Questions

1. What approach was used by the city of Medville to estimate the overall project cost?

2. Define the scope of this project.

3. Do you think the city made a wise decision to use this approach for cost estimation? Why do you think so?

Chapter Review and Discussion Questions

1. Define analytics.

2. What is the difference between analytics and analysis?

3. What are advantages of using analytics in project management?

4. How can analytics be used in project selection and prioritization?

5. Describe briefly the 7 Cs of project stakeholder management.

6. What are the characteristics of normal distribution in terms of standard deviation?

7. When can Poisson distribution be used for project management? Provide some examples.

8. Which statistical distribution is used for three-point estimation in project management?

9. Describe briefly the various stages of the DMAIC cycle.

10. What does PDSA stand for?

11. What is the primary purpose of using the Lean Six Sigma approach in project management?

12. List some of the applications of the AHP approach.

13. What is the *empirical rule* in normal distribution?

14. The mean duration of the activities of a project is 10 days with a standard deviation of 2 days. Using the empirical rule estimate the percentage of project activities with duration between 7 and 10 days.

15. Solve the preceding problem using Excel's NORMDIST function.

Bibliography

Anbari, F.T. (1997). *Quantitative Methods for Project Management.* 59th Street, New York: International Institute for Learning, Inc.

Borror, C. (2009). "The Define Measure Analyze Improve Control (DMAIC) Process." Retrieved February 14, 2015, from http://asq.org/learn-about-quality/six-sigma/overview/dmaic.html

Deltek. (2013, September 11). "Deltek wInsight Analytics: Avoid Surprises and Quickly Discover Trends and Issues in Your Earned Value Data." Retrieved February 14, 2015, from http://www.deltek.com/~/media/pdf/productsheets/govcon/winsight-ipm-ps.ashx

Ghera, B. (2011). "Project and Program Management Analytics." Retrieved February 10, 2015, from http://www.pmi.org/~/media/PDF/Knowledge-Shelf/Gera_2011(2).ashx

Goodpasture, John C. (2003). *Quantitative Methods in Project Management.* Boca Raton, Florida, USA: J. Ross Publishing.

Larson, R. and Farber, E. (2011). *Elementary Statistics: Picturing the World,* 5th ed. Upper Saddle River, New Jersey: Pearson.

Mavenlink. (2013). "Using Analytics for Project Management." Retrieved February 11, 2015, from http://blog.mavenlink.com/using-analytics-for-project-management

MDH QI Toolbox. (2014). "PDSA: Plan-Do-Study-Act." Minnesota Department of Health. Retrieved February 15, 2015, from http://www.health.state.mn.us/divs/opi/qi/toolbox/pdsa.html

Pollard, W. (n.d.). *BrainyQuote.com.* Retrieved October 5, 2015, from BrainyQuote.com Web site: http://www.brainyquote.com/quotes/authors/w/william_pollard.html.

Project Management Institute (2014). *A Guide to the Project Management Body of Knowledge* (PMBOK® Guide), 5th ed. Newton Square, Pennsylvania: Project Management Institute (PMI).

Quora. (2014). What is the difference between "Business Analytics" and "Business Analysis"? Retrieved September 4, 2015, from http://www.quora.com/What-is-the-difference-between-Business-Analytics-and-Business-Analysis

Ramakrishnan, Dr. (2009). "CRM and Stakeholder Management." 20th SKOCH Summit, Hyatt Regency, Mumbai, July 16-17 2009.

Saaty, T.L. (2008). "Decision Making with Analytic Hierarchy Process." *International Journal of Services Sciences,* 1 (1), pp. 83–98.

2

Data-Driven Decision-Making

Learning Objectives

After reading this chapter, you should be familiar with

- Common project management decisions
- Characteristics of a good decision
- Factors influencing decision-making
- Analysis paralysis
- Importance of a decisive project manager
- Automation of decision-making process
- Predictive versus prescriptive analytics
- Data-driven decision-making process flow
- Benefits of data-driven decision-making
- Challenges associated with data-driven decision-making

> "There is nothing like first-hand evidence."
> —*Sherlock Holmes*

Strong project management and leadership skills are not the only prerequisites for the ability of a project manager to deliver a successful project. His or her ability to make complex project decisions in a timely manner is also one of the "must have" skills because there is a strong positive correlation between the quality of project decisions and the project success. Being able to select the best course of action based on careful evaluation of various alternatives by analyzing the underlying tangible and intangible criteria is the only way a project manager can lead the project to achieve the stipulated objectives.

Decisions are ubiquitous throughout the project life cycle (PLC). For instance, decisions must be made

- To undertake the project
- To move forward from one stage of the PLC to the next
- To hire or not hire a project human resource
- To buy or build
- To select the best supplier from multiple alternatives
- To approve or reject a project risk
- To approve or reject a change request
- To accept or reject a deliverable

Characteristics of a Good Decision

An action must follow a decision made. If the action is missing, the decision made is useless and the effort leading to that decision is wasted.

The following are the characteristics of a good decision:

- Considers all factors influencing the situation
- Based on the "win-win" approach?
- Incorporates appropriate tools and techniques
- Involves the right participants from beginning to end
- Considers viewpoints of all parties involved
- Transparent to all parties involved; no hidden agenda exists
- Utilizes a 360-degree analytical approach to include tangibles (measurable data) as well as intangibles (such as intuition and subjectivity)
- Based on high-quality predictive analysis (intelligent anticipation) because the results of decisions made today will be noticeable in the future and the future involves uncertainty. For example, Hewlett-Packard's decision to undertake a project to launch its tablet product "touchpad" resulted in a product that died right after its birth because by the time the project was completed and the touchpad was launched, the marketplace was already flooded with lower cost and higher quality tablets.

Decision-Making Factors

Decision-making depends on multiple factors including knowledge, skills, tangibles, intangibles, pragmatism, and decision-making methodology.

Knowledge: Knowledge pertains to the information needed to make a decision. For decisions to be feasible and effective, all parties involved in the decision-making process must have knowledge of the information about the situation and the context of the situation.

Skills: Decision-makers must have skills to use their knowledge and experience to acquire and intelligently analyze the information pertaining to the situation about which the decision is being made.

Tangibles: Tangibles include directly measured or observed qualitative and quantitative data such as hard facts or evidences pertaining to the situation.

Intangibles: Intangibles in decision-making refers to decision-makers' intuitions and subjective approach.

Measuring Project Manager Soft Competencies: Quantifying the Subjective Information for Measurement

For fully informed decision-making both subjective and objective information should be considered. The subjective information is often collected via surveys but until some criteria are developed, many decision-makers do not know how to take the subjective information into account.

Gregory J. Skulmoski et al. shared in their article published in the March 2010 issue of *Project Management General* how the subjective answers to a survey questions about an information systems project manager's soft skills were quantified. They wrote, "During the pilot testing of the interview questions, the research participants had some difficulty discussing competence broadly and deeply...the interviewees were provided with a list of competencies by project phase (initiation, planning, implementation, and closeout) to rank. They were given 25 points to use to rank and weight the competencies within the list. They could distribute their 25 points within each category in any way they felt appropriate."

Pragmatism: A pragmatic approach allows the decision-makers to accept less-than-perfect results. The quest to achieve a perfect outcome often paralyzes decision-making efficiency. Pragmatism is the factor in the decision-making process that takes into account the practical realities (such as politics, regulations, financial constraints, cost-benefit tradeoff, urgency, and so on) of the project environment and helps prevent analysis paralysis.

Analysis Paralysis (Over-Analysis of the Information)

Data analysis for project decision-making is important but it should not become "analysis paralysis" where project managers just keep spinning the wheels in analysis and can't make a clear decision. When they do finally make a decision due to being forced up against the wall by certain critical project deadlines, they end up making poor decisions.

The level of analysis should match the complexity of the situation. For example, a project manager does not need to collect and analyze a massive amount of data just to make decision whether to buy a projector for presentations or not; however, he or she must perform a thorough analysis before deciding which vendor to award the project solution integration contract to.

Decision-Making Methodology: Effective decision-making involves the use of proper tools, technologies, and methodologies, which include brainstorming, facilitation, meetings, negotiation, research, cost-benefit analysis, alternative analysis, communication techniques, and so on.

Brainstorming allows for a fear-free environment for free flow of ideas from all participants. Tight facilitation keeps the meeting discussions focused on the subject matter of interest for quicker and effective decision-making. Well-researched alternatives processed through cost-benefits–based alternative analysis enable the decision-maker to select the best possible alternative. Effective communication techniques help with stakeholder engagement and exchange of information among the participants in the decision-making process.

Importance of Decisive Project Managers

An integral part of a project manager's day-to-day project management job is to make a variety of often time-sensitive important project decisions. Thus, a project manager's decisiveness attribute alone has the potential to steer the project ship toward the destination or toward destruction.

The mind map in Figure 2.1 captures the key reasons why project managers' decisiveness is important in project management.

Figure 2.1 Importance of Decisive Project Managers

Time Is of the Essence

Right and rational decisions made by a project manager in a timely[1] manner are critical for the progress of a project. "Rational" means the decisions being made are logical and properly thought through. A project manager's strong project management knowledge and soft skills enable him or her to make rational decisions in a timely manner. Also, it is important that the key stakeholders are involved in the decision-making process and that their consent is given due consideration. However, when the team takes a significant amount of time to arrive at a consensus, the project manager should take control in making a decision so that the project can move forward because time is of the essence.

Lead by Example

Leading by example is an important and effective skill of a project manager to motivate the project team. By being able to make effective project decisions in a timely manner, the project manager sets an example for the rest of the team that right decisions need to be made in right time frame by involving the right people.

Establish Credibility

The ability of a project manager to be decisive and make things happen on the project helps her establish her credibility among the project team members as a strong leader. Indecisive project managers can lose credibility as strong project leaders and the project team members may soon lose confidence in their ability to steer the project ship in the right direction.

---

[1] "Timely" does not mean that the decisions are made in haste with their quality compromised.

Resolve Conflicts and Other Project Problems

Projects typically have to deal with lots of uncertainty and involve multiple diverse stakeholders. They involve a variety of conflicts and project problems. The project manager's responsibility ultimately is to handle and resolve those conflicts and problems effectively to keep the project on track to success. This often requires a project manager to be able to make quick and rational decisions to find a win-win resolution. Unexpected situations cannot be proactively planned for. Therefore, resolving conflicts and problems pertaining to these unexpected situations requires that a project manager be able to think quickly and clearly under pressure to make the best possible decisions after weighing the pros and cons of various alternatives.

Avoid Analysis Paralysis

We discussed the concept of *analysis paralysis* earlier in this chapter under "Pragmatism." Many project managers often hesitate to make decisions and they fall into this trap. They keep over-analyzing the same set of information without arriving at a decisive conclusion. An alternative-analysis-based decision-making approach can enable the project manager to make quicker and correct decisions and avoid analysis paralysis by evaluating:

- The pros and cons of pursuing each alternative
- The opportunity cost of not pursuing an alternative
- SWOT (Strengths, Weaknesses, Opportunities, and Threats) analysis of each alternative

Automation and Management of the Decision-Making Process

The project decision-making process, when automated and effectively managed, can produce effective and efficient decisions that are critical to the success of a project.

Project decision-making is an ongoing process. Decisions made throughout the stages of the PLC not only impact the domain within which the decisions are made but they also impact other decisions in various other domains of the project. This complexity of the wide array of project decisions requires some level of automation of the project decision-making process. Some methodologies or approaches that can be used to automate and manage the decision-making process, include the following:

- **Predictive analytics:** This involves data mining to analyze historical data to identify certain patterns or trends in data that can help make data-driven predictive decisions to mitigate the risks due to uncertainty of the future.

- **Optimization techniques (prescriptive analytics):** These help with optimizing the allocation and use of scarce project resources within project constraints.

- **Statistical analytics:** This presents statistical techniques to analyze probability for decision-making.

- **Big data:** Big data refers to data-sets that are too large and/or complex to use traditional methods for searching, capturing, analyzing, archiving, securing, and distributing data. Big data makes use of various advanced computational techniques such as predictive analytics to assist in automating the data-driven decision-making process.

- **Analytic Hierarchy Process:** This is an effective approach to multi-criteria-driven decision-making.

The automation of the decision-making process is hard to achieve if project managers keep delaying decision-making in continued quest for perfection. Experts recommend the application of the 80–20 rule in decision-making. According to Butler Analytics, "Eighty percent of the benefit will come from twenty percent of the rules."

An efficient, reliable, consistent, and fact-based decision-making process is very important in any organization. It is specifically more critical in environments such as banking, insurance, and other financial services where the volume of decisions to be made is very high and/or the decision-making process is repetitive.

Data-Driven Decision-Making

Data-driven decision-making is defined as the process of making decisions not just on the basis of gut feeling or intuition but also by taking the actual facts or data into consideration. The mind map in Figure 2.2 outlines seven steps to data-driven decision-making.

Data-Driven Decision-Making—Pathway to Gaining the Competitive Advantage

In his article in *Harvard Business Review* (*HBR*), Walter Frick (2014) refers to the 2012 report by Andrew McAfee and Erik Brynjolfsson in *HBR* that highlights the benefits of data-driven decision-making, "Companies in the top third of their industry in the use of data-driven decision making were, on average, 5% more productive and 6% more profitable than their competitors." To reinforce his stance, Frick further quotes comments from McAfee's other post on HBR, "Data and algorithms have a tendency to outperform human intuition in a wide variety of circumstances." Also, the data-driven approach minimizes the risks generally associated with the process of making decisions.

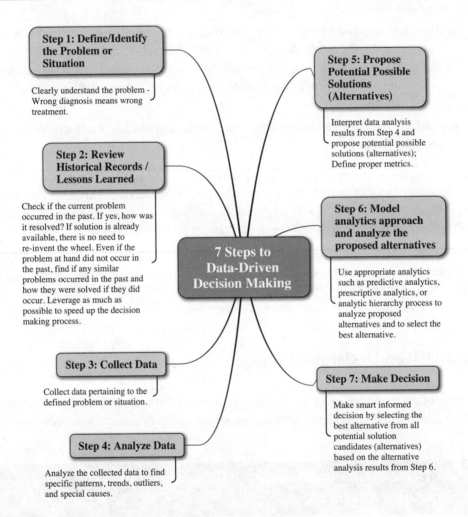

Figure 2.2 Seven Steps to Data-Driven Decision-Making

Data-Driven Decision-Making Process Challenges

Although data-driven decision-making provides numerous benefits, it is not without challenges. Project managers must consider these challenges while planning for the data-driven decision-making processes to achieve the desired results. The following are common challenges associated with this process:

- **Magnitude and complexity of the data:** The higher the magnitude and complexity of the data, the more difficult and time consuming is the security, storage, and processing of the data.

- **Sources of the data:** Sources of data determine the type of data collected. Incorrect sources means incorrect data and hence incorrect decisions, as discussed in the next section, "Garbage In, Garbage Out."

- **Quality of the data:** Uniform data (attributes) pertaining to various alternatives must be compared to mimic apple-to-apple comparison for fair alternative analysis. Also, the quality of the data collected must be adequate to bring forth the true value of a given alternative. The collected data is not always all good and sorting out good data from the bad is a must but is not an easy task, as says Alexey Shelushkov in one of the 2014 blog posts on itransition.com, "Not all data that glitters is gold. Data has to be exact, correct and uniform in order to be the yardstick to measure the business potency of this or that decision."

- **Personnel analytical skills:** Inadequate analytical skills of data analyst personnel will certainly pose a challenge in ensuring the accuracy, quality, and efficiency of the analysis.

- **Tools and technologies:** The speed, accuracy, and quality of data collection, storage, analysis, and interpretation processes depend on the available tools and technologies, particularly when the data in question is large and complex. Inadequacy or lack of appropriate tools and technology certainly pose a challenge to data-driven decision-making.

- **Shelf-life of the data:** Data collected that is not processed in a timely manner may become stale and no longer useful. For example, data pertaining to the technology in use today may not be worth analyzing two years from now when this technology becomes obsolete and is replaced by another technology.

Garbage In, Garbage Out

The quality of data-driven decisions is determined by the type[2] and quality of the data collected and by the manner in which the collected data is analyzed, interpreted, and used for decision-making.

Data for decision-making is collected through various means such as measurements, observations, conversations, and surveys. The quality of the data collected through conversations and surveys depends on the types of data-related questions asked from the responders. In his article "Keep Up with Your Quants," published in the July 2013 issue of *HBR*, Thomas H. Davenport identifies the following six questions that should be asked to collect the good type and quality of data:

- What was the source of your data?
- How well do the sample data represent the population?
- Does your data distribution include outliers? How did they affect the results?
- What assumptions are behind your analysis? Might certain conditions render your assumptions and your model invalid?
- Why did you decide on that particular analytical approach? What alternatives did you consider?
- How likely is it that the independent variables are actually causing the changes in the dependent variable? Might other analyses establish causality more clearly?

Summary

The mind map in Figure 2.3 summarizes tthe data-driven decision-making process.

---

[2] The type of data collected refers to the metrics used to collect data. Due diligence must be used to select the good (right) metrics. According to Frick (2014), "Good metrics are consistent, cheap, and quick to collect. But most importantly, they must capture something your business cares about."

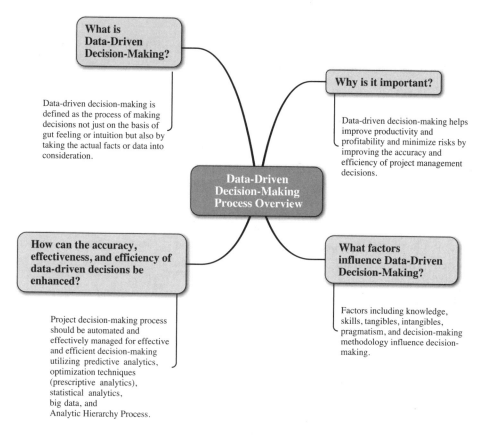

What is Data-Driven Decision-Making?

Data-driven decision-making is defined as the process of making decisions not just on the basis of gut feeling or intuition but also by taking the actual facts or data into consideration.

Why is it important?

Data-driven decision-making helps improve productivity and profitability and minimize risks by improving the accuracy and efficiency of project management decisions.

Data-Driven Decision-Making Process Overview

How can the accuracy, effectiveness, and efficiency of data-driven decisions be enhanced?

Project decision-making process should be automated and effectively managed for effective and efficient decision-making utilizing predictive analytics, optimization techniques (prescriptive analytics), statistical analytics, big data, and Analytic Hierarchy Process.

What factors influence Data-Driven Decision-Making?

Factors including knowledge, skills, tangibles, intangibles, pragmatism, and decision-making methodology influence decision-making.

Figure 2.3 Data-Driven Decision-Making Process Summary

Key Terms

Analysis Paralysis

Analytic Hierarchy Process (AHP)

Big Data

Cost-Benefits Tradeoff

Earned Value Management (EMV)

Intangibles

Pragmatism

Predictive Analytics

Prescriptive Analytics

Project Life Cycle (PLC)

SWOT Analysis

Tangibles

Case Study: Kheri Construction, LLC

In this case study, Kheri Construction, LLC uses the data-driven decision-making process to resolve the issue of high staff turnover.

Background

Kheri Construction (KC), LLC is a Dallas, Texas–based premier commercial construction company. The company has a reputation for successfully completing on-time and under-budget mega-million dollar projects in the state of Texas. The large portfolio of the projects completed by the company includes multi-story skyscrapers, multi-lane highways, railroad tracks, and shopping malls.

In the spring of 2011, KC was awarded a contract by the Texas state government to implement a large and complex highway reconstruction project in Houston. The company hired a limited-term (LT) project manager, Emma Veronica, and the project was initiated.

Problem

The project performance was measured primarily via the popular Earned Value Management (EVM). One year into the project, the periodic EVM analysis results over the year revealed that the project's schedule and budget have not been on track. The main reason, according to Emma, was the high turnover of the project staff. High turnover of the project staff (average 52.7% annual) had become a big issue on the project. The project would invest huge resources in training the new employees to bring then onboard quickly, many of whom would leave the project pre-maturely. The project would hire more temporary people to fill the vacancies but they had to be trained from scratch and there was a lengthy lead time before the new hires were able to contribute any significant value to the project. This staff turnover cycle had become a norm and it was hurting the project and KC in turn badly.

Eventually, KC Project Director James Rodriguez realized that the water was over the company's head and something needed to be done. He decided to engage an outside consultant, Rick Albany, to investigate the situation and suggest the best possible remedial solution.

Initial Investigation

The first logical step Rick took toward investigation was to review KC's historical organizational project artifacts[3] to understand whether the company had encountered a similar situation before. After reviewing archived artifacts including lessons learned, issue logs, risk databases, and decision logs for three weeks, Rick found that the staff turnover rate started ramping up exponentially since 2008 and it became worst while the project was being investigated. He noticed that nothing was done to address the situation all along. He also found that KC used to have mostly permanent staff prior to the economic downturn impact it faced in 2008. That was a bad year for KC that pushed the company very close to filing bankruptcy. That led the company to lay off most of its permanent staff. Thereafter, the company changed its hiring strategy to hire all new personnel on a LT basis (depending upon the length of the project the personnel were being hired for). During the planning stage of the project, Emma, the project manager suggested to KC management that the company should consider hiring at least some key positions on a permanent basis to maintain business continuity due to the long-term nature of the project. Emma's suggestion, however, was overruled by the KC management. Therefore, the project was staffed with mostly LT positions.

Further Root Cause Analysis (RCA)

Rick invited key project stakeholders[4] for a brainstorming session to find the root cause(s) and potential remedies for the issue of turnover. With Rick facilitating, the brainstorming session was conducted. Rick decided to use a fishbone diagram, affinity diagram, and Pareto chart to capture and analyze the data. First he captured the raw inputs from the brainstorming session participants, as shown in Figure 2.4.

---

[3] "The historical organizational project artifacts refer to an organization's historical artifacts archived from other similar projects completed previously. Leveraging lessons learned, historical information, tools, and other artifacts from previously done similar projects can save the project at hand a lot of time and money." Source: Singh, H. (2014). *Mastering Project Human Resource Management,* 1st ed. Upper Saddle River, New Jersey: Pearson FT Press.

[4] "Key stakeholders are stakeholders with high power, influence on the project, and interest in the success or failure of the project." Source: Singh, H. (2014). *Mastering Project Human Resource Management,* 1st ed. Upper Saddle River, New Jersey: Pearson FT Press.

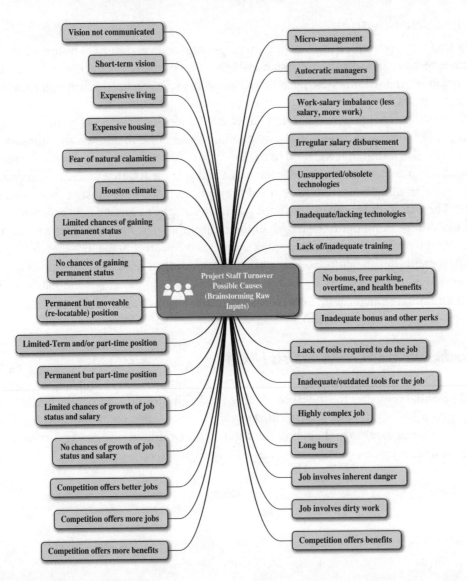

Figure 2.4 Brainstorming Raw Inputs

After capturing the raw inputs from all brainstorming participants, Rick used an affinity diagram,[5] shown in Figure 2.5, to categorize them. He identified the following categories:

---

[5] The affinity diagram is typically used after a brainstorming session to organize a large number of ideas into relevant categories for ease of analysis.

- Tools and technologies
- Compensation
- Competition
- Nature of job

- Management
- Working/living conditions
- Tenure
- Future prospects

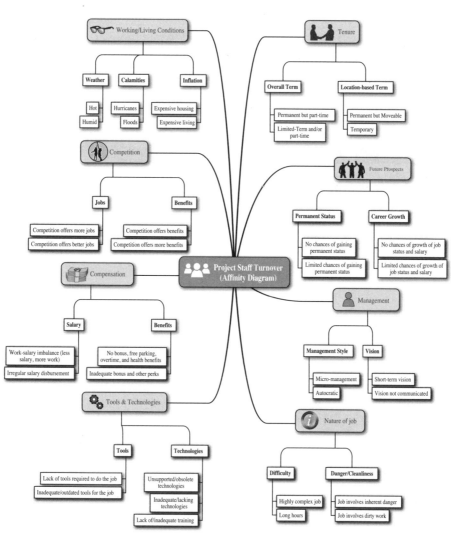

Figure 2.5 Affinity Diagram Displaying Categories of Various Causes for Staff Turnover

In the next step, Rick transferred the categorized information from the affinity diagram to a fishbone[6] or cause-and-effect diagram, shown in Figure 2.6, and discussed it with the key stakeholders participating in the brainstorming session.

All participants anonymously approved the possible causes identified in the fishbone analysis. Rick suggested that the KC human resources department frame exit interview questions based on the "identified possible causes" and ask them from all the personnel leaving the project over the next three months. He also suggested asking similar questions to the existing staff as well to understand what would motivate them to stay.

After three months, the collected data was analyzed. Table 2.1 captures the percentage of votes for the criticality of each type (category) of possible cause.

Table 2.1   Percentage of Votes for Each Area of Criticality

Category	% Votes
Tools and technologies	11.7
Compensation	15.0
Competition	1.2
Nature of job .	2.6
Management	5.2
Working and living conditions	3.3
Tenure	46.4
Future Prospects	14.6

Rick used Microsoft Excel to develop a Pareto chart, shown in Figure 2.7, to focus KC management on the areas that needed the most attention.

---

6 The fishbone diagram (also known as a cause-and-effect diagram or Ishikawa diagram) is used to help identify various causes that lead to certain effects.

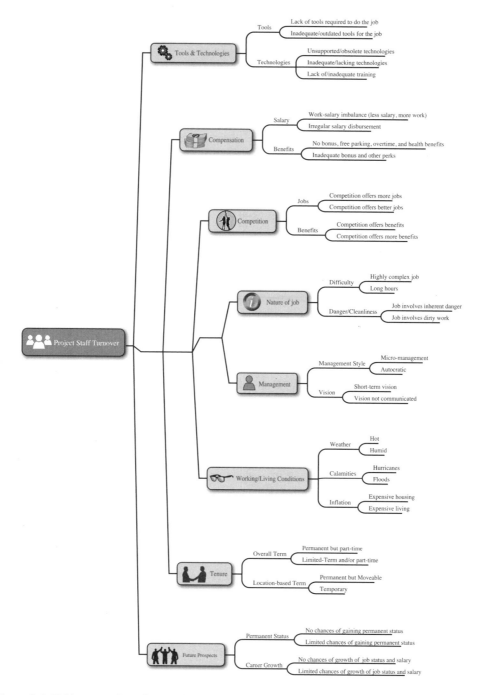

Figure 2.6 Fishbone Analysis for Possible Causes for Staff Turnover

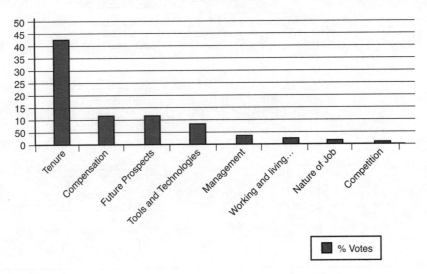

% Votes

Figure 2.7 Pareto Chart Highlighting Most Critical Areas Needing Improvement

Based on the analysis, the top four areas that demanded immediate attention included tenure, compensation, future prospects, and tools and technologies. Rick outlined the following alternatives going forward:

Alternative 1: Do nothing and live with the status quo.

Alternative 2: Convert the key project positions to permanent full-time.

Alternative 3: Convert the key project positions to permanent full-time, offer competitive compensation, improve job tools and technologies, ensure appropriate training, and improve opportunities for growth.

Decision-Making

Rick performed a comprehensive alternative analysis and discussed cost versus benefits for each alternative with KC management, which then decided to pursue alternative 3.

Action Plan

KC management drafted the following action plan to implement alternative 3:

- Make all key project positions (such as project director, project manager, project scheduler, business analysts, project cost analysts, and project quality analysts) permanent full-time

- Adjust paygrades to competitive levels

- Improve benefits (for example, match 401k contributions up to 3%, resume sabbatical leaves, fund Christmas breakfast and company picnics, and initiate a rewards and recognition program)

- Upgrade staff laptops to better models

- Implement SharePoint and Project Server for improvement in collaboration, productivity, and project management

- Ensure appropriate training for the project staff to learn new tools and technologies, to improve productivity in the current job, or to prepare for promotional opportunities

- Enhance opportunities for career growth within the organization (for example, start a Leadership Academy program to provide special leadership training to the employees who have desire and aptitude for the leadership positions)

Results

KC started observing the positive results within a month after the action plan was implemented. After one year of the plan implementation, the annual staff turnover rate dropped from average 52.7% to merely 8.6%, an 83.68% improvement.

Case Study Questions

1. What data analytics tools did Rick Albany use to capture and analyze the data in this case?

2. What is fishbone analysis? How does it help in decision-making?

3. How effective was data-driven decision-making in this case?

Chapter Review and Discussion Questions

1. Define data-driven decision-making.

2. List some of the key decisions made during the project life cycle.

3. What is meant by the term *analysis paralysis?*

4. What are the advantages of using data-driven decision-making in project management?

5. What methodologies or approaches can be used to automate and manage the process of decision-making?

6. What is the difference between predictive and prescriptive analytics?

7. What is meant by *garbage in, garbage out*?

8. Define *pragmatism.*

9. What are typical steps in a data-driven decision-making process?

10. Discuss some challenges associated with the data-driven decision-making process.

Bibliography

BI Insights. (2013). "6 Steps to Becoming a Data-Driven Decision Maker." Retrieved March 7, 2015, from http://businessintelligence.com/bi-insights/6-steps-to-becoming-a-data-driven-decision-maker/

Butler Analytics. (2015). "Decision Oriented Business Process Management." Retrieved March 8, 2015, from http://butleranalytics.com/wp-content/uploads/Decision-Oriented-Business-Process-Management.pdf

Davenport, T. H. (2013). "Keep Up with Your Quants," *Harvard Business Review.* Retrieved March 10, 2015, from https://hbr.org/2013/07/keep-up-with-your-quants

Ferris, B. (2012). "Why You Need to Be a Decisive Project Manager." Retrieved March 9, 2015, from http://cobaltpm.com/why-you-need-to-be-a-decisive-project-manager/

Frick, W. (2014). "An Introduction to Data-Driven Decisions for Managers Who Don't Like Math," *Harvard Business Review.* Retrieved March 6, 2015, from https://hbr.org/2014/05/an-introduction-to-data-driven-decisions-for-managers-who-dont-like-math

Pitagorsky, G. (2013). "Decision Making - A Critical Success Factor." Retrieved March 8, 2015, from http://www.projecttimes.com/george-pitagorsky/decision-making-a-critical-success-factor.html

Rouse, M. (2012). "What Is Decision Management?" Definition from WhatIs.com. Retrieved March 9, 2015, from http://whatis.techtarget.com/definition/decision-management

Shelushkov, A. (2014). "Gaining Competitive Advantage with Data-Driven Decision Making." Retrieved March 8, 2015, from http://www.itransition.com/blog/gaining-competitive-advantage-with-data-driven-decision-making/

Singh, H. (2014). *Mastering Project Human Resource Management,* 1st ed. Upper Saddle River, New Jersey: Pearson FT Press.

Skulmoski, G.J. et al. (2010). "Information Systems Project Manager Soft Competencies: A Project-Phase Investigation." *Project Management Journal,* 41(1): p. 63.

Villanova University. (2015). "Importance of a Decisive Project Manager." Retrieved March 6, 2015, from http://www.villanovau.com/resources/project-management/importance-of-project-manager-decisiveness/#.VRTnafnF-7w

3

Project Management Framework

Learning Objectives

After reading this chapter, you should be familiar with

- Project definition and characteristics
- Project constraints
- Project success criteria
- Why projects fail
- Project versus operations
- Project, program, and portfolio management
- Project Management Office (PMO)
- Project life cycle
- Project management life cycle
- Systems (software) development life cycle
- Project processes
- Work Breakdown Structure (WBS)

"All things are created twice; first mentally, then physically. The key to creativity is to begin with the end in mind, with a vision and a blue print of the desired result."
—*Stephen Covey, Author of The Seven Habits of Highly Effective People*

Because the discussion in this book focuses on project management analytics, you must clearly understand the context or environment (project management framework[1]) within which the project management analytics knowledge is targeted. This chapter defines some key project management terms in addition to providing you an overview of the project management framework, including the Project Life Cycle (PLC), Project Management Life Cycle (PMLC), Systems (Software) Development Life Cycle (SDLC), and the project management processes.

What Is a Project?

A project is a temporary[2] endeavor taken on to create a unique product, service, process, or outcome. It is a temporary endeavor because it has a definite start and a definite end. It also uses a specific scope and budget, and it involves a particular set of operations targeted to achieve an unusual goal.

A project is initiated when a unique business need has to be fulfilled and a project manager is authorized (via the approval of a project charter[3]) to undertake the efforts to fulfill that business need. A project ends for various reasons, such as

- The project objectives have been met.
- The project is terminated (prematurely) due to lack of confidence that the project objectives can be met.

---

[1] "Project management framework (PM framework) is a subset of tasks, processes, tools, and templates used in combination by the management team to get insight into the major structural elements of the project in order to initiate, plan, execute, control, monitor, and terminate the project activities throughout the management life cycle. PM framework allows using various methodologies and approaches to plan and schedule the major phases of the lifecycle. Regardless of the type, size, and nature of project, a typical PM framework includes micro and macro phases, templates and checklists, processes and activities, roles and responsibilities, training material and work guidelines—all this information is organized and systematized into a structure allowing managers and planners to control progress of their projects throughout the lifecycle."

Source: McConnell, E. (2010). http://www.mymanagementguide.com/project-management-framework-definition-and-elements/

[2] Not necessarily short in duration

[3] *Project Management Body of Knowledge (PMBOK)* 5th edition, defines the project charter as "the document issued by the project initiator or sponsor that formally authorizes the existence of a project and provides the project manager with the authority to apply organizational resources to project activities. It documents the business needs, assumptions, constraints, the understanding of the customer's needs and high-level requirements, and the new product, service, or result that it is intended to satisfy...."

Source: Project Management Institute (PMI). (2014). *A Guide to the Project Management Body of Knowledge,* 5th edition.

- The project is terminated because the need for the project no longer exists.
- The project is terminated because the client (customer, sponsor,[4] or champion) wants to do so.

Characteristics

The following characteristics of a project will help to enhance the understanding of its definition:

- **It's unique:** A project has a well-defined objective. For example, firms like HP and Intel undertake multiple projects to design, develop, and roll out new product lines, and each product line is unique.

- **It has a temporary nature:** A project is temporary by nature because it has a definite start and a definite end. For example, a shopping mall construction project in a neighborhood was initiated in June 2010 and was completed in December 2011.

- **It consumes resources[5]:** Specific resources are needed to complete the project tasks. The project resources include people (human resources), materials, and equipment. For example, people with a diverse skillset (such as plumbers, framers, roofers, painters, and so on), materials (such as wood, concrete, tiles, nails, paint), and equipment (such as a concrete mixer, nail gun, saw, hammer, ladder, paint sprayer) are needed to complete the construction of a new home.

- **It uses progressive elaboration:** When a project is started, the detailed information on all aspects of the project is not available. Thus, it is planned based on the best possible estimates derived from the limited information that is available during the initial planning. Thereafter, the project plans are updated when more details become available as the project progresses through its life cycle. This process is called *progressive elaboration.*

- **It needs a sponsor:** Active support, direction, and funding from the project sponsor are the primary requirements for the success of a project.

- **It's a risky endeavor:** A project is a risky endeavor because it involves uncertainty. For instance, the project objectives might not be clear, a project might be delayed, or a project might face financial uncertainty.

---

[4] A project sponsor is an executive, external to the project, who manages, administers, monitors, and funds the project and authorizes the project manager to undertake the project.

[5] Project human resources (people), equipment, and raw materials needed to complete the project work

Constraints

Every project has a defined scope (performance),[6] schedule (time),[7] and budget (cost).[8] These three project parameters are referred to as the *triple constraints* of the project. These triple constraints are often illustrated by an equilateral triangle (also known as the *Iron Triangle*), as shown in Figure 3.1. The key characteristics of this triangle is that a change in one of the three constraints will affect at least one other constraint. A project manager must balance these constraints as well as the project quality[9] for the success of the project. This balancing act often involves negotiations between the project manager and the project sponsor or owner customer (project owner).

Figure 3.1 Triple Constraints of a Project

See the nearby sidebar for an illustration of triple constraints.

Project Triple Constraints Illustrated...

Kheri Construction, LLC, a premier construction company of San Francisco, California, won a bid to construct three commercial buildings for a client. The scope, schedule, and budget parameters for these three buildings were as follows:

---

6 *Scope* defines the work that must be done to complete the project.
7 *Schedule* represents the duration of the project.
8 *Budget* represents the estimated cost of completing the project.
9 *Quality* stands for how well a product or service meets the pre-defined specifications or requirements and how satisfied the customer is.

	Scope	Schedule	Budget
Building 1	3000 sq. ft.	6 months	$300K
Building 2	4000 sq. ft.	8 months	$400K
Building 3	5000 sq. ft.	10 months	$500K

Two months into the project, the client asked Kheri Construction Project Manager Bill Anderson to make the following changes to the scope, schedule, and budget:

	Scope	Scope Change	Schedule	Schedule Change	Budget	Budget Change
Building 1	3000 sq. ft.	*Increase by 500sq. ft.*	6 months	-	$300K[1]	-
Building 2	4000 sq. ft.	-	8 months	*Reduce by 2 months*	$400K	-
Building 3	5000 sq. ft.	-	10 months	-	$500K	*Reduce by $100K*

[1] 1K = 1000

Bill (the project manager) analyzed the client request and responded as follows:

1. To add 500 sq. ft. to the existing scope for building 1:

    a. Increase budget for building 1 by $80K, or

    b. Increase budget for building 1 by $40K AND extend schedule for building 1 completion by one month OR negotiable combination of both.

2. To compress schedule for building 2 by two months:

    a. Reduce scope for building 2 by 600 sq. ft., or

    b. Increase budget for building 2 by $120K.

3. To reduce budget for building 3 by $100K:

    a. Reduce scope for building 3 by 800 sq. ft., or

    b. Extend schedule for building 3 completion by three months, or

    c. Negotiable combination of both.

Success Criteria

In his blog "Why Projects Fail," Robert Goatham (2015) explains the project success criteria in terms of multiple layers of project success. According to him, a project meets the success criteria when

- It meets its defined objectives.
- Its product is successful (creates value).
- Project management is successful (the project is executed efficiently).

Figure 3.2 illustrates the layers of project success criteria. The bottom line is that a project is said to be successful when

- The product outcome or solution (product or service) is acceptable to the customer.
- The project solution was delivered on time.
- The project solution was delivered within budget.

Why Projects Fail

Even the projects with great underlying concepts can fail if they are not planned and managed effectively. The following are the key reasons why some projects fail:

- Lack of project sponsor commitment and support.
- Not starting the project with the end in mind. In other words, not knowing the vision or not articulating the vision to the project stakeholders[10] can leave them wondering where the project is heading and can erode their support.
- Not involving the key stakeholders in decision-making can lead to the lack of support from them.
- Unclear expectations, roles, and responsibilities can erode the sense of responsibility and accountability.
- Lack of career growth opportunities, lack of respect and trust, favors, and poor conflict resolution can bring the team morale down.

---

[10] A *project stakeholder* is an individual or an organization that can be impacted by the project outcome negatively or positively *or* can impact the project outcome negatively or positively.

- Poor stakeholder analysis and poor requirements analysis can lead to overlooking some key stakeholders and incorrect and/or incomplete requirements, which can in turn lead to detrimental scope creep[11] during the life of the project.

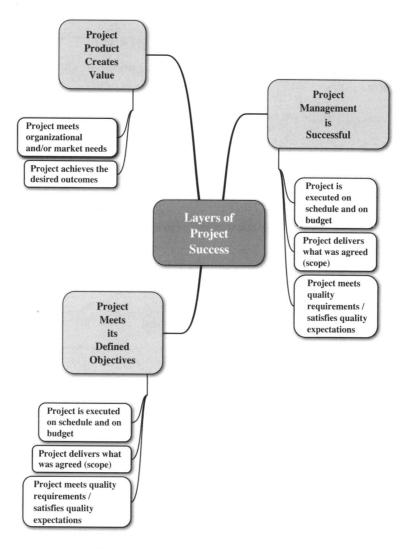

Figure 3.2 Project Success Criteria

---

[11] "Project scope creep refers to the unwanted growth in the project scope primarily due to poor stakeholder identification and analysis, incorrect and/or incomplete requirements collection and analysis, and poor scope management. It can be detrimental to the project." *Source:* Singh, H. (2014). *Project Human Resource Management*, 1st ed. Upper Saddle River, New Jersey: Pearson FT Press.

- Not following a standard project management methodology.
- Poor estimation of project scope, schedule, and budget.
- Poor general project management skills of the project manager.

How Is a Project Different from Operations?

Although they have some similarities, projects and operations are different. The following are the similarities:

- Resources are finite for both.
- Both require proper planning, execution, and control to be successful.
- Both require human resources to carry out the work.

Now as far as differences between projects and operations are concerned, Table 3.1 summarizes the key differences between both.

Table 3.1   Project versus Operations

Project	Operations
A project is a temporary endeavor.	Operations involve ongoing day-to-day work.
A project's activities[12] deliver a unique result.	Operational activities are repeatable.
A project's outcome involves change.	Operations' outcome is consistent and predefined.

Examples of projects include the following:

- Construction of a railroad track for high-speed rail between Sacramento and Los Angeles
- Information technology infrastructure refresh in a data center
- Remodel a household kitchen

---

[12] Project activities or tasks are defined as the actions undertaken to accomplish the project work. They constitute the smallest units of the project work breakdown structure (WBS) for which the resources, cost, and duration can be assigned to.

All these efforts possess the characteristics of a project, because

- They are unique and temporary with a definite start and end.
- The outcome of these efforts involve change.
- They require completion of some work (scope).
- They involve consumption of financial resources (budget).
- It will take certain period of time to complete them (schedule).

Examples of operations include:

- Invoice processing at a company
- Payroll processing at a company
- Daily office cleanup by the janitorial staff
- Daily mail sorting at a post office

All these efforts possess the characteristics of operations because they involve repeatable and ongoing day-to-day work.

Project versus Program versus Portfolio

Some people often get confused with these similar-sounding words—project, program, and portfolio. The following subsections will provide you a quick rundown of the differences among the three.

Project

A *project* transforms an idea into a unique outcome to realize the strategic goals and objectives of the project and the organization. *Project management* involves the application of knowledge, skills, tools, and techniques to planning, organizing, directing, and controlling the project activities to achieve the intended results (project goals and objectives) within the constraints of scope, time, and budget.

Program

A *program* is a group of related projects that are managed together to realize some benefits or efficiencies. Program examples include:

- A large IT firm launches a program for implementing an enterprise-level data center consisting of various related projects:
  - A project for application design, development, and deployment

- A project for database design, development, and deployment
- A project for server and storage virtualization
- A project for networking solution design, development, and deployment
- A government agency sponsors a program called Child Welfare Services that consists of several related projects:
  - Case Management System project for Child Protective Services
  - Young Children Healthcare project
  - Nutrition Project for Underprivileged Children

Program management helps the projects in a program achieve their cost, schedule, performance, and quality objectives by allowing them to share the common pool of resources and leverage lessons learned among a group of related projects, especially when the magnitude and complexity of the work undertaken are very high.

A *program manager* is an individual who manages a program and provides leadership, coaching, and direction to the project managers managing individual related projects under the program umbrella. A program manager meets with these project managers periodically to review the information pertaining to each project and assess the status[13] of the overall program.

Portfolio

A *project portfolio* (or simply *portfolio*) is a collection of all the projects (related or unrelated) of an organization that is managed to achieve a common business result.

Portfolio examples include:

- All projects and programs under a Project Management Office (PMO)
- All enterprise server, storage, and networking projects in an IT company

Project Portfolio Management (PPM) is the centralized management of a portfolio of projects and programs that contribute to the entire enterprise's success. The key objective of PPM is to determine the optimum mix of the resources for cost effectiveness and to achieve operational efficiencies.

---

[13] The program/project status is a snapshot of the condition of the program/project at a point in time. It is usually represented as the variance between the actual and the planned progress.

A *portfolio manager* is an individual who monitors and manages a portfolio. More specifically, a portfolio manager is a driving force behind the proper selection and prioritization of various projects, programs, and processes that make up the portfolio. In addition, a portfolio manager participates in portfolio review, assesses portfolio performance, ensures timely communication of the portfolio status to diverse stakeholders, supports various components of the portfolio, and ensures that portfolio goals and objectives are aligned with the organizational strategic goals and objectives.

Project Management Office (PMO)

The PMO or Project Office governs, oversees, and coordinates the selection, prioritization, and management of the projects in an organization. In addition, the PMO keeps top management informed about the status of all approved projects. More specifically, the activities of the PMO include but are not limited to the following:

- Providing guidance to the project managers
- Defining project selection criteria
- Identifying the project management framework, methodology, tools and technology, and best practices for the projects under its control
- Defining and enforcing project management policies, procedures, templates, and governance documents

Project Life Cycle (PLC)

By definition, a project is a temporary endeavor with definite start and definite end. From its start to its end, a project goes through *multiple stages* or *phases*. This journey through various stages or phases in a sequential manner is called the *project life cycle*. It is just like the human life cycle because humans also have a definite start (birth) and definite end (death) and they go through various life stages or phases (such as infancy, childhood, youth, middle age, and old age) from birth to death.

The traditional approach divides the project life cycle into four stages or phases: definition, planning, executing, and closing. The new approach, as suggested by Archibald, et al. (2012), has added two more stages or phases to the traditional PLC. The revised PLC is shown in Figure 3.3.

Project Life Cycle

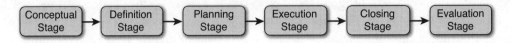

Figure 3.3 Project Life Cycle (PLC)

Conceptual Stage

The conceptual stage is when the project concept or idea is conceived because of

- The need to solve a problem
- The need to improve the status quo
- The motive to innovate something new

This stage is very crucial because an ill-conceived idea can result in a failed project. Thus, the concept should be well-researched and validated for feasibility and alignment with the organizational strategic goals and objectives. The key activities performed in this stage include

- Identifying business need
- Identifying business strategic goals and objectives
- Defining the approach
- Defining measureable business value
- Developing business case
- Performing alternative analysis, the criteria for which include
  - Feasibility analysis based on technology, funding, social constraints, laws and regulations, and so on
  - Cost-benefits analysis
  - Risks
  - Scoring based on various financial models such as net present value (NPV), return on investment (ROI), payback period, breakeven analysis, and so on
- Proposing the best alternative

The key deliverables[14] from this stage include:

- Business case, also known as Feasibility Study Report (FSR)
- FSR approval

Definition Stage

The definition stage of the PLC involves developing the approved project concept from the conceptual stage. It provides more details around the project concept in terms of project description; business justification; resources (human resources, materials, and equipment); and high-level information on the project scope, schedule, and budget. These details help remove most of the vagueness about the original project idea by providing clarity on the project roadmap and expectations.

The key activities performed in this stage include, among other things,

- Defining the purpose of the project
- Aligning the project with strategic goals and objectives of the business
- Developing a high-level overview of the proposed solution
- Defining a high-level scope
- Developing a high-level draft schedule
- Defining key deliverables
- Estimating the budget
- Identifying and analyzing stakeholders

The key deliverables from this phase include:

- Project charter
- Statement of work (SOW[15])
- Stakeholder register[16]

---

[14] A *project deliverable* refers to a tangible and measurable outcome as a result of the execution of a project process that must be produced to complete the project or a part of the project.

[15] An SOW contains the project goals, high-level requirements, and pricing. In other words, it is a description of the contracted work that must be completed within contractual terms and conditions.

[16] A stakeholder register is a document that contains the information about all project stakeholders including stakeholders' names, department/organization, titles, contact information, roles, power, interests, influence, requirements, and expectations. This document is used by the project manager for stakeholder management.

Planning Stage

The planning stage starts when the project charter is approved. During this stage, the project scope (work) is decomposed (broken down) into manageable chunks of work called *work packages*. The work packages are further broken down into project *activities*, which are sequenced and assigned estimated duration and resources to form the project schedule. Also, in this stage various control documents (also known as project plans) are developed that include the baseline project performance information against which the actual project performance is measured periodically throughout the PLC.

The specific key activities performed in this stage include the following:

- Collecting, analyzing, and validating business requirements
- Defining detailed scope
- Defining a baseline project schedule
- Defining a baseline project budget
- Identifying project team members
- Identifying roles and responsibilities
- Defining an escalation process
- Developing a risk register
- Developing an issues register/log
- Estimating required resources
- Developing a quality plan
- Developing a communication plan

The key deliverables from this stage include:

- Business requirements
- Requirements traceability matrix (RTM)
- Responsibility assignment matrix (RAM)
- Quality plan
- Communication plan
- Project organizational structure
- Project schedule
- Project budget
- Work breakdown structure (WBS)

Execution Stage

The execution stage is the overarching stage to the underlying three substages—design, development, and implementation (or *DD&I*). During this stage, the *actual* project work pertaining to design, development, and implementation of the project solution(s) is performed as was planned in the planning stage. Actual work performance is monitored and measured against the baseline performance standards established in the planning stage and if there is any unacceptable discrepancy, it is appropriately handled by making the necessary adjustment. Project deliverables are produced in this stage which are reviewed for quality (correctness) and scope (completeness) against the acceptance criteria outlined in the project plans. The key activities performed in this stage include the following:

- Conducting procurements
- Acquiring resources
- Designing and developing solutions
- Testing and validating solutions
- Measuring project performance
- Performing change control
- Managing schedules
- Managing quality
- Managing risks
- Resolving issues
- Producing deliverables
- Verifying deliverables against the acceptance criteria
- Implementing verified deliverables
- Developing and distributing project progress status reports

The key deliverables from this phase include:

- Project deliverables (work products)
- Project status reports

Closing Stage

The customer acceptance and signing off of all project deliverables triggers the start of the closing stage of the PLC. The key activities performed in this stage include the following:

- Accepting and signing off project deliverables
- Settling all payment accounts (invoices)
- Closing all project records
- Capturing lessons learned
- Archiving project documents
- Releasing project human resources

The key deliverables from this phase include:

- Completed project scope
- Customer acceptance document
- Lessons learned document
- Final project report

Evaluation Stage

The key activities performed in this phase include the following:

- Conducting the post-mortem
  - What went well?
  - What went wrong?
  - What could be done better?
- Receiving feedback
- Communicating

The key deliverables from this phase include generating a project evaluation report.

Project Management Life Cycle (PMLC)

The *PMLC* term is not used often and most people confuse it with the PLC. Typically, PMLC represents the project management processes that repeat in every phase of the project. The five process groups of the *PMBOK Guide* (initiating, planning, executing, monitoring and controlling, and closing) can be considered to be stages of the PMLC because processes in these process groups are repeated in every phase or stage of the PLC. The project is managed by performing a group of processes throughout these stages.

Figure 3.4 illustrates project management life cycle for a typical Information technology (IT) project.

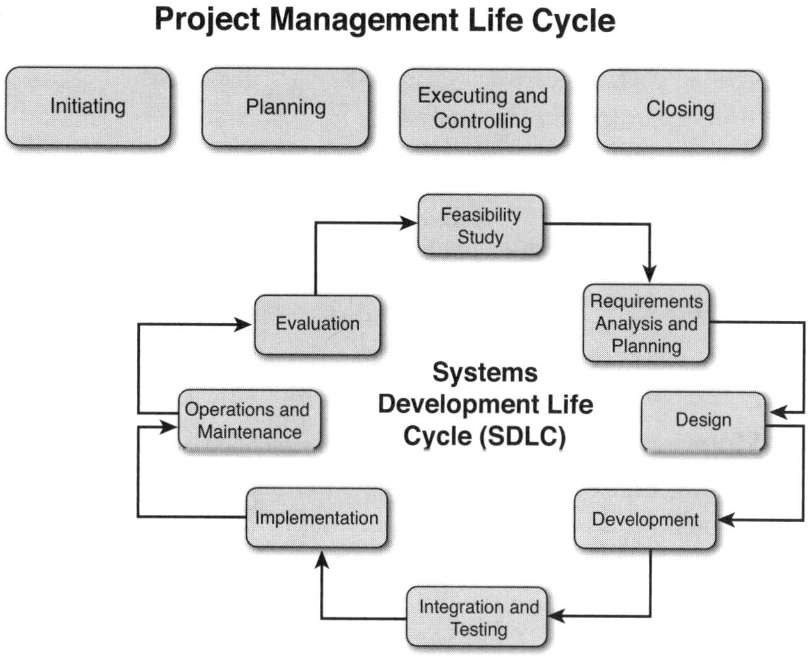

Project Management Life Cycle

Figure 3.4 IT Project Management Life Cycle

Initiating Stage

An approved business case or FSR leads to the initiating stage. During this stage, the project is officially started with the approval of the project charter and appointment of the project manager. Both the project sponsor and the project manager develop the project charter by consulting experts and referring to the organization's archive of the historical project artifacts. The project charter includes high-level information on, but not limited to, the project scope, key milestones,[17] project risks, assumptions, and constraints. The key activities performed in this stage include the following:

---

[17] A project *milestone* represents a significant event in a project and is commonly used to monitor the progress of the project. A milestone is also referred to as a task or activity with zero duration and can be spotted as a diamond-shaped symbol in the GANTT chart of an MS Project schedule.

- Assigning a project manager
- Developing and getting approval for the project charter, which include
  - Obtaining authorization to start the project
  - Defining the purpose of the project
  - Assigning the initial budget
  - Performing key stakeholder analysis
  - Identifying and documenting high-level milestones, risks, assumptions, and constraints

Deliverables from this stage include the following:

- Project charter
- Stakeholder register

Planning Stage

During the planning stage of the PMLC, a number of plans are developed that contain the instructions on how to perform various activities throughout the PLC. The project plans are developed based on the best possible estimates of the scope, schedule, and budget. Once completed and approved, these plans provide the baseline to measure the project performance against. The *project management plan* (or PM plan) is an overarching plan that either contains the rest of the plans or contains the references to the rest of the plans. The key activities performed in this stage include but are not limited to the following:

- Developing the project management plan
- Creating the work breakdown structure (WBS)
- Developing the project schedule
- Determining the project budget
- Developing the quality management plan
- Developing the human resource management plan
- Developing the communication management plan
- Developing the risk management plan
- Developing the procurement management plan
- Developing the stakeholder management plan

The key deliverables from this stage include the following:

- Project management plans
- Project scope statement
- Baselined project schedule
- Baselined project budget
- Risk register
- Issue log
- Decision log
- Change log

Executing and Controlling Stage

The executing and controlling PMLC stage is where the project plans developed during the planning stage are executed and the actual project work is performed. These plans provide the project manager guidance to direct and manage the project work and to monitor and control the project performance. The project performance entails the project work, process, and human resources performance and refers to the measured or observed *actual* performance of the project with respect to the *planned* project scope, schedule, cost, and quality. The variance between the planned performance (as outlined in the project plans) and the actual performance could trigger a change request (CR), which is typically handled by a Change Control Board (CCB).

The key executing activities performed include the following:

- Executing the project management plan
- Acquiring, developing, and managing project human resources
- Obtaining and managing project non-human resources
- Performing quality assurance
- Managing communications
- Conducting procurements
- Managing stakeholder engagement
- Implementing changes approved by the CCB—see the nearby sidebar

The key monitoring and controlling (or simply controlling) activities performed include:

- Measuring project performance
- Measuring, observing, and controlling the quality of project deliverables
- Managing change requests related to the triple constraints (scope, schedule, and budget)
- Updating the risk register, risk response plan, and corrective actions
- Disseminating project status information to project stakeholders

Change Control

Change requests (CRs) are generated as a result of

- The variance between the actual and planned project performance, *or*
- Special enhancement requests

The *change control process* handles the CRs. During this process, the Change Control Board (CCB; usually made of key project stakeholders) panel reviews all change requests and makes decisions. The CCB review results in one of the following three possibilities:

- CR is rejected
- CR is sent back to the submitter for additional information if the submitted request was found to be incorrect and/or incomplete *or*
- CR is approved

The key deliverables from this stage include the following:

- Project deliverables[18]
- Project work performance information (progress status reports)
- Project communications
- Change management log

---

[18] Project deliverables refer to the products, services, or results that need to be delivered to meet the project requirements.

Closing Stage

The closing stage of the project management life cycle is initiated when

- The delivered project scope is verified[19] and validated[20] *or*
- The project is terminated prematurely due to some business or other reasons

This stage refers to the management of the closure of the project itself or the closure of a phase of the project. The key activities performed in this stage include:

- Completing all remaining project activities
- Obtaining acceptance (sign-off) for all project deliverables
- Closing procurements and pay all invoices
- Capturing lessons learned[21]
- Archiving project documents
- Releasing the project team

A Process within the PMLC

You learned earlier that a project transforms an idea into a viable and unique product, service, or deliverable. This transformation is the result of the execution of multiple processes during the course of the project. A process within the project framework is a mechanism of converting a set of inputs to outputs (deliverables) by using certain tools and technologies as shown in Figure 3.5. The *PMBOK Guide*, 5th edition, process map contains 47 processes for managing a project.

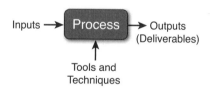

Figure 3.5 Project Management Process

---

[19] Checked for correctness

[20] Checked for completeness

[21] Capture lessons learned even if the project is terminated prematurely so that the future projects can avoid the same or similar pitfalls that were encountered by the project being terminated.

Work Breakdown Structure (WBS)

To manage the high-level project scope, it is broken down into manageable chunks of work called the work *packages*. The process of breaking down the scope is also called *decomposition of the scope*. The tree structure obtained as a result of the decomposition is called the work breakdown structure (WBS). The work packages are generally further decomposed into smaller components called activities or tasks. The activities should be small enough so that they can be managed effectively and large enough so that appropriate resources, cost, and duration can be assigned to them. The project activities are then sequenced and assigned resources, cost, and duration for developing the estimated schedule and time-phased budget. Figure 3.6 shows the partial WBS for a typical home construction project.

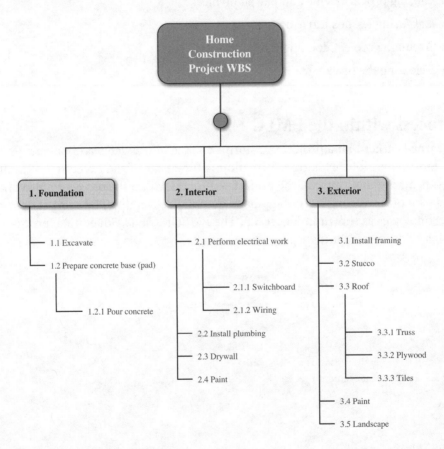

Figure 3.6 WBS for a Home Construction Project

Systems Development Life Cycle (SDLC)

According to Taylor (2004) "the project life cycle encompasses all the activities of the project, while the systems development life cycle focuses on realizing the product requirements." As discussed earlier in this chapter, a project progresses through various stages of its life cycle, referred to as the *PLC*. Similarly, an information system goes through various logically sequenced stages or phases of its development life cycle, referred to as the *SDLC*. Thus, the SDLC represents the *product life cycle* for an IT project. It is also called the software development life cycle because the IT projects are not only related to systems or hardware but they can be related to software as well.

The SDLC falls under the executing stage of the PLC or the PMLC because the information system design, development, and implementation (DD&I) activities occur during this stage of the PLC/PMLC.

Figure 3.7 illustrates the various stages of the SDLC.

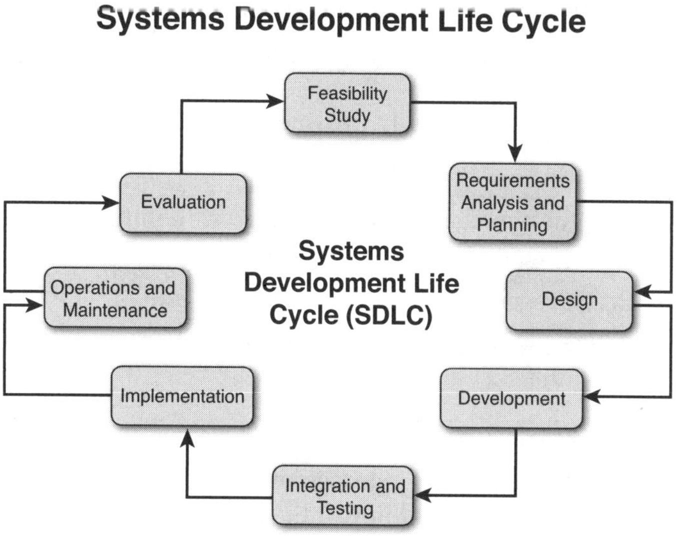

Systems Development Life Cycle

Figure 3.7 Systems Development Life Cycle (SDLC)

Feasibility Study

A feasibility study is conducted to determine the viability of the solution being developed. For the success of the project and the product, conducting this study carefully with thorough research and alternative analysis is essential.

Alternative analysis determines the feasibility of each alternative based on the following criteria:

- Alignment with organizational strategic goals and objectives
- Technical feasibility; that is, practicality of the solution as well as the availability of technology and technical resources needed to produce the solution
- Economic feasibility; that is, profitability
- Legal and/or political feasibility
- Opinions of key stakeholders such as employees, consultants, clients, or vendors
- Competitor benchmarking
- Cost benefits analysis (CBA)
- Resource requirements and availability
- Complexity assessment
- Risk assessment
- Scoring based on various financial models such as net present value (NPV), return on investment (ROI), payback period, breakeven analysis, and so on.

Upon completion, the feasibility study provides you enough information to decide whether to

- Stay with the status quo; that is, do not proceed with improvement of the existing system or development of the new system
- Proceed with improvement of the existing system *or*
- Proceed with development of the new system

Requirements Analysis and Planning

The requirements analysis and planning stage of the SDLC pertains to analysis of the end-user requirements as well as planning for the information system DD&I activities.

The specific end-user requirements are collected, analyzed, validated for correctness and completeness, and documented. There are many ways to collect the end-user requirements, such as telephonic or face-to-face interviews, targeted surveys, joint application development (JAD[22]), general observations, quality databases, organizational reports, and so on.

---

[22] "JAD (Joint Application Development) is a methodology that involves the client or end user in the design and development of an application, through a succession of collaborative workshops called JAD sessions." —Margaret Rouse (http://searchsoftwarequality.techtarget.com/definition/JAD)

The planning involves making sure that the scope, schedule, and budget are clearly defined as well as the supporting tools and technologies lined up for the information system DD&I work.

Design

The design stage provides detailed information about the features and operations of the system including the following:

- System specifications
- Process maps
- Blueprints or layouts
- Business rules
- Dummy or pseudocode

Development

All modules, units, or subassemblies of the system—for example, software functions, hardware units, or hardware units with software (firmware)—are developed during the development stage of the SDLC.

Integration and Testing

In the integration and testing stage of the SDLC, all individually developed units are first tested at the unit-level to validate their functional and performance specifications as standalone units. These units are then integrated into a complete (comprehensive) system or solution. For example, if the solution being produced involves IT infrastructure, all servers, storage, databases, networking, and software applications are first tested at the unit-level and then they are integrated to form a complete IT infrastructure solution. The complete solution is then tested to check for

- Interoperability[23]
- Bugs or errors related to system integration and/or compatibility
- Functionality and performance specifications of the integrated solution

---

[23] "Interoperability describes the extent to which systems and devices can exchange data, and interpret that shared data." HIMSS (2013).

Implementation

During the implementation or deployment stage, the solution is rolled out into the production to perform the actual business transactions.

Operations and Maintenance

During the operations and maintenance stage of the SDLC, the system operation is continually monitored to ensure that it performs optimally in accordance with its functional and performance specifications. Preventive maintenance steps (for example, application software updates, firmware updates, security updates, system patches, operating system kernel tuning, and so on) are performed from time-to-time to keep the system operating in optimum health. Also, appropriate corrective actions are taken if deviation from the expected performance standards is detected based on the continuous evaluation of the system performance.

Evaluation

The evaluation stage of the SDLC is an important stage that should not be overlooked. This is a post-implementation stage during which the implemented system is evaluated for the expected:

- Sustainability
- Reliability
- Safety standards
- Capability for meeting the business requirements
- Functional performance

In addition to the evaluation activities outlined in the preceding, post-mortem of the work performed during the design, development, and implementation stages is also performed and lessons learned are captured for future reference or for implementing immediate corrective actions to the processes, if needed.

Summary

The mind map in Figure 3.8 summarizes the project management framework.

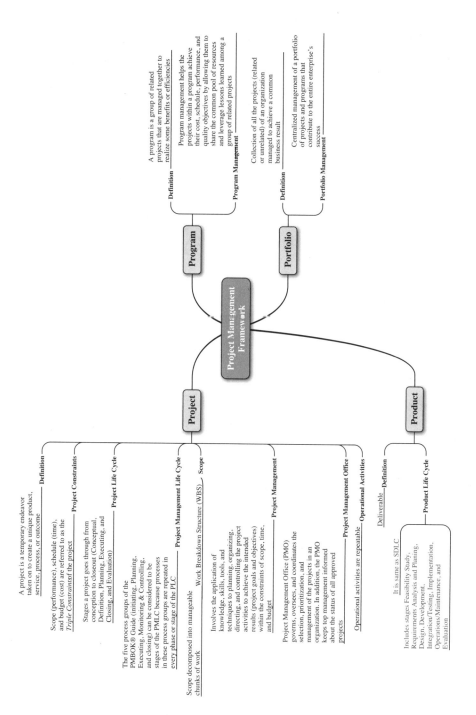

Figure 3.8 Project Management Framework Summary

The following text appears as nodes within the figure:

Project

Definition — A project is a temporary endeavor taken on to create a unique product, service, process, or outcome

Project Constraints — Scope (performance), schedule (time), and budget (cost) are referred to as the *Triple Constraints* of the project

Project Life Cycle — Stages a project goes through from conception to closeout (Conceptual, Definition, Planning, Executing, and Closing, and Evaluation)

Project Management Life Cycle — The five process groups of the PMBOK® Guide (initiating, Planning, Executing, Monitoring & Controlling, and closing) can be considered to be stages of the PMLC because processes in these process groups are repeated in every phase or stage of the PLC

Scope / **Work Breakdown Structure (WBS)** — Scope decomposed into manageable chunks of work

Project Management — Involves the application of knowledge, skills, tools, and techniques to planning, organizing, directing, and controlling the project activities to achieve the intended results (project goals and objectives) within the constraints of scope, time, and budget

Project Management Office — Project Management Office (PMO) governs, oversees, and coordinates the selection, prioritization, and management of the projects in an organization. In addition, the PMO keeps top management informed about the status of all approved projects

Operational Activities — Operational activities are repeatable

Program

Definition — A program is a group of related projects that are managed together to realize some benefits or efficiencies

Program Management — Program management helps the projects within a program achieve their cost, schedule, performance, and quality objectives by allowing them to share the common pool of resources and leverage lessons learned among a group of related projects

Portfolio

Definition — Collection of all the projects (related or unrelated) of an organization managed to achieve a common business result

Portfolio Management — Centralized management of a portfolio of projects and programs that contribute to the entire enterprise's success

Product

Deliverable / **Definition** — It is same as SDLC

Product Life Cycle — Includes stages Feasibility Study, Requirements Analysis and Planning, Design, Development, Integration/Testing, Implementation, Operations/Maintenance, and Evaluation

Project Management Framework (central node)

Key Terms

Change Control Board

Cost-Benefit Analysis

Deliverable

Interoperability

Milestone

Portfolio Management

Program Management

Progressive Elaboration

Project Charter

Project Life Cycle

Project Management

Project Management Framework

Project Management Life Cycle

Project Management Office

Project Management Plan

Project Sponsor

Project Success Criteria

Requirements Traceability Matrix

Responsibility Assignment Matrix

Scope Creep

Stakeholder

Statement of Work

Systems Development Life Cycle

Triple Constraints

Case Study: Life Cycle of a Construction Project

This case study will illustrate the life cycle of a typical project.

Background

Singh Construction, LLC is a medium-sized construction company located in Corona, a city in Southern California. The company's Chief Executive Officer is Surinder Singh, a Licensed General Contractor.

Singh Construction Company had a humble beginning. Surinder Singh started this company in 1987 and started working on small jobs in residential building maintenance and renovation. Due to the company's high-quality work and superb customer service, it quickly gained a reputation for being one of Southern California's top-ten building maintenance companies. The company enjoyed an exponential growth during the '90s housing boom and earned enough reputation and credibility to win large commercial construction projects.

Challenge

The company's growth did not come without a challenge. Its small office in Surinder Singh's home garage was not adequate to handle the increased volume of work. Not only did the company need a bigger main office but it needed a mobile office at the job site as well.

Project Concept and Definition

The challenge of the lack of adequate office facilities gave rise to an urgent need to find a solution to meet that challenge. To facilitate a quicker solution, the company engaged a local consulting firm, Pathlawa Consulting, which offered two possible alternatives—one entailed expansion of the existing home office and the other was to rent an office in downtown Los Angeles. In addition, the consulting firm suggested buying a mobile trailer office for the construction site. After performing alternative analysis, the consulting firm recommended in its feasibility study report that the expansion of the existing home office would be the better of the two alternatives.

Planning

Pathlawa project manager James Xiong talked to Surinder Singh and captured his requirements for the renovation. Based on the agreed-upon requirements, the expansion of the existing office would include the expansion of a home office from a one-car garage space to a three-car garage space (the entire garage), installation of a dedicated air-conditioning unit, insulation of the garage door, and installation of garage cabinets and office furniture. It also included setup of the local area network of one server, two desktop computers, storage array, laser printer, and a plotter (to print construction project drawings). The total cost of the renovation work was estimated to be about $160,000 plus $80,000 for the mobile trailer office. The duration of this entire project was estimated to be 10 months. James put together a project management plan and developed a time-phased (spanning over 10 months) budget that included $20,000 for contingencies. A fixed price contract was signed with interior design company Hi-Tech Designs to design the new office layout.

Execution

The actual project work pertaining to design, development, and implementation of the proposed solution was started after all baseline planning activities were completed and signed off by Hi-Tech Designs and Surinder Singh.

Design

Hi-Tech Designs completed the new office layout design in a month. It was a two-part design: the first part included the design of the office itself and the second part included the design of the computer local area network.

Development

The delays in the new office design approvals by the city delayed the start of development activities by two weeks. Thereafter, as the development (construction) activities ramped up, more issues started to emerge. It was discovered that when the garage was closed, there was not enough natural light in the office, which Surinder Singh wanted. Thus, the scope was augmented to cut the side wall and install a window. This increase in scope resulted in an elongated project schedule and increase in project cost. The construction part of the new office was completed two months later than the planned completion date. But when the city inspector came to inspect the renovated site, he found that no permit was acquired to install a big side window into the garage. The need to get a permit for the window delayed the implementation stage.

Implementation

It took two weeks to obtain the permit for the window, which delayed implementation of the solution—that is, setup of the office furniture, installation of the computer network, and starting normal business operations from the office. The mobile office trailer was purchased as planned.

Closing

Finally, the construction work was completed and signed off by the city inspector and approved by the sponsor (Surinder Singh). The project was completed; however, actual expenditures exceeded the budget and the actual completion date exceeded the scheduled completion date. All costs pertaining to the change orders as well as to the schedule delays were charged to the Singh Construction Company's account. The project was closed after all bills were paid, work was accepted and signed off, and lessons learned were documented and archived.

Evaluation

Singh Construction retained another independent consultant to conduct the post-project evaluation. The evaluation results revealed that a better job could have been done in project planning to avoid schedule delays, cost overruns, and scope creep.

Case Study Questions

1. Was the project in this case conceived and defined well?
2. Define the scope of this project.
3. Was the project planned well?

4. What were some challenges encountered during the management of this project?

5. Did this project meet the success criteria discussed in this chapter?

Chapter Review and Discussion Questions

1. What is a project management framework?

2. What is a project?

3. What is meant by the *Iron Triangle* of a project?

4. Why do some projects fail?

5. What is project management? How is it different from program and portfolio management?

6. Describe the various stages of the project life cycle.

7. Describe the difference between the project life cycle and the systems development life cycle.

8. Define the process within the project management framework.

9. What is a work breakdown structure? What role does it play in project management?

10. Briefly describe various stages of the systems development life cycle.

Bibliography

Adams, J. R. and Barndt, S. E. (1978, Dec.). "Organizational Life Cycle Implications for Major Projects." *Project Management Quarterly*, IX (4), pp. 32-39.

Ajam, M. (2014). "What is the difference between the project life cycle and the project management life cycle?" Retrieved March 22, 2015, from http://blog.sukad.com/20140109/difference-between-project-life-cycle-and-project-management-life-cycle/

Angelo State University IT Project Office. (2014). "Project Lifecycle." Retrieved March 21, 2015, from https://www.angelo.edu/services/project_management/lifecycle.php

Archibald, R.D., Di Filippo, I., and Di Filippo, D. (2012). "The six-phase comprehensive project life cycle model including the project incubation/feasibility phase and the post-project evaluation phase." *PM World Journal*, 1(5), pp. 1-40.

Coolman, A. (2014). "15 Project Management Quotes to Live By (Infographic)." Retrieved October 6, 2015, from https://www.wrike.com/blog/15-project-management-quotes-to-live-by-infographic/

ENS-INC. (2014). Project Management. Retrieved March 22, 2015, from http://www.ens-inc.com/services/projectmanagement/

Goatham, R. (2015). "Why Projects Fail." Retrieved April 6, 2015, from http://calleam.com/WTPF/?page_id=2213

HIMSS. (2013). "What is Interoperability?" Retrieved March 17, 2015, from http://www.himss.org/library/interoperability-standards/what-is-interoperability

Kapur, G.K. (2005). *Project Management for Information, Technology, Business, and Certification,* 1st ed. Upper Saddle River, New Jersey: Pearson.

Marchewka, J.T. (2003). *Information Technology Project Management,* 1st ed. Hoboken, New Jersey: John Wiley & Sons.

McConnel, E. (2010). "Project Management Framework: Definition and Basic Elements." Retrieved October 20, 2015, from http://www.mymanagementguide.com/project-management-framework-definition-and-elements/.

Method123. (2014). "Project Management Life Cycle." Retrieved March 18, 2015, from http://www.method123.com/project-lifecycle.php

Pinto, J.K. (2013). *Project Management: Achieving Competitive Advantage,* 3rd ed. Upper Saddle River, New Jersey: Pearson.

Project Management Institute. (2014). *A Guide to the Project Management Body of Knowledge (PMBOK® Guide),* 5th ed. Newton Square, Pennsylvania: Project Management Institute (PMI).

Rouse, M. (2007). "What Is JAD (Joint Application Development)?" Definition from WhatIs.com. Retrieved March 18, 2015, from http://searchsoftwarequality.techtarget.com/definition/JAD

Singh, H. (2014). *Project Human Resource Management,* 1st ed. Upper Saddle River, New Jersey: Pearson FT Press.

Taylor, J. (2004). *Managing Information Technology Projects.* New York: AMACOM, p.39.

Watt, A. (2014). "Project Management." Retrieved March 20, 2015, from http://opentextbc.ca/projectmanagement/

Whitten, J.L., and Bentley, L.D. (1997). *Systems Analysis and Design Methods,* 4th Edition, New York: McGraw Hill.

4

Statistical Fundamentals I: Basics and Probability Distributions

Learning Objectives

After reading this chapter, you should be familiar with

- Types of data
- Data versus information
- Population versus sample
- Probability, outcome, sample space, and event
- Classical versus empirical probability
- Conditional probability
- Statistical study
- Central tendency (mean, median, and mode)
- Discrete versus continuous random variables
- Expected value of a random variable
- Mean, variance, and standard deviation
- Empirical rule of standard deviation
- Binomial probability distribution
- Poisson and normal distributions
- Central limit theorem
- Confidence intervals—point versus interval estimates

"Cognitive psychology tells us that the unaided human mind is vulnerable to many fallacies and illusions because of its reliance on its memory for vivid anecdotes rather than systematic statistics."

—Steven Pinker: American experimental psychologist, cognitive scientist, linguist, and popular science author

Uncertainty is inherent in all projects. You need data to make informed decisions in today's complex, uncertain, and fast-changing business environment. You might have access to any amount of data but unless data is properly collected, stored, analyzed, and interpreted, you cannot accomplish informed project decision-making goals. Fortunately, statistics provide us with statistical tools and techniques to achieve our goals.

"Statistics provide managers with more confidence in dealing with uncertainty in spite of the flood of available data, enabling managers to more quickly make smarter decisions and provide more stable leadership to staff relying on them," says John T. Williams of Demand Media. According to John, statistical analysis can enable managers to focus on the big picture and in turn make reasonably correct and unbiased business decisions. In addition, because a picture is worth a thousand words, statistical data plotted graphically can paint a picture of the entire business case and can be used by the project managers to support their arguments while negotiating or when they find themselves cornered.

The purpose of this chapter is to introduce you to the basics of statistical theory. This information will lay the groundwork for Chapter 8, "Statistical Applications in Project Management."

NOTE

Scattered, fragmented, and unorganized *data*, when properly organized and analyzed, becomes information.

Information, when properly interpreted, becomes knowledge.

Knowledge, when properly used, enables informed, effective, and rational *decision-making*.

Statistics Basics

Before you embark on your journey to learn how to apply statistics in your day-to-day decision-making process as a project manager, you must first understand the basics of statistics. The following subsections will introduce you to some common statistical terms and fundamental concepts that are used throughout this book.

Terms to Know

The following are some common statistical terms you should be familiar with:

- **Data:** Raw (unanalyzed) results of measurements and observations constitute data. It can be qualitative or quantitative.

  - **Qualitative data:** Qualitative data refers to a quality or attribute. It is non-numerical and descriptive, which can only be observed or felt but not measured. For example:

    - The project manager surveyed all project stakeholders to assess their satisfaction, and most of the stakeholders responded that they were dissatisfied with the way the project had been managing the stakeholder engagement.

    - The pizza is fresh, hot, and tasty.

    - He is tall.

    - The bag is heavy.

  - **Quantitative data:** Refers to quantity or numbers. It is numerical and can be measured. For example:

    - The project manager surveyed 60 project stakeholders to assess their satisfaction, and 62% of the stakeholders responded that they were dissatisfied with the way the project had been managing the stakeholder engagement for the past 10 months.

    - The pizza is 18 inch, has 14 slices, has a temperature of 160° F, and costs $23.50.

    - He is 6'2" tall.

    - The bag weighs 20 pounds.

- **Information:** Analyzed and organized data becomes information.

- **Statistics:** Statistics is referred to as the methodology of gathering, organizing, analyzing, and interpreting data for decision-making.

- **Population:** This includes all measurements or observations that are of interest; for example, all stakeholders of a project.

- **Sample:** This is a subset of the population—for example, the project stakeholders or subjects selected to take part in a survey.

- **Probability trial:** This is an experiment conducted to collect responses or specific measurements from selected subjects; for example, rolling a die.

- **Outcome or result:** This is an output obtained after conducting a single probability trial; for example, obtaining 6 after rolling a die.

- **Sample space:** This is a collection of all possible outcomes or results of a probability experiment; for example, {1, 2, 3, 4, 5, 6}.
- **Event:** This is a specific set of select outcomes of a probability trial and is a subset of the sample space. For example, {1, 3, 5} is an event representing all odd outcomes of rolling a die experiment with a set of possible outcomes (sample space) given by {1, 2, 3, 4, 5, 6}.

Classical or Theoretical Probability

In classical or theoretical probability, each outcome of a probability experiment or trial is equally likely to occur:

P(Classical) = Number of outcomes in an event / Total number of all outcomes in a sample space

Example Problem 4.1

A probability experiment consists of rolling a die. Find the probability of the occurrence of event {2}, {3}, and {> 3}.

Empirical or Statistical Probability

In empirical or statistical probability, each outcome of a probability experiment or trial is not equally likely to occur; rather, the probability of occurrence of each outcome is dependent upon the result of a probability experiment.

P(Empirical) = Frequency of occurrence of an event / Total frequency of occurrence of all events in a sample space

Example Problem 4.2

To figure out the root cause of the high turnover of the project staff, a project launched an anonymous survey last week to select project stakeholders. The project manager just looked at the latest survey results and found that 120 responses are in so far, as shown in Table 4.1. How likely is it that the next response will indicate that "Limited Term" nature of positions is the main reason behind the high turnover?

Table 4.1   Staff Turnover Reasoning Survey Responses

Response	Frequency of Occurrence, f
Limited Term (LT)	66
Lack of Career Growth Opportunities	38
Micromanagement	16
Sum of all frequencies of occurrence	$\Sigma f = 120$

Probability Range

The range of probabilities includes all probabilities between 0 (0%) and 1 (100%), both extremes inclusive.

$$0 \leq P(E) \leq 1$$

Conditional Probability

Conditional probability is the occurrence of a certain event after the occurrence of another event.

It is denoted by $P(X \mid Y)$, which implies probability of occurrence of event X, given that event Y already occurred.

Example Problem 4.3

The Project Management Office (PMO) in a large organization studied 42 historical projects to understand the correlation between the occurrence of project scope creep and the quality of requirements. Table 4.2 shows the results of the study.

Table 4.2 Project Scope Creep versus Requirements Quality

Scope Creep Status	High Quality Requirements (*Meet all criteria*)[1]	Poor Quality Requirements (*Do not meet one or more criteria*)	Total
Scope Creep Occurrence Significant	4	20	24
Scope Creep Occurrence Insignificant	16	2	18
Total	20	22	42

Calculate the probability that the project will suffer from significant scope creep, given that the project has poor quality requirements.

Designing a Statistical Study

A statistical study involves the collection and analysis of data and can be designed by following these steps:

1. Identify the topic (variable) of interest and domain (population) of study.
2. Develop a detailed plan for collecting data. If you use a sample, make sure the sample is representative of the population.
3. Collect the data.
4. Describe the data using descriptive statistics techniques.
5. Analyze the data using statistical techniques.
6. Interpret the data and make decisions about the population using inferential statistics.
7. Interpret the analysis results.
8. Make decisions based on the interpretation of the analysis results.

Data Collection for a Statistical Study

The type of statistical study is determined by the methodology used for data collection, which can involve surveys, experiments, or observations, or any combination of the three.

Now, let's briefly discuss the three types of data collection techniques:

---

[1] Requirements cover all stakeholders, and they are complete, correct, documented, approved, and signed-off.

Surveys   Most of us can recall receiving occasional junk mail from random marketing companies asking us to answer questionnaires about our household structure, consumer goods consumption habits, tastes and preferences, and our feedback on certain products and services. These questionnaires are what are called statistical surveys. They are used to collect quantitative information (factual or just opinions) from the target population, called a *sample* in statistical language.

Experiments   Experiments are conducted to collect the factual data via measurements of the experiments' results. The sample population is studied for its response to a controlled mix of certain variables. Multiple trials are usually conducted using the following options and the results are remeasured:

> *Option 1:* Keep sample population composition constant and manipulate the variable mix.

> *Option 2:* Keep variable mix constant and manipulate sample population composition.

An example of the use of experiments for data collection is a drug company's experiments to collect data by measuring the target diabetic population's response to the use of a new drug.

Observations   In this technique of data collection, data is collected by simply observing the sample population without any type of influence or experimental manipulation.

For example, data collected from a sample student population to study the correlation between attending the instructor-led PMP[2] exam prep training and passing the exam on the first attempt is observational data collection. The sample student population in this example would involve the students who recently passed their PMP exam in their first attempt. The mode of data collection could be a survey questionnaire given to both students who took the exam without any instructor-led training and those who took the exam after attending a formal instructor-led training program.

Measures of Central Tendency

A measure of central tendency represents a central (typical) value for a probability distribution. It is measured by calculating the mean, median, and mode of a probability distribution.

---

[2] PMP stands for the Project Management Professional exam given by the Project Management Institute (PMI). PMP credentials are globally known and accepted. More information is available at the PMI website: http://www.pmi.org/.

Mean

The mean of a probability distribution is equal to the sum of all possible values in the distribution divided by the total number of values in the distribution. It is often referred to as the arithmetic average of a probability distribution.

If Σx is the sum of all data values in the distribution (for example, $x1 + x2 + x3 + ...$), then

$$\text{Population mean } \mu = \frac{\Sigma x}{N}$$

$$\text{Sample mean } \bar{x} = \frac{\Sigma x}{n}$$

where N = total number of data values in a probability distribution for a population, and n = total number of data values in a probability distribution for a sample.

Example Problem 4.4

The number of project risks reported per month for the past six months are listed here. What is the mean number of risks reported over this period?

72 32 97 27 88 82

The mean has both advantages and disadvantages. It is a reliable measure because all data values in the probability distribution are used to calculate the mean, and it can be used for both continuous and discrete quantitative data. However, the mean can be influenced by outliers (a data value that is far off from the rest of data values) in the probability distribution.

Example Problem 4.5

The number of project risks reported per month for the past six months are listed here:

72 32 97 27 88 482

What is the mean of the number of risks reported over this period?

Median

The median is the value that exists in the middle of an ordered data set:

- For an odd number of values, the median is the middle value.

- For an even number of values, the median is the mean of the two data values in the middle.

Example Problem 4.6

The number of project risks reported per month for the past seven months are listed here. What is the median of the number risks reported over this period?

72 32 97 27 88 82 62

Example Problem 4.7

The number of project risks reported per month for the past six months are listed here. What is the median of the number risks reported over this period?

72 32 97 27 88 82

The median has advantages and disadvantages. It is less affected by outliers and skewed data than the mean and is usually the preferred measure of central tendency when the distribution is not symmetrical. However, the median cannot be identified for categorical nominal data, because it cannot be logically ordered.

Mode

The mode is the value that occurs most frequently in a data set.

If no data value occurs more than once, the data set does not have a mode. If two data values have the same frequency of occurrence in the data set, then each of the two values is a mode and this type of data set is called *bimodal*.

Example Problem 4.8

What is the mode of the following two data sets?

Data set A: 27 32 97 27 88 82

Data set B: 27 32 97 27 88 32

Unlike the median and the mean, the mode can be calculated for both qualitative and quantitative data. However, the mode may not always reflect the central tendency of the probability distribution; for example, consider the following ordered data set:

27 27 32 72 82 88 97

The center of this distribution is 72, but the mode is 27, which is quite lower than the central value 72.

Which Measure of Central Tendency Is the Best—Mean, Median, or Mode?

As you learned earlier, the mean, median, and mode all have pros and cons. However, the mean is considered to be the best measure of central tendency (despite the possibility of outliers in the probability distribution) because it takes into account all the data values. The influence of the outliers on the mean can be reduced by performing regression analysis on the data values.

Weighted Mean

A weighted mean is calculated by using the data values that have different weights assigned to them.

$$\bar{x} = \frac{\Sigma x \cdot w}{\Sigma w}$$

where w is the weight of each data value x.

The PERT (Program Evaluation and Review Technique) three-point estimation technique to estimate the duration of a project activity is an example of weighted mean or average. According to this estimation technique, the estimated duration of a project activity is obtained by calculating the weighted mean of the pessimistic, realistic (most likely), and optimistic values of the duration using the below formula:

Duration = (P + 4R + O) / 6

where P is the pessimistic value, R is the realistic value, and O is the optimistic value. The realistic or most likely estimate is weighted 4 times more than the pessimistic and the optimistic estimates.

Example Problem 4.9

Calculate the estimated duration of a project activity using the three-point estimation technique using the following data:

Pessimistic estimate = 12 days

Most likely estimate = 8 days

Optimistic estimate = 4 days

Range

Range is the difference between the maximum and minimum values in a quantitative data set.

For example, consider the following data set:

27 32 19 31 41 44 22 34 45 27

To find the range of this data set, first sort it in the ascending order.

19 22 27 27 31 32 34 41 44 45

Range = Maximum Value – Minimum Value = 45 – 19 = 26

Probability Distribution

The assignment of a probability to each of the possible outcomes of a random statistical experiment is called a probability distribution.

Random Variable

The outcome of a probability distribution represented in numerical form is called a random variable, denoted by the letter x. An example of a random variable would be the number of support calls a company's call center received in 24 hours.

Discrete versus Continuous Random Variables

Table 4.3 summarizes the difference between a discrete and continuous random variable.

Table 4.3 Discrete versus Continuous Random Variables

Comparison Factors	Discrete	Continuous
Type	**Discrete**	**Continuous**
Characteristics	Possible outcomes are finite and countable (data can take only certain values)	Possible outcomes are infinite and uncountable (data can take any value in an interval)
Probability	$0 \leq P(x) \leq 1$ and $\Sigma P(x) = 1$ Means that the probability of each possible outcome is between 0 and 1 with 0 and 1 inclusive and the sum of all probabilities is equal to 1.	$P(a \leq X \leq b) = \int_a^b fx(x)\,dx$ and $\int_{-\infty}^{\infty} fx(x)\,dx = 1$ Means that the probability of each possible outcome of a continuous variable X is between the interval a and b with a and b inclusive, and it is calculated by integrating its probability density function over the interval $[a,b]$. The sum of all probabilities (the integration of the probability density function) is equal to 1.
Probability Density Function	$P(X = x)$	$\int_a^b fx(x)\,dx$
Examples	Number of cars a car salesperson sells in a day Number of times tails will appear when a coin is tossed six times	Duration of a random telephone call (it could be any number of seconds) Volume of milk in a one gallon bottle (it could be any amount within a gallon)

Example Problem 4.10

A project manager sent out a survey to 50 stakeholders and gave them a score to respond with from 1 to 5 (1 was extremely dissatisfied, 3 was neutral, and 5 was extremely satisfied) for the way the project had been managing the stakeholder engagement. What type of probability distribution would it be? Develop a probability distribution for the random variable x and plot the distribution based on the responses received in Table 4.4.

Table 4.4 Survey Results

Score, X	Response Frequency, f
1	8
2	11
3	14
4	10
5	7

Mean of a Discrete Probability Distribution

The mean of a discrete probability distribution can be found by multiplying each value of the random variable x by its corresponding probability $P(x)$ and then adding all the products.

It is denoted by the Greek letter μ.

$$\mu = \Sigma x P(x)$$

Variance of a Discrete Probability Distribution

The variance of a discrete probability distribution, denoted by σ^2, can be found by using this formula:

$$\sigma^2 = \Sigma (x - \mu)^2 P(x)$$

Standard Deviation of a Discrete Probability Distribution

The standard deviation of a discrete probability distribution, denoted by σ, can be found by taking the square root of the variance.

$$\sigma = \sqrt{\sigma^2}$$

Example Problem 4.11

A project manager sent out a survey to 50 stakeholders and gave them a score to respond with from 1 to 5 (1 was extremely dissatisfied, 3 was neutral, and 5 was extremely satisfied) for the way the project had been managing the stakeholder engagement. Find the mean, variance, and standard deviation of the probability distribution based on the responses received in Table 4.5.

Table 4.5 Survey Results

Score, X	Response Frequency, f
1	8
2	11
3	14
4	10
5	7

Expected Value of a Random Variable

The mean value of a random variable is known as its expected value (EV).

For a discrete random variable, EV can be calculated by adding the products of all possible values of that random variable by their corresponding probabilities of occurrence.

$$E(X) = \mu = \Sigma x P(x)$$

For a continuous random variable, EV can be calculated by integrating the products of all possible values of that random variable by their corresponding probability densities $f(x)$ of occurrence.

$$E(x) = \int_{-\infty}^{\infty} x(fx)\,dx$$

EV can help a project manager make an optimal decision (choice) in an uncertain environment.

Example Problem 4.12

The number of project risks (probability density of random variable x) submitted to the risk database each month is given by Table 4.6.

Table 4.6 Probability Density of Random Variable P(x)

Value of Random Variable, x	Probability Density of Random Variable, P(x)
0	0.05
4	0.10
8	0.17

Value of Random Variable, x	Probability Density of Random Variable, $P(x)$
10	0.28
14	0.20
16	0.12
20	0.08

Find the number of risks that the risk manager should expect to be submitted each month.

Example Problem 4.13

Sigma PMC, a project management consulting company, is looking to buy a projector for its training center. The price of the brand-new projector that the company wants to buy is $800. To save money, the company president John Gill decides to buy the projector through a raffle sale conducted by the State of California surplus inventory warehouse. Twenty raffle tickets are available to buy at $20 each for drawings of three projectors at $600, $400, and $200, respectively. John buys one ticket. What is the expected value of his gain?

Mean, Deviation, Variance, and Standard Deviation of the Population

To calculate the mean of the population data values, you use

$$\mu = \frac{\Sigma x}{N}$$

where N = total number of values in the population data set.

Deviation of Each Data Value of the Population

The deviation of each data value of the population is the difference between any data value of the population and the mean of all values in the population data set.

$$\sigma = x - \mu$$

Population variance is

$$\sigma^2 = \frac{\Sigma(x - \mu)^2}{N}$$

Population standard deviation is

$$\sigma = \sqrt{\frac{\Sigma(x - \mu)^2}{N}}$$

Example Problem 4.14

The contract manager of a project received bids for a project management tool as follows. Find the mean, population variance, and standard deviation of the bids.

45 48 49 42 47 (in thousands)

Mean, Deviation, Variance, and Standard Deviation of the Sample

To calculate the mean of a sample, use

$$\bar{x} = \frac{\Sigma x}{n}$$

where n = total number of values in the sample data set.

For deviation of each value of the sample data set, use

$$x - \bar{x}$$

And for variance, use

$$s^2 = \frac{\Sigma(x - \bar{x})^2}{n - 1}$$

To calculate the standard deviation, use

$$s = \sqrt{\frac{\Sigma(x-\bar{x})^2}{n-1}}$$

Standard Deviation Empirical Rule (or 68 – 95 – 99.7 Rule)

The standard deviation for data with a symmetrical distribution (bell-shaped curve, as shown in Figure 4.1) exhibits that

- Approximately 68% of the data falls within one standard deviation from the mean.
- Approximately 95% of the data falls within two standard deviations from the mean.
- Approximately 99.7% of the data falls within three standard deviations from the mean.

Standard Score (or Z-Score)

Denoted by z, Standard or z-score = (Data Value – Mean of all Data Values in the distribution) / Standard Deviation:

$$z = \frac{(x-\mu)}{\sigma}$$

Example Problem 4.15

The average monthly PMO office supplies expense is $450 with a standard deviation of $75. What is the z-score corresponding to an expense of $850?

Mean, Variance, and Standard Deviation of a Binomial Distribution

The following are the characteristics of a binomial distribution:

- A binomial experiment involves a fixed number of trials and all trials are independent of each other.
- Each trial has only two outcomes: a success or a failure.

- A success is equally likely for each of the trials.
- A random variable is used to track the number of successful trials.

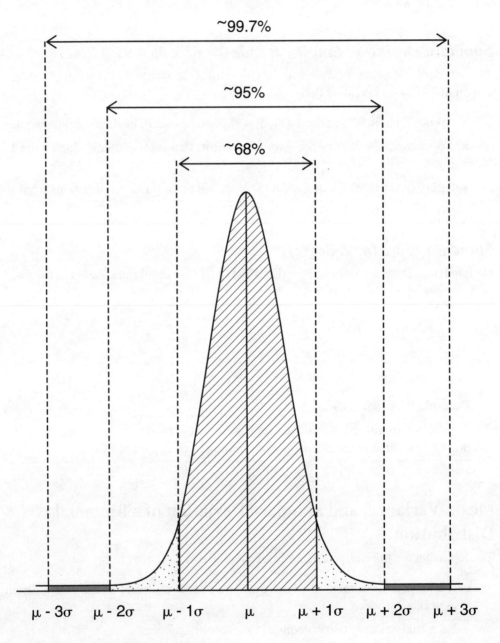

Figure 4.1 Standard Deviation Empirical Rule

Example Problem 4.16

About 10% of the project team members work at least one hour overtime every day. The project manager randomly selects seven team members. What is the probability that exactly two team members work at least one hour overtime every day?

In a binomial experiment, if

> the number of times the trial is repeated is denoted by *n*, and
>
> the probability of success in one trial is *p* = *P(Success)*, and
>
> the probability of failure in one trial is *q* = *P(Failure)*

then

> **Mean** (Binomial) is denoted by $\mu = np$,
>
> **Variance** (Binomial) is denoted by $\sigma^2 - npq$, and
>
> **Standard Deviation** (Binomial) is denoted by $\sigma = \sqrt{npq}$

Example Problem 4.17

Over the past six months, 26% of the project tasks were observed to be completed late. Assuming 20 working days in the month of March, find the mean, variance, and standard deviation for the number of late tasks in March.

Poisson Distribution

The following are the characteristics of a Poisson distribution:

- The experiment in a Poisson experiment involves counting the number of times an event would occur in an interval of area, volume, or time.
- The event is equally likely to occur for each of the intervals.
- The number of occurrences in one interval has no dependency on the number of occurrences in other intervals.

$$P(x) = \frac{\mu^x \cdot e^{-\mu}}{x!}$$

where, $e \sim= 2.718$ and μ = mean of the total number of occurrences

Example Problem 4.18

The average (mean) number of late project tasks per month during the last quarter is 12. What is the probability that 10 project tasks will be late in any given month?

Normal Distribution

Normal distribution is the most important and most commonly used continuous probability distribution in statistical analysis. According to Larson and Farber (2011), "If a random variable x is normally distributed, you can find the probability that x will fall in a given interval by calculating the area under the normal curve for that interval."

The following are the characteristics of a normal distribution:

- The bell-shaped normal curve is symmetric about the mean μ.
- The total area under the normal curve is equal to one.
- The mean, mode, and median of a normal distribution are equal.
- The normal curve exhibits maximum peak at the mean and slopes down as it moves away from the mean. It appears to be touching the x-axis as it keeps moving away from the mean but it never does touch the x-axis.

Figure 4.2 depicts the graph of a normal distribution (also known as the normal curve).

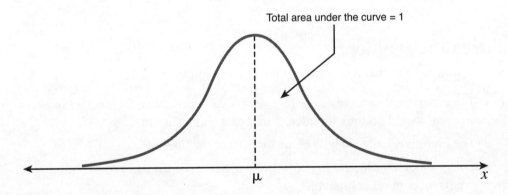

Figure 4.2 Normal Distribution

Standard Normal Distribution

A normal distribution that has mean 0 and standard deviation 1 is called a standard normal distribution. The following formula converts the value of random variable x of normal distribution into a z-score for use in the standard normal distribution.

z = (Data Value – Mean of all Data Values in the distribution) / Standard Deviation

$$z = \frac{(x - \mu)}{\sigma}$$

The following are the characteristics of the standard normal distribution:

- The cumulative area under the standard normal curve is never 0 but very close to 0 when the z-score is close to (–3.49).

- The cumulative area under the standard normal curve is close to 1 when the z-score is close to 3.49.

- As the z-scores increase, the cumulative area also increases.

- At z-score $z = 0$, the cumulative area is 0.5.

Figure 4.3 illustrates these characteristics of the standard normal distribution.

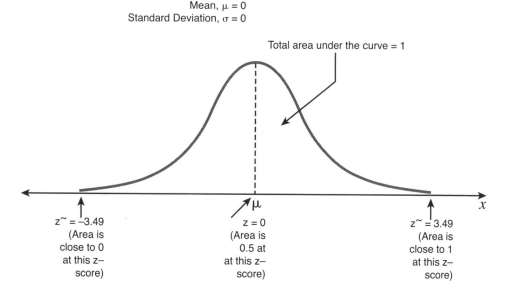

Figure 4.3 Standard Normal Distribution

You can use the standard normal table (see Appendix A, "Standard Normal Distribution Table") to find the cumulative area under a standard normal curve for any z-value. Figure 4.4 shows an excerpt of the standard normal table.

STANDARD NORMAL DISTRIBUTION: Table Values Represent AREA to the LEFT of the Z score									
Z	.00	.01	.02	.03	.04	.05	.06	.07	.08
0.0	.50000	.50399	.50798	.51197	.51595	.51994	.52392	.52790	.53188
0.1	.53983	.54380	.54776	.55172	.55567	.55962	.56356	.56749	.57142
0.2	.57926	.58317	.58706	.59095	.59483	.59871	.60257	.60642	.61026
0.3	.61791	.62172	.62552	.62930	.63307	.63683	.64058	.64431	.64803
0.4	.65542	.65910	.66276	.66640	.67003	.67364	.67724	.68082	.68439
0.5	.69146	.69497	.69847	.70194	.70540	.70884	.71226	.71566	.71904
0.6	.72575	.72907	.73237	.73565	.73891	.74215	.74537	.74857	.75175
0.7	.75804	.76115	.76424	.76730	.77035	.77337	.77637	.77935	.78230
0.8	.78814	.79103	.79389	.79673	.79955	.80234	.80511	.80785	.81057

Figure 4.4 Excerpt of the Standard Normal Table

Example Problem 4.19

The data published by a state information technology department in the United States indicates that typical data centers refresh their computing infrastructure on average every 5 years with a standard deviation of 1 year. What is the probability that one of the data centers will refresh its infrastructure after 4 years of usage? Assume the probability distribution to be normal.

The Central Limit Theorem

If sample size $n \geq 30$, with population mean = μ and standard deviation = σ then the sampling distribution of the sample means will be approximately equal to a normal distribution. The quality of the approximation will be directly proportional to the size of the sample.

If the population is already normally distributed, then the sampling distribution of the sample means is normally distributed for all sample sizes:

$$\mu_{\bar{x}} = \mu$$

Variance $\sigma_{\bar{x}}^2 = \dfrac{\sigma^2}{n}$

The standard deviation (also known as standard error of the mean) is

$$\sigma_{\bar{x}} = \frac{\sigma}{\sqrt{n}}$$

Confidence Intervals

A confidence interval is an interval estimate with range of values specifying probability or confidence that the value of a parameter of interest lies within it.

Point Estimate versus Interval Estimate

A point estimate of a parameter of interest is a single value of a statistic,[3] whereas an interval estimate specifies a range for the probability of having the parameter of interest within it as shown in Figure 4.5. The point estimate is more accurate.

For example, the point estimate of the population mean μ is the sample mean $\bar{x}$.

An interval estimate may contain a point estimate. For example, consider the following range of values as the interval estimate. If the value of the point estimate is 6.5, it is within the interval estimate.

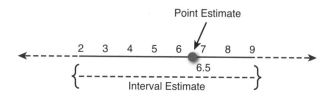

Figure 4.5 Point versus Interval Estimate

Level of Confidence

The level of confidence, denoted by the letter c, indicates the probability that an interval estimate contains the parameter of interest. For example, if the level of confidence is given to be 78%, then there is a 78% probability that the parameter of interest (the population mean μ) lies in the interval.

Sampling Error = point estimate $\bar{x}$ – population mean μ

Margin of Error, denoted by E = error tolerance (also known as maximum error of estimate)

$$E = z_c \sigma_{\bar{x}}$$

$$E = \frac{z_c \sigma^*}{\sqrt{n}}$$

---

[3] A single piece of data in a large collection of data values obtained from a statistical study is called a *statistic*.

Note: *Population standard deviation σ can be replaced with the sample standard deviation, s if sample size $n \geq 30$.

Identifying Confidence Intervals

The procedure to identify the confidence interval for the population mean depends on the sample size and/or the availability or unavailability of the population standard deviation σ.

To find the confidence interval when the sample size is large ($n \geq 30$), follow these steps:

1. Find $\bar{x}$, the sample statistic using (if σ is not available):

$$\bar{x} = \frac{\Sigma x}{n}$$

2. If population standard deviation σ is available, use it; otherwise, substitute it by the sample standard deviation:

$$s = \sqrt{\frac{\Sigma(x - \bar{x})^2}{n-1}}$$

3. Using the z-table (standard normal table) in Appendix A, find the critical value z_c for the given confidence interval.

4. Calculate the margin of error:

$$E = z_c \frac{\sigma}{\sqrt{n}}$$

5. Finally, find the left and right extremes (end points) of the confidence interval $(\bar{x} - E)$ and $(\bar{x} + E)$, respectively.

Example Problem 4.20

A project manager wants to estimate the average (mean) duration of all project activities. In a random sample of 40 activities, the mean duration is found to be 360 days. The standard deviation is 3 days, and the population is normally distributed. Develop a 90% confidence interval of the population mean duration.

How do you find the confidence interval when the sample size is small ($n < 30$)?

The procedural steps are very similar to the previous case with large sample size ($n \geq 30$). The key differences are that the small sample case uses degrees of freedom (d.f.) and the t-table to calculate the critical value t_c.

1. Find $\bar{x}$ and s, the sample statistics, using the following:

$$\bar{x} = \frac{\Sigma x}{n}$$

$$s = \sqrt{\frac{\Sigma(x - \bar{x})^2}{n-1}}$$

2. Identify the degrees of freedom using this:

   d.f. = n – 1

3. Using the t-table (standard normal table) in Appendix A, find the critical value t_c for the given confidence interval.

4. Calculate the margin of error:

$$E = t_c \frac{s}{\sqrt{n}}$$

5. Finally, find the left and right extremes (end points) of the confidence interval ($\bar{x} - E$) and ($\bar{x} + E$), respectively.

Summary

The mind map in Figure 4.6 summarizes the overview of the data-driven decision-making process.

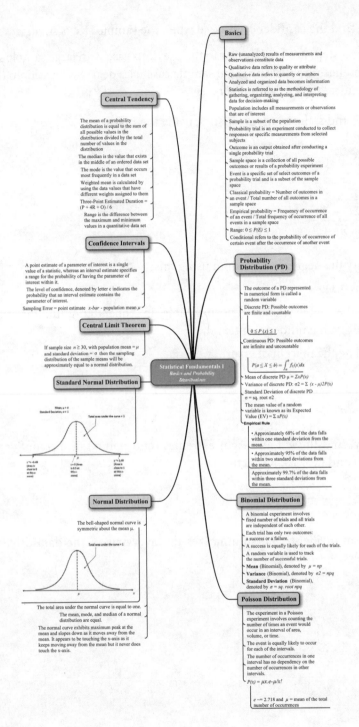

Figure 4.6 Statistical Fundamentals I Summary

Key Terms

Binomial Distribution

Central Limit Theorem

Central Tendency

Classical Probability

Conditional Probability

Confidence Interval

Continuous Random Variable

Data

Degrees of Freedom

Discrete Random Variable

Empirical Probability

Empirical Rule

Event

Expected Value

Interval Estimate

Information

Knowledge

Level of Confidence

Outcome

PERT

Point Estimate

Poisson Distribution

Population

Probability Trial

Qualitative Data

Quantitative Data

Sample

Sample Space

Standard Deviation

Standard Normal Distribution

Statistics

Variance

Weighted Mean

Solutions to Example Problems

Example Problem 4.1 Solution

$P(2) = 1/6 = 0.167$

$P(3) = 1/6 = 0.167$

$P(>3) = P(\{4, 5, 6\}) = 3/6 = 0.5$

Example Problem 4.2 Solution

$P(Limited\ Term) = f / \Sigma f = 66/120 = 0.55\ (55\%)$

Example Problem 4.3 Solution

Applying conditional probability $P(X \mid Y)$:

Given: The project has poor quality requirements.

There are 22 total projects in the study that have poor quality requirements out of which 20 projects have significant scope creep occurrence.

Thus, $P(X | Y) = P$(High Scope Creep | Poor Quality Requirements) $= 20/22 = 0.91$ (91%)

This implies that the project is 91% likely to suffer scope creep, given that it has poor quality requirements.

Example Problem 4.4 Solution

The sum of monthly project risks is

$\Sigma x = 72 + 32 + 97 + 27 + 88 + 82 = 398$

You can find the mean number of risks by dividing the sum of risks reported over six months by the total number of data values (equal to the number of months in the observation period).

$$\bar{x} = \frac{\Sigma x}{n}$$

Thus, the mean number of risks = 398/6 ~= 66

Example Problem 4.5 Solution

The sum of monthly project risks is

$\Sigma x = 72 + 32 + 97 + 27 + 88 + 482 = 798$

You can find the mean number of risks by dividing the sum of risks reported over six months by the total number of data values (equal to the number of months in the observation period).

$$\bar{x} = \frac{\Sigma x}{n}$$

Thus, the mean number of risks = 798/6 = 133

In this example, 482 is an outlier, which causes the mean to be skewed toward it. The mean 133 is far off from the majority of the data values in the sample.

Example Problem 4.6 Solution

First order the values:

27 32 62 72 82 88 97

This data set has an odd number of values. The median in this ordered data set is the middle value, which is 72.

Example Problem 4.7 Solution

First order the values:

27 32 62 72 82 88

This data set has an even number of values. The median in this ordered data set is the mean of the two data values in the middle, which is

$= (62 + 72)/2 = 67$

Example Problem 4.8 Solution

First order the data sets:

Data set A: 27 27 32 82 88 97

Data set B: 27 27 32 32 88 97

Because the mode is the most commonly occurring value in a probability distribution, the mode for data set A is 27 (occurring twice), and data set B is bimodal with two modes 27 and 32 (both occur twice).

Example Problem 4.9 Solution

Estimate Type	Value, x	Weight, w	x.w
Pessimistic	12	1 (0.17%)	12*1 = 12
Most Likely	8	4 (0.66%)	8*4 = 32
Optimistic	4	1 (0.17%)	4*1 = 4
		$\Sigma w = 6$ (100%)	$\Sigma x.w = 12 + 32 + 4 = 48$

Estimated duration,

$$\bar{x} = \frac{\Sigma x \cdot w}{\Sigma w}$$

$= 48/6 = 8$ days

Example Problem 4.10 Solution

This probability distribution would be discrete due to the finite number of responses. Follow these steps:

1. Find the relative frequency of each score by dividing the frequency of each score by the total number of stakeholders who participated in the survey.

   $P(1) = 8/50 = 0.16$

   $P(2) = 11/50 = 0.22$

   $P(3) = 14/50 = 0.28$

   $P(4) = 10/50 = 0.20$

   $P(5) = 7/50 = 0.14$

   The following table shows the probability distribution:

x	1	2	3	4	5
P(x)	0.16	0.22	0.28	0.20	0.14

2. Validate the discrete probability distribution.

   This is a valid discrete probability distribution because $0 \leq P(x) \leq 1$, and

   $\Sigma P(x) = 0.16 + 0.22 + 0.28 + 0.20 + 0.14 = 1$

3. Plot the distribution (depicted in Figure 4.7).

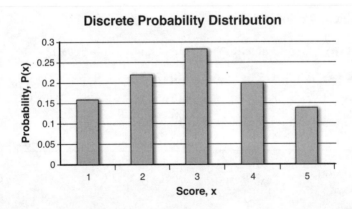

Figure 4.7 Plotting the Discrete Probability Distribution

Example Problem 4.11 Solution

Find the relative frequency of each score by dividing the frequency of each score by the total number of stakeholders who participated in the survey.

$P(1) = 8/50 = 0.16$

$P(2) = 11/50 = 0.22$

$P(3) = 14/50 = 0.28$

$P(4) = 10/50 = 0.20$

$P(5) = 7/50 = 0.14$

The following table shows the probability distribution and other calculations:

X	1	2	3	4	5
$P(x)$	0.16	0.22	0.28	0.20	0.14
$xP(x)$	0.16	0.44	0.84	0.80	0.70
$(x - \mu)^2$	$(1 - 2.94)^2 = 3.76$	$(2 - 2.94)^2 = 0.88$	$(3 - 2.94)^2 = 0$	$(4 - 2.94)^2 = 1.12$	$(5 - 2.94)^2 = 4.24$
$(x - \mu)^2 P(x)$	0.60	0.19	0	0.22	0.59

Mean $\mu = \Sigma xP(x) = 0.16 + 0.44 + 0.84 + 0.80 + 0.70 = 2.94$

Variance $\sigma^2 = \Sigma(x - \mu)^2 P(x) = 0.60 + 0.19 + 0 + 0.22 + 0.59 = 1.6$

Standard Deviation $\sigma = \sqrt{\sigma^2} = \sqrt{1.6} = 1.26$

Example Problem 4.12 Solution

Because X is a discrete random variable, the expected value is given by:

$E(X) = \mu = \Sigma xP(x)$

$E(X) = (0 \times 0.01) + (4 \times 0.10) + (8 \times 0.17) + (10 \times 0.28) + (14 \times 0.20) + (16 \times 0.12) + (20 \times 0.08)$

$E(X) = 10.88 \sim= 11$ risks per month

Example Problem 4.13 Solution

Follow these steps:

1. Find the gain for each possible outcome.

    Gain for the $600 projector = $800 – $500 = $300

    Gain for the $400 projector = $800 – $400 = $400

    Gain for the $200 projector = $800 – $200 = $600

    Gain for winning no raffle = $0 – $20 = –$20

2. Find probability density for each possible outcome

Gain, x	$300	$400	$600	–$20
P(x)	1/20	1/20	1/20	17/20

3. Find the expected value:

$E(X) = \mu = \Sigma x P(x)$

$E(X) = (\$300 \times 1/20) + (\$400 \times 1/20) + (\$600 \times 1/20) + (-\$20 \times 17/20)$

$E(X) = \$48$

Thus, John should expect to gain an average of $48 for each raffle ticket he buys.

Example Problem 4.14 Solution

Here $N = 5$.

Mean can be calculated using the formula:

$$\mu = \frac{\Sigma x}{N}$$

$$= 231/5 = 46.2$$

Population Variance

Bid, x	Deviation squared, $(x - \mu)^2$
45	$(45 - 46.2)^2 = 1.44$
48	$(48 - 46.2)^2 = 3.24$
49	$(49 - 46.2)^2 = 7.84$
42	$(42 - 46.2)^2 = 17.64$
47	$(47 - 46.2)^2 = 0.64$

$$\sigma^2 = \frac{\Sigma(x - \mu)^2}{N}$$

$$= (1.44 + 3.24 + 7.84 + 17.64 + 0.64) / 5$$

$$= 6.16 \text{ or } 6.16 \times 1000 = \$6,160$$

Population Standard Deviation can be calculated with the following formula:

$$\sigma = \sqrt{\dfrac{\Sigma(x-\mu)^2}{N}}$$

$$= \sqrt{6.16} = 2.48 \text{ or } 2.48 \times 1000 = \$2,480$$

Example Problem 4.15 Solution

$z = (x - \mu) / \sigma = (850 - 450) / 125 = 3.2$

Example Problem 4.16 Solution

This is an example of a binomial experiment, where:

The number of times the trial is repeated is $n = 7$.

The probability of success in one trial is $p = P(Success) = 0.10$.

The random variable to track the number of successes is $x = 2$.

The probability of this random variable can be calculated using the binomial probability distribution table (provided in Appendix C) as shown in Figure 4.8.

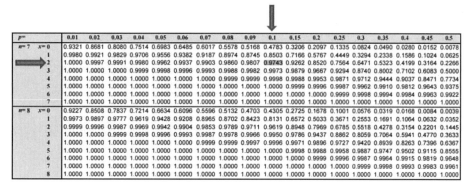

Figure 4.8 An Excerpt from the Binomial Probability Distribution Table

The probability that exactly two team members work at least one hour overtime every day = 0.9743 = 97.43%.

Example Problem 4.17 Solution

Mean: $\mu = np = 20 \times 0.26 = 5.2$

Variance: $\sigma^2 = npq = 20 \times 0.26 \times 0.74 = 3.85$

Standard Deviation: $\sigma = \sqrt{npq} = \sqrt{3.85} = 1.96$

This means that on average, approximately 5 project tasks were observed to be late in March with a standard deviation of approximately 2 tasks.

Example Problem 4.18 Solution

Here, μ (mean) = 12 and variable $x = 10$.

Applying the Poisson distribution formula,

$$P(x) = \frac{\mu^x \cdot e^{-\mu}}{x!}$$

$P(10) = 12^{10}.(2.718)^{-12}/10! = 0.105$ (or 10.5%)

Example Problem 4.19 Solution

$\mu = 5, \sigma = 1, x = 4$

Figure 4.9 presents the plot for this normal distribution.

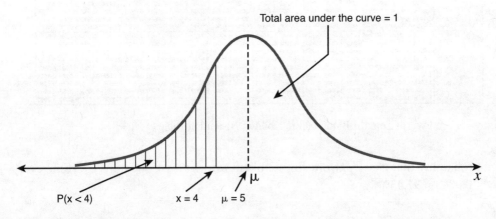

Figure 4.9 Normal Distribution

Using the following formula, convert the variable x into a z-score for standard normal distribution.

$$z = \frac{(x-\mu)}{\sigma}$$

$$= (4 - 5) / 1 = -1.0$$

For standard normal distribution, $\mu = 0$ and $\sigma = 1$. Figure 4.10 presents the plot for this standard normal distribution.

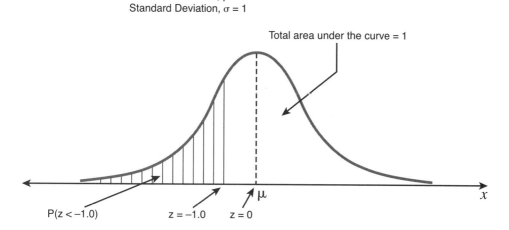

Figure 4.10 Standard Normal Distribution

Using the standard normal distribution z-table shown in Figure 4.11, the cumulative area under the standard normal curve is 0.15866.

STANDARD NORMAL DISTRIBUTION: Table Values Represent AREA to the LEFT of the Z score.

Z	.00	.01	.02	.03	.04	.05	.06	.07	.08	.09
-3.9	.00005	.00005	.00004	.00004	.00004	.00004	.00004	.00004	.00003	.00003
-3.8	.00007	.00007	.00007	.00006	.00006	.00006	.00006	.00005	.00005	.00005
-3.7	.00011	.00010	.00010	.00010	.00009	.00009	.00008	.00008	.00008	.00008
-3.6	.00016	.00015	.00015	.00014	.00014	.00013	.00013	.00012	.00012	.00011
-3.5	.00023	.00022	.00022	.00021	.00020	.00019	.00019	.00018	.00017	.00017
-3.4	.00034	.00032	.00031	.00030	.00029	.00028	.00027	.00026	.00025	.00024
-3.3	.00048	.00047	.00045	.00043	.00042	.00040	.00039	.00038	.00036	.00035
-3.2	.00069	.00066	.00064	.00062	.00060	.00058	.00056	.00054	.00052	.00050
-3.1	.00097	.00094	.00090	.00087	.00084	.00082	.00079	.00076	.00074	.00071
-3.0	.00135	.00131	.00126	.00122	.00118	.00114	.00111	.00107	.00104	.00100
-2.9	.00187	.00181	.00175	.00169	.00164	.00159	.00154	.00149	.00144	.00139
-2.8	.00256	.00248	.00240	.00233	.00226	.00219	.00212	.00205	.00199	.00193
-2.7	.00347	.00336	.00326	.00317	.00307	.00298	.00289	.00280	.00272	.00264
-2.6	.00466	.00453	.00440	.00427	.00415	.00402	.00391	.00379	.00368	.00357
-2.5	.00621	.00604	.00587	.00570	.00554	.00539	.00523	.00508	.00494	.00480
-2.4	.00820	.00798	.00776	.00755	.00734	.00714	.00695	.00676	.00657	.00639
-2.3	.01072	.01044	.01017	.00990	.00964	.00939	.00914	.00889	.00866	.00842
-2.2	.01390	.01355	.01321	.01287	.01255	.01222	.01191	.01160	.01130	.01101
-2.1	.01786	.01743	.01700	.01659	.01618	.01578	.01539	.01500	.01463	.01426
-2.0	.02275	.02222	.02169	.02118	.02068	.02018	.01970	.01923	.01876	.01831
-1.9	.02872	.02807	.02743	.02680	.02619	.02559	.02500	.02442	.02385	.02330
-1.8	.03593	.03515	.03438	.03362	.03288	.03216	.03144	.03074	.03005	.02938
-1.7	.04457	.04363	.04272	.04182	.04093	.04006	.03920	.03836	.03754	.03673
-1.6	.05480	.05370	.05262	.05155	.05050	.04947	.04846	.04746	.04648	.04551
-1.5	.06681	.06552	.06426	.06301	.06178	.06057	.05938	.05821	.05705	.05592
-1.4	.08076	.07927	.07780	.07636	.07493	.07353	.07215	.07078	.06944	.06811
-1.3	.09680	.09510	.09342	.09176	.09012	.08851	.08691	.08534	.08379	.08226
-1.2	.11507	.11314	.11123	.10935	.10749	.10565	.10383	.10204	.10027	.09853
-1.1	.13567	.13350	.13136	.12924	.12714	.12507	.12302	.12100	.11900	.11702
-1.0	(.15866)	.15625	.15386	.15151	.14917	.14686	.14457	.14231	.14007	.13786
-0.9	.18406	.18141	.17879	.17619	.17361	.17106	.16853	.16602	.16354	.16109

Figure 4.11 An Excerpt from Standard Normal Distribution z-Table

Thus, $P(x < 4) = P(z < -1.00) \sim= 0.1587$

Example Problem 4.20 Solution

1. Find $\bar{x}$, the sample statistic, using (if σ is not available):

   N/A as σ is available

2. If population standard deviation σ is available, use it; otherwise, substitute it by the sample standard deviation:

   σ is available = 3

3. Using the z-table (standard normal table) in Appendix A, find the critical value z_c for the given confidence interval as shown in Figure 4.12.

   $z_c = 1.645$

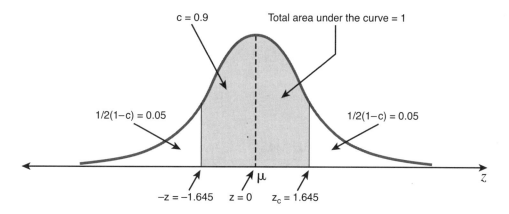

Figure 4.12 Critical Values for Standard Normal Distribution

4. Calculate the margin of error:

$$E = z_c \frac{\sigma}{\sqrt{n}}$$

$$= 1.645 \, (3/\sqrt{40}) \sim= 0.78$$

5. Finally, find the left and right extremes (end points) of the confidence interval $(\bar{x} - E)$ and $(\bar{x} + E)$, respectively.

$$\bar{x} - E = 360 - 0.78 = 359.22$$

$$\bar{x} + E = 360 + 0.78 = 360.78$$

Point estimate $\mu = 360$.

Because $359.22 < \mu < 360.78$, there is 90% confidence that the mean duration of all project activities lies between 359.22 and 360.78.

Chapter Review and Discussion Questions

1. Define *data, information,* and *knowledge.*

2. Give two examples each of qualitative and quantitative data.

3. The PMO of an organization launched an anonymous survey to select project stakeholders to gauge their level of satisfaction. A week after the survey was launched, the PMO manager looked at the responses received thus far and found

that 46 responses had been received as shown in the following table. How likely is it that the next response will be "Most Satisfied?"

Response	Frequency of Occurrence, f
Most Satisfied	16
Neutral	18
Least Satisfied	12
	$\Sigma f = 46$

4. What is central tendency? Out of mean, median, and mode, which one is the best for decision-making?

5. Find the mean, median, and mode of the following data set:

   22 22 31 67 34 78 79

6. Find the estimated duration of a project activity with the following data:

   ■ Pessimistic duration = 9 days

   ■ Realistic duration = 6 days

   ■ Optimistic duration = 3 days

7. Differentiate between discrete and continuous random variables. Provide one example for each.

8. Singh Construction, LLC is competing for one of the three California state government projects A, B, and C. The costs to prepare these three bids for projects A, B, and C are $1,500, $1,200, and $1,000, respectively. All three contracts are of one-year duration each. The cost to enter the bidding contest is $100 for each bid. According to the rules of the bidding contest, a company can bid on any number of projects but can win only one contract. Singh Construction is submitting bids for all three projects and is hoping to win the bid for one of them. The expected net earnings from these three contracts A, B, and C are $200,000, $160,000, and $100,000, respectively. Calculate the expected value of the company's gain.

9. Calculate the mean, population variance, and standard deviation for the following data set:

   55 48 49 52 47 50

10. What is the empirical rule of standard deviation?

11. About 30% of the project tasks have at least two-day slack.[4] The project manager randomly selects 10 tasks. What is the probability that exactly 4 tasks have at least two-day slack?

12. Describe the characteristics of a Poisson distribution.

13. The average number of cumulative project overtime hours per month during the last quarter is 12. What is the probability that there is 10 hours' worth of overtime in any given month?

14. What is the mean and standard deviation of a standard normal distribution?

15. Describe the central limit theorem. Is a bigger and bigger sample size a good thing per this theorem?

16. What is an interval estimate?

17. A project manager wants to estimate the average (mean) overtime hours for each month. In a random sample of 20 project team members, the mean number of overtime hours per month is found to be 80. The standard deviation is 10 hours, and the population is normally distributed. Construct a 90% confidence interval of the population mean duration.

Bibliography

Amiryar, H. (2014). "PERT Three Point Estimation Technique." Retrieved March 20, 2015, from http://www.pmdocuments.com/2012/09/17/pert-three-point-estimation-technique/

Anbari, F.T. (1997). *Quantitative Methods for Project Management*. New York: International Institute for Learning, Inc.

Goodpasture, J. C. (2003). *Quantitative Methods in Project Management*. Boca Raton, FL, USA: J. Ross Publishing.

Holsinger, K. (2013). Decision Making Under Uncertainty: Statistical Decision Theory. Retrieved March 22, 2015, from http://darwin.eeb.uconn.edu/eeb310/lecture-notes/decision.pdf

Lane, D., and Ziemer, H. (2014). "What Is Central Tendency?" Retrieved March 23, 2015, from http://onlinestatbook.com/2/summarizing_distributions/what_is_ct.html

Larson, R., and Farber, E. (2011). *Elementary Statistics: Picturing the World*, 5th ed. Upper Saddle River, New Jersey: Pearson.

---

[4] In project management, *slack* (also called *float*) represents the units of time by which a project task can be delayed without impacting either the overall project schedule (called *total float*) or the succeeding tasks (called *free float*).

Pepe. (2002). "Statististical Probability Distribution Tables." Retrieved March 20, 2015, from http://pegasus.cc.ucf.edu/~pepe/Tables

Pinker, S. (2014). "Statistics Quotes." Retrieved March 22, 2015, from http://www.brainyquote.com/quotes/quotes/s/stevenpink547593.html?src=t_statistics

Roberts, D. (2012). "Statistical Studies." Retrieved March 24, 2015, from http://www.regentsprep.org/regents/math/algtrig/ats1/statsurveylesson.htm

Williams, J. (2015). "The Importance of Statistics in Management Decision Making." Retrieved March 24, 2015, from http://smallbusiness.chron.com/importance-statistics-management-decision-making-4589.html

WyzAnt Resources. (2014). "Expected Values of Random Variables." Retrieved March 20, 2015, from http://www.wyzant.com/resources/lessons/math/statistics_and_probability/expected_value

5

Statistical Fundamentals II: Hypothesis, Correlation, and Linear Regression

Learning Objectives

After reading this chapter, you should be familiar with:

- Null and alternative hypotheses
- Types of statistical hypothesis tests
- *z*-test process
- *t*-test process
- Interpretation of hypothesis test–driven decisions
- Correlation and causation
- Linear regression
- Multiple regression

> "Hypothesis tests are procedures for making rational decisions about the reality of effects."
>
> —*David W. Stockburger, Professor at Missouri State University*

Decision-making is part of our day-to-day personal and professional life. For example, choosing an investment portfolio, selecting a project, hiring an employee, or selecting a vendor all require a rational decision for selecting the best possible candidate from several alternatives. If the decision is made without validating the completeness and correctness of the information associated with the selected alternative, it may be a risky and irrational decision. Statistical hypothesis testing allows us not to take the things for granted, rather it makes us validate the claim (alternative) for correctness before making the final decision on it. For data-driven rational decision-making, implementing the appropriate procedures to test an alternative for its likelihood or probability of being successful if selected is imperative.

This chapter provides an introduction to hypothesis testing for the mean, proportions, variance, and standard deviation along with some discussion on the basics of statistical correlation and linear regression.

What Is a Hypothesis?

Merriam-Webster dictionary provides a generic definition of the hypothesis as "an idea or theory that is not proven but that leads to further study or discussion." It refers to a theory that may or may not be true, but generally accepted as highly probable in the absence of the valid factual information, to explain an observed phenomenon. For example, kids who watch too much television lose their ability to concentrate.

A hypothesis is called a *research or scientific hypothesis* when it represents a knowledgeable and testable statement that can be researched or investigated for validity on some point of interest. If an experiment is conducted for investigation, then this hypothesis is called an *experimental hypothesis*. The research or scientific hypothesis generally involves an *if-then* relationship—for example, *if* instructor-led training is taken, *then* the chances of passing the project management professional (PMP) credentials exam will be enhanced.

A *statistical hypothesis* is expressed as a statement associated with various probability distributions and involving statistical parameters such as median, mode, range, mean, variance, standard deviation, etc. It is generally developed by using the research or scientific hypothesis as a baseline. It involves anticipation of the results based on two scenarios: one if the research or scientific hypothesis is true and the other if the research or scientific hypothesis is false. This process leads to two forms of *statistical hypotheses* called the *null hypothesis* (H_0) and the *alternative hypothesis* (H_a), which are explained in the section "Statistical Hypothesis Testing."

Much like a scientific hypothesis does not become a law of nature until it is proven to be correct and valid by repeated testing, a statistical hypothesis is subject to rejection until its acceptability is determined via testing for correctness. "Testing a hypothesis is trying to determine if your observation of some phenomenon is likely to have really occurred based on statistics," says Sirah Dubois, an eHow contributor. The testing method used to test whether a hypothesis is true or false on the basis of statistical inference is called a *statistical hypothesis test*.

Statistical Hypothesis Testing

> "There are two possible outcomes: if the result confirms the hypothesis, then you've made a measurement. If the result is contrary to the hypothesis, then you've made a discovery."
>
> —*Enrico Fermi, Italian scientist*

Before discussing statistical hypothesis testing, let's first look at a hypothesis test because there is difference between *test* and *testing*. While *testing* is a process, a *test* is a single event within the overall testing process. A testing process may contain multiple tests.

Hypothesis Test

A hypothesis test is a statistical test used to confirm that there is enough evidence in a data sample to prove the correctness or incorrectness of a claim or to infer that a condition is true for the population as a whole. A hypothesis test is also known as a test of significance because it tests the observed data for its statistical significance.

Look at the following example scenario and explanation for more clarification.

> *According to the survey posted by a staffing firm on its website, the mean annual salary of a business analyst in the Houston, Texas, area is $52,000.*

To test this claim or hypothesis, a data sample can be taken that includes some subjects in the Houston, Texas, area. If the data sample mean is found to differ enough from the mean posted by the staffing firm, you can conclude that the staffing company's hypothesis is wrong.

Hypothesis Testing

Statistical hypothesis testing (also known as confirmatory data analysis) is used to determine whether the actual experimental findings are able to refute the perceptions made via educational guesses. In other words, hypothesis testing involves the use of statistical tests to determine the probability of whether an unproven claim or hypothesis is true or not. Two hypotheses are used—one that represents the claim and the other that contradicts that claim. If one of the hypotheses is determined to be true, the other must be false and vice versa.

The comprehensive hypothesis testing process involves the following seven logical steps:

1. State the null hypothesis (H_0) and the alternative hypothesis (H_a).
2. Specify the level of significance (α).

---

3. Determine the critical values (z_c or t_c).

4. Calculate the test statistic.

5. Determine the p-value.

6. Make a decision.

7. Draw a conclusion.

The following section discusses these steps in more detail.

Step 1: State the Null Hypothesis (H_0) and the Alternative Hypothesis (H_a)

The first step in a hypothesis testing process is formulating the null and alternative hypotheses.

The *null hypothesis* (H_0) assumes that the observations are the result of pure chance. It is characterized by containing a statement of equality ≤, =, or ≥. The notation H_0 is pronounced as *H naught*.

The *alternative hypothesis* (H_a) is a complement of the null hypothesis, which means if H_0 is false, H_a will be true and vice versa. It is characterized by containing a statement of inequality >, ≠, or <. The notation H_a is pronounced as *H sub-a*.

There are some errors associated with hypothesis test–based decision-making. Commonly, the hypothesis test is begun assuming that the equality condition in the null hypothesis is true. After the test is complete, a decision is made either to reject the null hypothesis or to fail to reject the null hypothesis. Because this decision is made based on the test of a data sample (not of the entire population), the decision made may be erroneous.

The two types of errors associated with this decision-making are

- **Type I error:** This type of error occurs when a "true" null hypothesis is rejected.

- **Type II error:** This type of error occurs when a "false" null hypothesis is not rejected.

The American Legal System Uses Hypothesis Testing to Make Decisions in Criminal Cases

Null hypothesis (H_0): The defendant is assumed innocent until proven guilty. **Alternative hypothesis (H_a):** The jury tries to prove that beyond a reasonable doubt, the defendant is guilty.

"Beyond a reasonable doubt," if the jury produces the guilty verdict, the null hypothesis is rejected; otherwise, the jury fails to reject the null hypothesis.

The American legal system works on the assumption that convicting an innocent person (example of type I error) is more harmful than not convicting the guilty (example of type II error).

Step 2: Specify the Level of Significance (α)

In this step you select a level of significance or a probability threshold below which the null hypothesis can be rejected. Common values are 5% and 1%.

Denoted by the Greek letter α, the level of significance signifies the probability of rejecting a null hypothesis that otherwise is true. In other words, it is the probability of making a type I error.

Usually, a small value (such as 0.01, 0.05, or 0.10) is used as the level of significance.

Step 3: Determine the Critical Values (z_c or t_c)

The distribution of the test statistic under the null hypothesis contains points beyond which the null hypothesis will be rejected. These points are called the *critical values* of the test statistic.

- The critical value z_c corresponds to the standardized test statistic z, where sample size n is large ($n >= 30$).
- The critical value t_c corresponds to the standardized test statistic t, where sample size n is small ($n < 30$).

Step 4: Calculate the Test Statistic

Calculate a test statistic to test the null hypothesis.

After stating the null and alternative hypotheses and determining the level of significance, take a random sample from the population and calculate the sample statistics.

The statistic (from sample) that is compared with the parameter in the null hypothesis (from population) is called the *test statistic*.

Step 5: Determine the p-Value

Step 5 involves determining the *p-value* or the *probability value,* which is the probability of obtaining a test statistic that is at least as significant as the one being observed, provided the null hypothesis is true. The magnitude of the p-value is inversely proportional to the evidence against the null hypothesis; that is, the larger the p-value, the weaker the evidence against the null hypothesis and vice versa.

Before you determine the p-value, you need to understand the nature of the statistic test being performed, which could be one of the following three types:

- Left-tailed test
- Right-tailed test
- Two-tailed test

The directional attribute of the tail of the test is determined by the region under the sample probability distribution curve that pertains to the alternative hypothesis H_a (remember, the alternative hypothesis favors the rejection of the null hypothesis).

In a left-tailed type of test, the H_a region is toward the left-hand side of the test statistic, as shown in Figure 5.1.

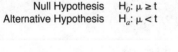

Null Hypothesis $H_0: \mu \geq t$
Alternative Hypothesis $H_a: \mu < t$

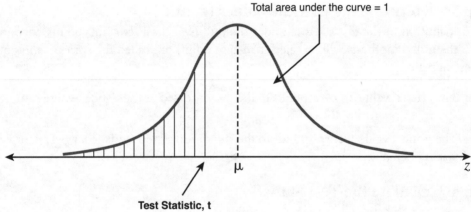

Figure 5.1 Left-tailed Test

In a right-tailed type of test, the H_a region is toward the right-hand side of the test statistic, as shown in Figure 5.2.

In a two-tailed type of test, the H_a region is the sum of the shaded areas on both the left- and right-hand sides of the sample probability distribution, as shown in Figure 5.3.

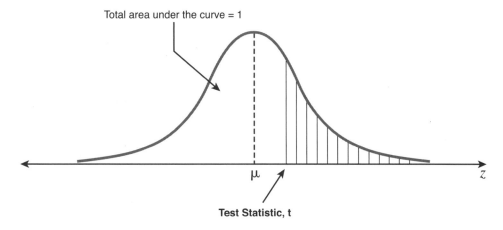

Null Hypothesis $\quad H_0: \mu \leq t$
Alternative Hypothesis $\quad H_a: \mu > t$

Total area under the curve = 1

μ

z

Test Statistic, t

Figure 5.2 Right-tailed Test

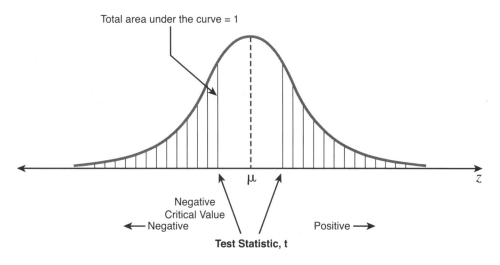

Null Hypothesis $\quad H_0: \mu = t$
Alternative Hypothesis $\quad H_a: \mu \neq t$

Total area under the curve = 1

μ

z

Negative
Critical Value
← Negative   Positive →

Test Statistic, t

Figure 5.3 Two-tailed Test

There are three scenarios to determine the probability value P:

- **Scenario 1: Left-tailed Test:** P = 2 times the area to the left-hand side of the negative test statistic
- **Scenario 2: Right-tailed Test:** P = 2 times the area to the right-hand side of the positive test statistic
- **Scenario 3: Two-tailed Test:** P = (Area to the left-hand side of the negative test statistic + Area to the right-hand side of the positive test statistic)

Step 6: Make a Decision

After completing steps 1 through 5, you will have enough information to make an informed decision.

To make a decision, compare the p-value determined in step 5 to the level of significance α from step 4.

- **Option 1:** If the p-value is less than or equal to α, then reject H_0.
- **Option 2:** If the p-value is greater than α, then fail to reject H_0.

Step 7: Interpret (Draw Conclusion)

The decision made in step 6 can be interpreted as follows:

Reject H_0 implies there is sufficient evidence to reject the claim.

Fail to reject H_0 implies there is not sufficient evidence to reject the claim.

NOTE

Accepting the null hypothesis H_0 is not the same as failing to reject it.

Failing to reject means the null hypothesis is assumed to be true from the very beginning of the test and it is continued to be assumed true in the absence of evidence that could prove it false.

Accepting the null hypothesis means it is proven to be true simply due to the fact that it has not been proven false.

Example Problem 5.1

A data center reports that the percentage of its infrastructure that needs to be refreshed in 5 years is 75%. You have decided to perform a hypothesis test for this claim. How would you interpret or draw a conclusion from your decision?

- You reject H_0.

- You fail to reject H_0.

Explain.

Rejection Region

The *rejection region* is the area under the distribution curve in which if a test statistic falls, the null hypothesis is rejected. A critical value z_c or t_c separates the rejection region from the rest of the area under the distribution curve.

You use critical values to determine the rejection region(s) as follows:

1. Specify the level of significance α.
2. Identify the critical value(s) z_c or t_c.

    - For a *left-tailed* hypothesis test, find the z-score that corresponds to area α.
    - For a *right-tailed* hypothesis test, find the z-score that corresponds to area $1 - \alpha$.

OR

    - For a *two-tailed* hypothesis test, find the z-score that corresponds to area between $\frac{1}{2}\alpha$ and $1 - \frac{1}{2}\alpha$.

3. Within the standard normal distribution, draw a vertical line at each of the critical values and shade the regions as follows:

    - For a *left-tailed* hypothesis test, shade the area to the left-hand side of the critical value.

    - For a *right-tailed* hypothesis test, shade the area to the right-hand side of the critical value.

    - For a *two-tailed* hypothesis test, shade the area to the left-hand side of the negative critical value and to the right-hand side of the positive critical value.

The shaded area is the rejection region as illustrated in Figure 5.4.

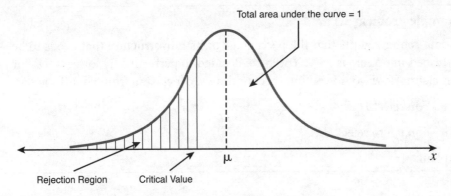

Total area under the curve = 1

Rejection Region   Critical Value

Rejection Region for a Left-tailed Test

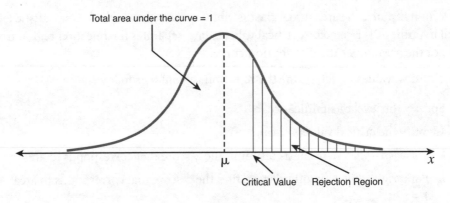

Total area under the curve = 1

Critical Value   Rejection Region

Rejection Region for a Right-tailed Test

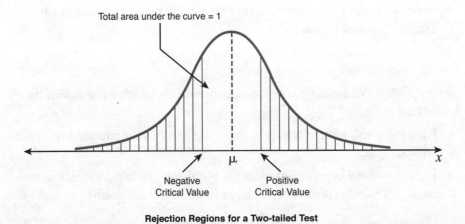

Total area under the curve = 1

Negative   Positive
Critical Value   Critical Value

Rejection Regions for a Two-tailed Test

Figure 5.4 Determining Rejection Region(s) via Critical Values

The z-Test versus the t-Test

When to use the z-test or when to use the t-test depends upon various factors, including the sample size n, the type of distribution, and the availability of the population standard deviation σ.

The z-Test

You use the z-test when

- The population distribution is normal and the population standard deviation σ is known, or
- The sample size n is large (≥ 30). In this case, the sample standard deviation s can be used in lieu of the population standard deviation σ.

The standardized test statistic is

$$z = \frac{\bar{x} - \mu}{\sigma / \sqrt{n}}$$

where $\bar{x}$ = test statistic of the sample mean and $(\sigma/\sqrt{n})$ = standard error $_x$.

Figure 5.5 encapsulates the process involving the z-test.

Example Problem 5.2

The Project Management Office in a large organization has decided to acquire the Service Oriented Architecture (SOA) based Project Portfolio Management (PPM) services from an outside vendor. The vendor claims that its mean time to respond to a support call is less than 30 minutes. A random survey of 32 service recipients from that vendor revealed a sample mean of 29.5% and a standard deviation of 3.5%. Is there enough evidence to support the claim at $\alpha = 0.01$? Use a p-value.

Example Problem 5.3

You are the manager of a Project Management Office (PMO). You receive a proposal for a project with a mean budget of $2.5M. You do not think that this estimate is correct. To validate your assertion, you review archived historical budget documents for 30 previously completed similar projects in the organization and

---

find the mean budget of the sample of 30 projects to be $2.2M with a standard deviation of $700,000. Is there enough evidence to support your claim at α = 0.05? Use a p-value.

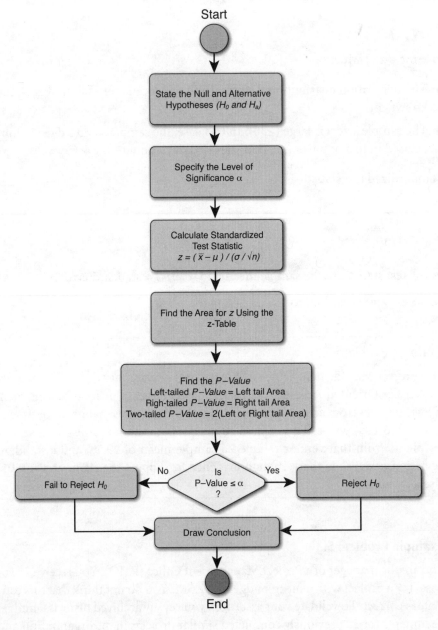

Figure 5.5 *z*-Test Process

Example Problem 5.4

Project managers in a large construction company claim that the mean salary of the company's project managers is less than that of its competitor's, which is $85,000. A random sample of 33 of the company's project managers has a mean salary of $83,500 with a standard deviation of $7,200. At $\alpha = 0.05$, test the project managers' claim.

The t-Test

You use the t-test when

- The population distribution is approximately normal and the population standard deviation σ is unknown, and
- The sample size n is small (<30)

The standardized test statistic is

$$t = \frac{\bar{x} - \mu}{s / \sqrt{n}}$$

where $\bar{x}$ = test statistic of the sample mean and the degrees of freedom,[1] $df = n - 1$.

Figure 5.6 encapsulates the process involving the t-test.

Example Problem 5.5

Data published by *U.S. News & Review* indicates that the mean salary of a project manager in the United States is $85,000. A random sample of 50 project managers around the country has a mean salary of $88,500 with a standard deviation of $7,200. At $\alpha = 0.05$, test the *U.S. News & Review's* claim.

---

[1] The degrees of freedom (*df*) in statistics refer to the number of values you can vary in your calculation. They are used in a *t*-test when sample size $n < 30$. See the usage procedure outlined in Figure 5.6.

Example: Consider the algebraic relationship: $(10 + 20 + a + b)/4 = 20$

Solving for unknowns *a* and *b* and rearranging: $a = 50 - b$

In this relationship, *a* is a dependent variable and *b* is an independent variable. Choosing a value for *b* will help you figure out the value of *a*. Thus, the degree of freedom in this case is 1.

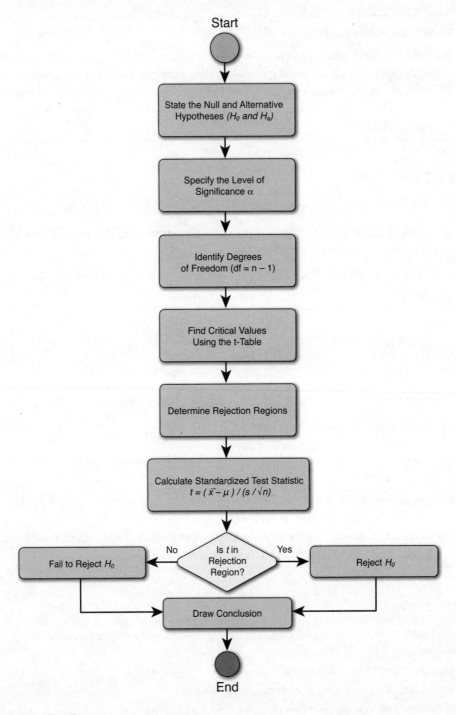

Figure 5.6 *t*-Test Process

Example Problem 5.6

You are a project manager in the process of developing the schedule for your project. A task lead on your project reports that to complete a particular task, it will take him at least 20 days. You suspect that his claim is not correct. To validate your assertion, you look at 10 similar tasks and determine that the mean duration is 18 days with a standard deviation of 2 days. Is there enough evidence to reject the team lead's claim at $\alpha = 0.05$? Assume the probability distribution to be normal.

Correlation in Statistics

Correlation between two random variables signifies some sort of relationship between two variables. To understand correlation within the context of statistics, you need to

1. Understand what a correlation is.
2. Understand the types of correlation.
3. Identify the correlation coefficient.
4. Test the population correlation coefficient.
5. Differentiate correlation from causation.

Types of Correlation

The following are various types of correlation:

- Linear correlation (negative and positive)
- No correlation
- Nonlinear correlation

To explain the preceding various types of correlation, assume two random variables x and y associated with one another via the following algebraic relationship:

$$y = f(x)$$

In this relationship, x is called the independent variable and y is called the dependent variable.

Linear Correlation

The correlation between the random variables x and y is said to be linear when the ratio of the change in the value of x to the change in the value of y is constant. In other words, certain change in the value of x will cause a proportionate change in the value of y (either in positive or in negative direction).

In *positive linear correlation*, a change in the value of variable x causes a proportionate change in the value of variable y in a positive direction; that is, as x increases, y also tends to increase. For example, the program cost for the wages of project managers doubles when the number of project managers is doubled, assuming all project managers are paid equally.

In *negative linear correlation*, a change in the value of variable x causes a proportionate change in the value of variable y in a negative direction; that is, as x increases, y tends to decrease. For example, a project task is completed twice as fast (in half of the originally estimated duration) when the number of resources working on that task is doubled.

No Correlation

No correlation between two variables x and y means the values of these random variables do not increase or decrease in tandem. This does not mean that x and y are independent; there might exist a nonlinear correlation between the two. For example, the gender of a project manager has no correlation to the success of a project.

Nonlinear Correlation

The correlation between the random variables x and y is said to be nonlinear when the ratio of the change in the value of x to the change in the value of y is not constant. In other words, a certain change in the value of x causes an out-of-proportion change in the value of y. For example, adding more resources to a project task does not always result in proportionate improvement in efficiency. Adding more resources beyond a certain point may create chaos and hence lead to an out-of-proportion decline in efficiency.

The preceding types of correlation can be illustrated using scatter plots, as shown in Figure 5.7.

Correlation Coefficient

A correlation coefficient measures the strength and the direction of a linear correlation. The sample correlation is represented by the symbol r, where

$$r = \frac{(n\Sigma xy - (\Sigma x) \cdot (\Sigma y))}{\sqrt{(n\Sigma x^2 - (\Sigma x)^2)} \cdot \sqrt{(n\Sigma y^2 - (\Sigma y)^2)}}$$

The population correlation coefficient is represented by the symbol ρ (rho).

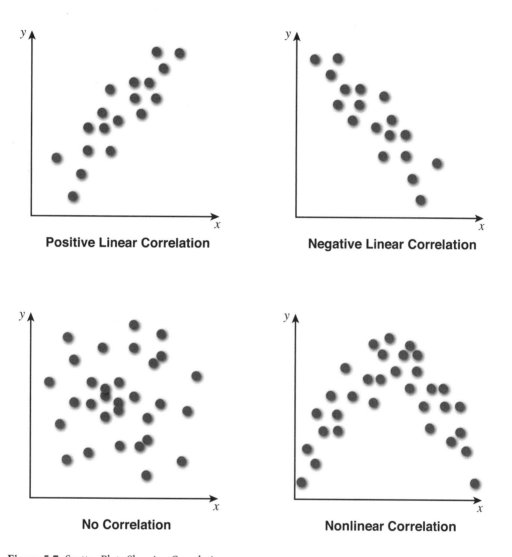

Figure 5.7 Scatter Plots Showing Correlations

Correlation and Causation

If two random variables are strongly correlated, it does not automatically mean that a cause-and-effect relationship exists between them.

However, there could be various possibilities, such as:

- x could cause y.
- y could cause x.
- A third variable could cause the relationship.
- A combination of several other variables could cause the relationship.
- Just a coincidence could cause the relationship.

Linear Regression

In the previous section on correlation, you learned about the possible relationships between the two random variables x and y. This section on linear regression is the continuation of the same discussion, where you will learn how to further analyze correlation scatter plots to help you make better decisions.

Linear regression is the process of finding a best-fitting straight line, called a *regression line*, through the points in a scatter plot.

The example plot in Figure 5.8 illustrates the process of linear regression. The regression line in this figure shows the predicted values for variable y for each possible value of x.

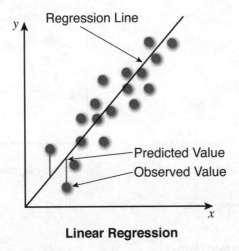

Linear Regression

Figure 5.8 Process of Linear Regression

The Regression Line Equation

The following is the equation of a regression line:

$$\hat{y} = mx + b$$

where $\hat{y}$ (called *y-hat*) = the predicted value of dependent variable y for a given value of independent variable x.

$$m = \text{slope of the regression line} = \frac{(n\Sigma xy - (\Sigma x)(\Sigma y))}{(n\Sigma x^2 - (\Sigma x)^2)}$$

b = y-intercept = $\bar{y} - m.\bar{x}$

$$= \Sigma y/n - m.\Sigma x/n$$

where $\bar{y}$ $\sqrt{x}$ and are the means of the values of variables y and x, respectively. Note that the regression line always passes through the coordinate $(\bar{x}, \bar{y})$.

Example: Table 5.1 shows the project staff training expenses and the staff performance (number of milestones completed per month) data for the past 6 months. Find the equation of the regression line for this data.

Table 5.1   Training Expenses and Staff Performance

Month	Training Expenses $ (x)	Number of milestones completed (y)
March 2015	2500	23
April 2015	1950	20
May 2015	2125	22
June 2015	2600	24
July 2015	1560	16
Aug 2015	2000	18

Solution: Table 5.2 tabulates the data for calculations.

Table 5.2 Data Analysis

x	y	xy	x^2	y^2
2500	23	57500	6250000	529
1950	20	39000	3802500	400
2125	22	46750	4515625	484
2600	24	62400	6760000	576
1560	16	24960	2433600	256
2000	18	36000	4000000	324
$\Sigma x = 12735$	$\Sigma y = 123$	$\Sigma xy = 266610$	$\Sigma x^2 = 27761725$	$\Sigma y^2 = 2569$

Sample size $n = 6$

$$m = \text{slope of the regression line} = \frac{(n\Sigma xy - (\Sigma x)(\Sigma y))}{(n\Sigma^2 - (\Sigma x)^2)}$$

$= (6(266610) - (12735)(123)) / 6(27761725) - (12735)^2$

$= 0.007575$

$b = \Sigma y/n - m.\Sigma x/n$

$= 123/6 - 0.007575(12735/6)$

$= 4.422158$

Thus, equation of the regression line is:

$\hat{y} = mx + b$

$= 0.007575x + 4.422158$

Using a Regression Equation to Predict y-Values

Figure 5.8 shows the scatter plot of a positive correlation between variables x and y and the regression line through the points of the scatter plot.

To find a predicted value of y for a given value of x, draw a vertical line from any point of the scatter plot (observed value of y) until it intersects the regression line. The point where that vertical straight line parallel to the y-axis meets the regression line represents the predicted value of y.

Prediction Error

The difference between the observed and predicted values of y for a given value of x on the regression line is called the *residual value*, which is also known as the prediction error. The closer an observed value is to the regression line, the smaller is the prediction error (the more accurate is the prediction).

Prediction Intervals

Assuming for any given value of x, the corresponding *y-values* are normally distributed and for any given values of y, the corresponding *x-values* are normally distributed, a prediction interval can be constructed.

Recall the equation of a linear regression

$\hat{y} = mx + b$

For a given value of x (x_0), the prediction interval for y is

$\hat{y} - E < y < \hat{y} + E$

where $\hat{y}$ = point estimate[2] (a single value of y in the interval), and the margin of error is calculated with the following

$$E = t_c s_e \sqrt{1 + \frac{1}{n} + \frac{n(x_0 - \bar{x})^2}{n\Sigma x^2 - (\Sigma x)^2}}$$

where n = sample size and c represents the probability that y is within the prediction interval.

t_c = critical value (obtained from t-table – using degrees of freedom = $n - 2$)

Standard error of estimate is given by

$$s_e = \sqrt{\frac{\Sigma(y_i - \hat{y}_i)^2}{n - 2}}$$

The following worked example will provide more clarification to these concepts.

Example: The regression equation for the project staff training expenses and the staff performance (number of milestones completed per month) is $\hat{y} = 0.007575x + 4.422158$ (from the preceding example).

1. Find the percentage of unexplained variation in the staff performance with respect to the variation in the training expenses.

2. Find the standard error of estimate.

---

[2] Discusssed in Chapter 4, "Statistical Fundamentals I"

---

3. Construct a 95% prediction interval for the staff performance with training expenses of $2000. Explain your conclusion.

Solution:

Part 1: First, find the correlation coefficient for the dataset in the preceding example using Microsoft Excel, as shown in Figure 5.9.

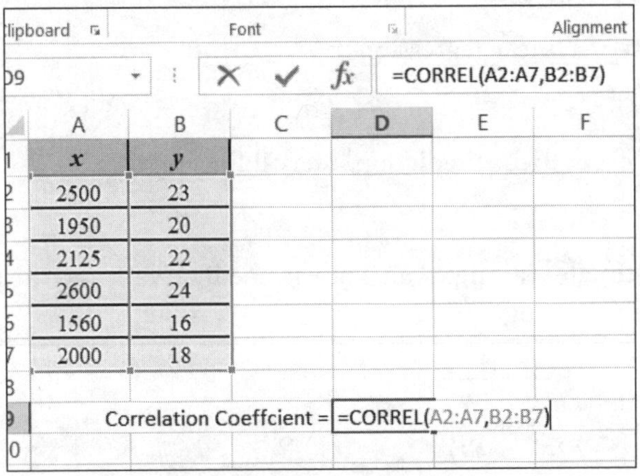

Figure 5.9 Finding the Correlation Coefficient Using Excel

The correlation coefficient $r = 0.940148$, and the coefficient of determination $r^2 = (0.940148)^2 = 0.883878$, which means that 88.4% of the variation in the staff performance can be determined or explained by the variation in the training expenses.

Thus, the undetermined or unexplained variation = $100 - 88.4 = 11.6$%.

Part 2: Now calculate the sum of the squared differences of each observed y-value and the corresponding predicted y-value as shown in Table 5.3.

Table 5.3 Table Title Here

x	y (Each value of y is y_i (observed))	$\hat{y}_i$ ($\hat{y}$ values (predicted) obtained by substituting x values in the regression line equation)	$(y_i - \hat{y}_i)2$
2500	23	23.359658	0.12935388
1950	20	19.193408	0.65059065
2125	22	20.519033	2.19326326
2600	24	24.117158	0.013726

x	y (Each value of y is y_i (observed))	$\hat{y}_i$ ($\hat{y}$ values (predicted) obtained by substituting x values in the regression line equation)	$(y_i - \hat{y}_i)2$
1560	16	16.239158	0.05719655
2000	18	19.572158	2.47168078
			5.51581111 (Unexplained Variation)

The standard error of estimate is caculated with this equation:

$$s_e = \sqrt{\frac{\Sigma(y_i - \hat{y}_i)^2}{n-2}}$$

$$= \sqrt{5.51581111} \ /(6-2))$$

$$= 1.174$$

This means that the standard error of estimate for the staff performance with respect to a particular training expense is about one milestone.

Part 3:

Point estimate $\hat{y} = 0.007575(2000) + 4.422158 = 19.5722$

Degrees of freedom, $df = n - 2 = 6 - 2 = 4$

From the t-Table in Appendix B, the critical value t_c for the 95% prediction interval = 2.447

Mean is $\bar{x} = (\Sigma x)/n = 12735/6 = 2122.5$

$\Sigma x^2 = 27761725$

The margin of error is calculated with the following:

$$E = t_c s_e \sqrt{1 + \frac{1}{n} + \frac{n(x_0 - \bar{x})^2}{n\Sigma x^2 - (\Sigma x)^2}}$$

$$= (2.447)(1.174)(\sqrt{(1 + 1/6 + (6(2000 - 2122.5)^2 / (6(271725) - (12735)^2))}$$

$$= 3.102806$$

Now, left endpoint of the prediction interval = $\hat{y} - E$ = 19.5722 – 3.102806 = 16.46939

Right endpoint of the prediction interval = $\hat{y} + E$ = 19.5722 + 3.102806 = 22.67501

Thus, the prediction interval is 16.469 < y < 22.675

This means that with 95% confidence, you can say that when the training expenses are $2000, the staff performance is between about 16 milestones and 23 milestones completed.

Predicting *y*-Values Using the Multiple Regression Equation

In the previous section, you learned about prediction based on a single independent variable. Practically, for better prediction, you need multiple independent variables to decide the value of the dependent variable. However, multiple independent variables increase the complexity of the regression equation and the use of technology (such as *Minitab*[3] or Microsoft Excel) becomes necessary to find and solve the regression equation.

The equation for the multiple regression is given by the following relationship:

$$\hat{y} = b + m_1 x_1 + m_2 x_2 + m_3 x_3 + \dots + m_k x_k$$

where x_1, x_2, x_3,..., x_k are independent variables, b is the y-intercept, and $\hat{y}$ is the dependent variable.

Example Problem 5.7

The human resources department of an organization uses multifactor criteria for candidate selection. The hiring manager wants to know how hiring scores are related to the performance in interview, professional experience, and education. She obtains data for eight scores from the human resources department, as shown in Table 5.4.

---

[3] A free trial of Minitab is usually available for download at http://www.minitab.com/.

Table 5.4 Multifactor Hiring Criteria

Score, y	Interview Points, x_1	Professional Experience, x_2	Education, x_3
47	20	10	17
38	18	6	14
28	9	7	12
30	5	9	16
44	16	12	16
29	14	1	14
27	10	5	12
37	12	8	17

a. Use Minitab software to find the multiple regression equation that models the data.

b. Calculate the predicted hiring score for a candidate who scored 20 points in the interview, has 10 years of professional experience, and possesses 16 years of education.

Summary

The mind map in Figure 5.10 summarizes this chapter on statistical fundamentals.

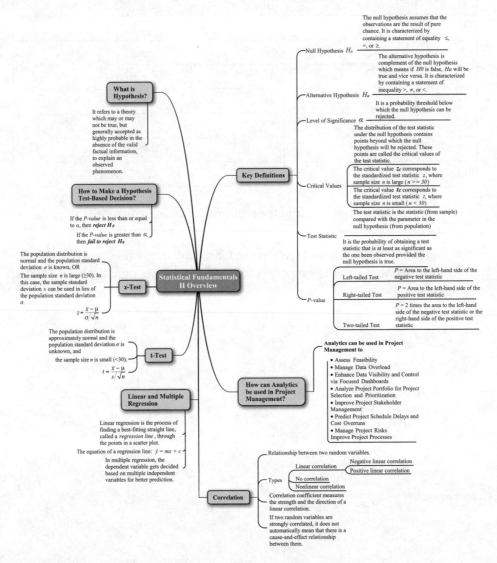

Figure 5.10 Statistical Fundamentals II Summary

Key Terms

Alternative Hypothesis

Correlation

Correlation Coefficient

Critical Value

Fail to Reject Claim

Hypothesis

Left-tailed Test

Level of Significance

Linear Correlation

Linear Regression

Multiple Regression

Null Hypothesis

Prediction Intervals

P-value

Regression Equation

Reject Claim

Rejection Region

Right-tailed Test

Test Statistic

t-Test

Two-tailed Test

z-Test

Solutions to Example Problems

Example Problem 5.1 Solution

In this example, the null hypothesis H_0 is the claim:

- Rejecting H_0 would be interpreted as "there is sufficient evidence that the claim is false."

- Failing to reject H_0 would be interpreted as "there is insufficient evidence that the claim is false."

Example Problem 5.2 Solution

Null Hypothesis H_0: $\mu \geq 30$ minutes

Alternative Hypothesis H_a: $\mu < 30$ minutes

Because H_a includes the "<" sign, a left-tail test is applicable in this scenario.

Level of significance $\alpha = 0.01$

The standardized test statistic is

$$z = \frac{\bar{x} - \mu}{\sigma / \sqrt{n}}$$

$$= (29.5 - 30) / (3.5 / \sqrt{32})$$

$$= -0.81$$

Using z-table, p-value = .2090

Because $0.2090 \geq 0.01$, the decision is *fail to reject H_0*.

Thus, at the 1% level of significance, you have sufficient evidence to conclude that the mean response time is less than 30 minutes.

Example Problem 5.3 Solution

Null Hypothesis H_0: $\mu = \$2.5M$

Alternative Hypothesis H_a: $\mu \neq \$2.5M$

Because H_a includes the "$\neq$" sign, a two-tail test is applicable in this scenario.

Level of significance $\alpha = 0.05$

The standardized test statistic is

$$z = \frac{\bar{x} - \mu}{\sigma / \sqrt{n}}$$

$$= (2.2 - 2.5) / (0.7 / \sqrt{30})$$

$$= -2.35$$

Using z-table, the area pertaining to $z = -2.35 = .0094$

Because this is a two-tail test, p-value = 2(z area) = 2(.0094) = .0188

Because $.0188 \geq 0.01$, the decision is *fail to reject H_0*.

Thus, at the 5% level of significance, you have sufficient evidence to conclude that the mean budget is $2.5M.

Example Problem 5.4 Solution

Null Hypothesis H_0: $\mu \geq \$85,000$

Alternative Hypothesis H_a: $\mu < \$85,000$

Because H_a includes the "<" sign, a left-tail test is applicable in this scenario.

Level of significance $\alpha = 0.05$

The standardized test statistic is

$$z = \frac{\bar{x} - \mu}{\sigma / \sqrt{n}}$$

$= (83500 - 85000) / (7200 / \sqrt{33})$

$= -1.20$

The negative value of z indicates that left-tail test is applicable in this scenario.

Using z-table, the area pertaining to $z = -1.20 = p\text{-}value = .1151$

Because $0.1151 \geq 0.01$, the decision is *fail to reject* H_0

At the 5% level of significance, you have sufficient evidence to support the project managers' claim that their mean salary is less than $85,000.

Example Problem 5.5 Solution

Null Hypothesis H_0: $\mu = \$85,000$

Alternative Hypothesis H_a: $\mu \neq \$85,000$

Because H_a includes the "$\neq$" sign, the two-tail test is applicable in this scenario.

Level of significance $\alpha = 0.05$

The standardized test statistic is

$$z = \frac{\bar{x} - \mu}{\sigma / \sqrt{n}}$$

$= (88500 - 85000) / (7200 / \sqrt{50})$

$= -3.43$

Using z-table, the area pertaining to $z = -3.43 = .0003$

Because this is a two-tail test, $p\text{-}value = 2(z \text{ area}) = 2(.0003) = .0006$

Because $.0006 < 0.01$, the decision is *reject* H_0.

Thus, at the 5% level of significance, you have sufficient evidence to reject the claim that project managers' mean salary is $85,000.

Example Problem 5.6 Solution

Null Hypothesis H_0: $\mu \geq 20$ days

Alternative Hypothesis H_a: $\mu < 20$ days

Because H_a includes the "<" sign, a left-tail test is applicable in this scenario.

Level of significance $\alpha = 0.05$

Degrees of freedom $(df) = 10 - 1 = 9$

Standardized test statistic

$= (18 - 20) / (2 / \sqrt{10})$

$= -3.16$

$$t = \frac{\bar{x} - \mu}{s / \sqrt{n}}$$

Using t-table, critical value t_c for $df = 9$ and $\alpha = 0.05$ is equal to -1.833

Because the test statistic falls within the rejection region, reject H_0.

Thus, at the 5% level of significance, there is sufficient evidence to reject the claim that the task will take at least 20 days to compete.

Example Problem 5.7 Solution

Part a.

Enter the y-values in C1 and x-values in C2, C3, and C4.

Select Regression, Regression from the Stat menu as shown in Figure 5.11.

Use the score (C1) as the response variable and the rest of the data (C2 to C4) as the predictors.

These steps give you the output shown in Figure 5.12.

The regression equation is

$y = 0.000000 + 1.00\ x_1 + 1.00\ x_2 + 1.00\ x_3$

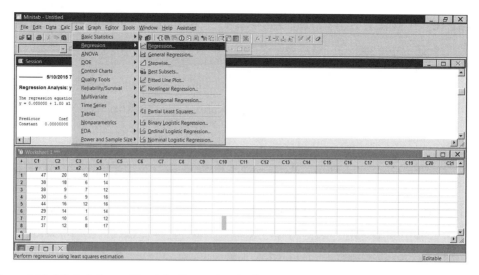

Figure 5.11 Minitab Screen Shot 1 for Regression Analysis

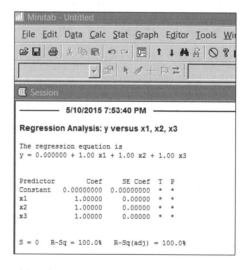

Figure 5.12 Minitab Screen Shot 2 for Regression Analysis

Part b.

Substitute interview points = 20, professional experience = 10 years, and education =16 years in the regression equation obtained in Part a.

$y = 0.000000 + 1\ (20) + 1\ (10) + 1\ (16) = 46$

The predicted hiring score for this candidate is 46.

Chapter Review and Discussion Questions

1. Define *hypothesis*. What is the difference between a null hypothesis and an alternative hypothesis?

2. What does "innocent until proven guilty" mean in the American legal system?

3. What is the difference between Type I and Type II errors associated with the hypothesis test?

4. What are the various types of statistical hypothesis tests? Explain.

5. A test manager claims the mean cost of test equipment is at least $8,025. State the null and alternative hypotheses.

6. Is testing the claim that at least 68% of the project managers have a PMP[4] a

   - Left-tailed test?
   - Right-tailed test?
   - Two-tailed test?

7. What is the difference between "reject H_0" and "fail to reject H_0"? Under what conditions would you reject H_0?

   - In a z-test
   - In a t-test

8. Outline the steps of a z-test process.

9. Outline the steps of a t-test process.

10. Find the standardized test statistic z for the following situation:

    Claim: $\mu > 55$ $s = 3.5$ $n = 30$

11. What is correlation? What are the different correlation types?

12. Is there always a "cause-and-effect" relationship between two strongly correlated random variables?

13. What is the significance of a prediction error?

14. Predict the cost of a project activity using the regression equation: $y = 200 + 10\,x_1 + 20\,x_2$

    Where x_1 is the level of difficulty and x_2 is the risk level. Predict the *y-value* for $x_1 = 12$ and $x_2 = 22$.

---

4 PMP stands for Project Management Professional.

Bibliography

Anbari, F.T. (1997). *Quantitative Methods for Project Management*. New York: International Institute for Learning, Inc.

Dubois, S. (2015). "The Importance of Hypothesis Testing." Retrieved April 9, 2015, from http://www.ehow.com/info_12094529_importance-hypothesis-testing.html

Fermi, E. (2014). "Enrico Fermi quote." Retrieved April 7, 2015, from http://www.brainyquote.com/quotes/quotes/e/enricoferm125836.html

Goodpasture, J.C. (2003). *Quantitative Methods in Project Management*. Boca Raton, Florida, J. Ross Publishing.

Groebner, D. et al. (2014). *Business Statistics: A Decision-Making Approach*, 9th ed. Harlow: Pearson.

Lane, D.M. (2014). "Introduction to Linear Regression." Retrieved April 10, 2015, from http://onlinestatbook.com/2/regression/intro.html

Larson, R. and Farber, E. (2011). *Elementary Statistics: Picturing the World*, 5th ed. Upper Saddle River, New Jersey: Pearson.

Ling, L. (2014). "Statistical Functions in Excel." Retrieved May 5, 2015, from http://www.comfsm.fm/~dleeling/statistics/excel.html

Merriam-Webster. (2015). "Hypothesis: Dictionary Meaning." Retrieved April 7, 2015, from http://www.merriam-webster.com/dictionary/hypothesis

Minitab. (2015). "Minitab for Regression Analysis." Retrieved May 8, 2015, from http://www.minitab.com/

NIST Handbook of Statistics. (2014). "What Are Statistical Tests?" Retrieved April 10, 2015, from http://www.itl.nist.gov/div898/handbook/prc/section1/prc13.htm

PennState. (2015). "Hypothesis Testing (Critical value approach)." Retrieved April 10, 2015, from https://onlinecourses.science.psu.edu/statprogram/node/137

San Jose State University. (2006). "Introduction to Hypothesis Testing." Retrieved September 7, 2015, from http://www.sjsu.edu/faculty/gerstman/StatPrimer/hyp-test.pdf

San Jose State University. (2007). "T-Table." Retrieved April 10, 2015, from http://www.sjsu.edu/faculty/gerstman/StatPrimer/t-table.pdf

Stockburger, D. W. (2014). "Hypothesis Testing." Retrieved April 8, 2015, from http://www.psychstat.missouristate.edu/introbook/sbk18.htm

Taylor, C. (2015). "What Is a Degree of Freedom?" Retrieved April 8, 2015, from http://statistics.about.com/od/Inferential-Statistics/a/What-Is-A-Degree-Of-Freedom.htm

Weisstein, E.W. (2015). "Hypothesis Testing." Retrieved April 7, 2015, from MathWorld—A Wolfram Web Resource. http://mathworld.wolfram.com/HypothesisTesting.html

6

Analytic Hierarchy Process

Learning Objectives

After reading this chapter, you should be familiar with

- Analytic Hierarchy Process (AHP)
- Using the AHP
- Decision hierarchy
- Saaty Scale
- Pairwise comparisons
- Alternatives and criteria prioritization
- Alternatives ranking
- Pros and cons of the AHP
- Tools related to the AHP

> "Not everything that counts can be counted and not everything that can be counted, counts."
>
> —*Albert Einstein*

Invented by Thomas L. Saaty in the 1970s, the AHP became very popular and useful for multi-criteria-based decision-making, especially in group environments. This structured methodology works through pairwise comparisons[1] of qualitative (subjective) as well as quantitative (objective) evaluation criteria and uses the priority scales driven by expert

---

[1] Pairwise comparison involves comparing multiple elements in pairs to determine which one in a pair is preferred over the other and by what weight (numerical value).

judgment for comparisons of the intangible factors (feelings and preferences) in the evaluation criteria.

This chapter introduces you to the fundamentals of the AHP by describing various building blocks of this process and uses examples and a case study to illustrate the underpinning concepts. The foundational knowledge gained from this chapter will help you understand the applications of the AHP discussed in Chapter 9, "Project Decision-Making with the Analytic Hierarchy Process (AHP)."

Using the AHP

Using the AHP approach involves systematically organizing, analyzing, and synthesizing the information pertaining to multi-criteria used in complex decision-making. The final decision is the selection of the best of multiple competing alternatives or the prioritization of various elements of a portfolio. For instance, the decision outcome could be the selection of the best project (based on certain criteria) from the list of multiple competing project ideas or it could be the prioritized[2] list of various projects in the portfolio.

The following steps outline the procedure for using the AHP:

1. Determine the criteria (and sub-criteria if any) to evaluate.

2. Develop the decision hierarchy with the decision goal at the top, various alternatives at the bottom, and various evaluation criteria and sub-criteria in the middle.

3. Perform the analysis:

   a. Perform pairwise comparison of the alternatives based on their strengths in meeting the evaluation criteria and determine priorities among them.

   b. Perform pairwise comparison of the criteria based on their importance in achieving the ultimate goal of the decision-making and determine priorities among them.

4. Synthesize the priorities from steps 2 and 3 to find the overall priority for each of the alternatives and assign a rank to each of the alternatives on the basis of its overall priority.

5. Make a decision by selecting the highest ranking alternative.

---

2 Prioritization of the projects in a portfolio is done so that limited resources can be shared by these projects in the order of priority (with highest priority being at the top of the prioritized list).

Determine the Evaluation Criteria

The criteria and optional sub-criteria for evaluation of the competing alternatives must be determined first.

For example, let's assume that you are trying to plan your next family vacation. Your goal is to choose the best alternative (vacation destination) from the list of potential alternatives (vacation destinations) that you have shortlisted after discussing with your family.

Your first step will involve determining various criteria against which you can evaluate all alternatives in order to pick the best one.

Suppose the vacation alternatives you have shortlisted include Hawaii, Florida, Las Vegas, and Lake Tahoe. Your criteria for evaluation of these alternatives might include the following:

- Water activities
- Night Life
- Theme parks
- Cost

Develop the Decision Hierarchy

The next step in using the AHP involves developing a decision hierarchy with the goal to be achieved at the top of the hierarchy, various alternatives at the bottom, and the evaluation criteria and sub-criteria in the middle, as shown in Figure 6.1.

Referring back to our vacation selection scenario, the following are examples of alternatives and the associated evaluation criteria:

- Alternative 1: Hawaii
- Alternative 2: Florida
- Alternative 3: Las Vegas
- Alternative 4: Lake Tahoe
- Evaluation Criterion 1: Water activities
- Evaluation Criterion 2: Night Life
- Evaluation Criterion 3: Theme parks
- Evaluation Criterion 4: Cost

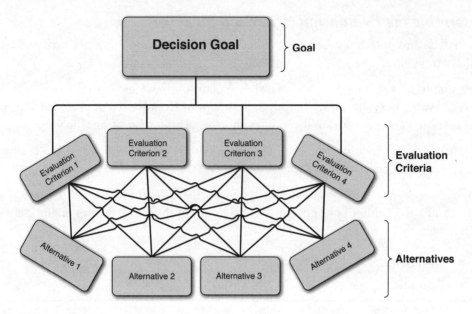

Figure 6.1 The AHP Decision Hierarchy

Perform the Analysis

After the hierarchy is developed, the next step is to evaluate various alternatives in terms of their respective strengths with regard to all factors in the evaluation criteria or sub-criteria. Subsequently, the factors in the evaluation criteria are assessed in terms of their importance in achieving the stipulated goal.

The nodes or elements of the decision matrix are assigned weights using the weighting scale, also known as the Saaty Scale, shown in Table 6.1. According to Saaty (2008), "The Analytic Hierarchy Process (AHP) is a theory of measurement through pairwise comparisons and relies on the judgments of experts to derive priority scales." Also, the AHP is a group decision-making technique. Thus, the weight assignment process uses expert judgment. The experts may include a project management core team, subject matter experts, or key stakeholders. For example, to assign weights to various factors of the vacation decision-making criteria, the experts or sources of information consulted might include travel agents, friends and family who have already traveled to one or more of the shortlisted vacation spots, the Internet, or even the tour books that are available from any location of the American Automobile Association (AAA).

Table 6.1 Saaty Scale

Intensity of Importance	Definition	Explanation
1	Equal importance	Two nodes (factors) contribute equally to the objective
3	Slightly more important	Experience and judgment slightly favor one factor over the other
5	Much more important	Experience and judgment strongly favor one factor over the other
7	Very much more important	Experience and judgment favor one factor over the other very strongly
9	Extremely more important	Experience and judgment favor one factor over the other extremely strongly
2, 4, 6, 8	Intermediate values	Experience and judgment moderately favor one factor over the other (Used when compromise is needed)

The weight assignment allows the pairwise comparison of various alternatives as well as various factors of the evaluation criteria and determines numerical priorities among them.

First, you need to determine how many pairwise comparisons you need to make using the *Saaty Scale* from Table 6.1. The number of comparisons needed depends on the number of alternatives under consideration and is determined by the formula,

Number of pairwise comparisons = $n(n-1)/2$

where n = number of alternatives being compared

In our hypothetical vacation selection scenario, we have four vacation alternatives to choose from, so $n = 4$, which gives us $4(4-1)/2 = 6$ pairwise comparisons.

The key underlying consideration in a pairwise comparison is determining which option in the pair you like more than the other and how much more. For example, let's look at our vacation destination selection scenario and use the relative scale (*Saaty Scale*) from Table 6.1. If you like option 1 more than option 2, then put a cross mark (X) between numbers 1 and 9 on the left side and if you like option 2 better than option 1, then put an X between numbers 1 and 9 on the right-hand side as illustrated in Table 6.2.

Table 6.2 Pairwise Comparisons for Vacation Destination Choices Based on Saaty Scale

		Comparison Scale									
Pair#	Option 1	9	7	5	3	1	3	5	7	9	Option 2
1	Hawaii			X							Florida
2	Hawaii		X								Las Vegas
3	Hawaii		X								Lake Tahoe
4	Florida							X			Las Vegas
5	Florida							X			Lake Tahoe
6	Las Vegas								X		Lake Tahoe

This pairwise comparison between the alternatives can be reformatted for better understanding and further analysis, as shown in Table 6.3.

Table 6.3 Pairwise Comparison Table Reformatted

Pair #	Option 1	Weight	Option 2	Weight	Explanation
1	Hawaii	5	Florida	1	Hawaii has more water activities than Florida.
2	Hawaii	7	Las Vegas	1	Hawaii has water activities but Las Vegas does not.
3	Hawaii	7	Lake Tahoe	1	Hawaii has more water activities than Lake Tahoe.
4	Florida	1	Las Vegas	5	Las Vegas has better night life and costs less.
5	Florida	1	Lake Tahoe	5	Lake Tahoe costs less and has some water activities.
6	Las Vegas	1	Lake Tahoe	7	Lake Tahoe has water activities but Las Vegas does not; Also Lake Tahoe costs less compared to Las Vegas.

The next step after pairwise comparisons is to perform the analysis of these comparisons by developing a comprehensive relative weight matrix.

For pairwise comparisons, weight assignment is relative; that is, a different weight is assigned to each entity (alternatives or criteria) in the pair depending on their relative strengths or importance as shown in the following relationships:

$$\text{Let Pairwise Comparison Matrix } A_{NxN} = \begin{pmatrix} W_1/W_1 & W_1/W_2 & \cdots & W_1/W_n \\ W_2/W_1 & W_2/W_2 & \cdots & W_2/W_n \\ \cdots & \cdots & \cdots & \cdots \\ W_n/W_1 & W_n/W_2 & \cdots & W_n/W_n \end{pmatrix}$$

and

$$\text{Weight Matrix } X_{Nx1} = \begin{pmatrix} W_1 \\ W_2 \\ \cdots \\ W_n \end{pmatrix}$$

Then

$$\begin{pmatrix} W_1/W_1 & W_1/W_2 & \cdots & W_1/W_n \\ W_2/W_1 & W_2/W_2 & \cdots & W_2/W_n \\ \cdots & \cdots & \cdots & \cdots \\ W_n/W_1 & W_n/W_2 & \cdots & W_n/W_n \end{pmatrix} \begin{pmatrix} W_1 \\ W_2 \\ \cdots \\ W_n \end{pmatrix} = \lambda \begin{pmatrix} W_1 \\ W_2 \\ \cdots \\ W_n \end{pmatrix}$$

Where W_1, W_2, ..., W_n are the relative weights corresponding to n number of alternatives under consideration.

This matrix can be expressed by the equation: $AX = \lambda X$

In this equation:

- λ represents the Eigen value of matrix A_{nxn}
- X is the right Eigen vector of matrix A_{nxn}
- "N" or "n" represents the number of Eigen values for matrix A_{nxn} and its Eigen vectors

Equation $AX = \lambda X$ implies $(A - \lambda I)X = 0$, which can be solved by finding its determinant. That is, $\det(A - \lambda)X = 0$, which implies $|A - \lambda I| = 0$

I represents the identity matrix. $I = \begin{pmatrix} 1 & & & \\ & 1 & & \\ & & \ldots & \\ & & & 1 \end{pmatrix}$

Now let's relate this to the vacation scenario.

The pairwise comparison for four vacation choices can be represented by the A_{4x4} matrix in Table 6.4.

Table 6.4 Vacation Destination Matrix

	Hawaii (W1)	Florida (W2)	Las Vegas (W3)	Lake Tahoe (W$_4$)
Hawaii (W$_1$)	W_1/W_1	W_1/W_2	W_1/W_3	W_1/W_4
Florida (W$_2$)	W_2/W_1	W_2/W_2	W_2/W_3	W_2/W_4
Las Vegas (W$_3$)	W_3/W_1	W_3/W_2	W_3/W_3	W_3/W_4
Lake Tahoe (W$_4$)	W_4/W_1	W_4/W_2	W_4/W_3	W_4/W_4

The diagonal elements of the matrix are always 1 and the other elements of the matrix can be determined based on the relative weights of the corresponding alternatives (see Table 6.5).

Table 6.5 Vacation Destination Comparison Scale

	Hawaii (W1)	Florida (W2)	Las Vegas (W3)	Lake Tahoe (W4)
Hawaii (W$_1$)	1	7/1	7/1	7/1
Florida (W$_2$)	1/7	1	1/5	1/5
Las Vegas (W$_3$)	1/7	5/1	1	1/7
Lake Tahoe (W$_4$)	1/7	5/1	7/1	1

From this analysis, you can observe that

- If your choice on the *comparison scale* in Table 6.5 is on the left-hand side of 1, you put the actual value of your choice in the cell.
- If your choice on the *comparison scale* is on the right-hand side of 1, you put the reciprocal of the actual value of your choice in the cell.

Synthesize and Rank Priorities

Finally, you synthesize the priorities pertaining to the alternatives and to the evaluation criteria to yield the overall numerical priorities for the alternatives. You then rank the alternatives on the basis of their numerical priorities and make a decision by choosing the highest ranked alternative.

Synthesizing

To determine the overall priorities of various alternatives with respect to the final goal, use the following synthesis procedure:

1. Multiply the priority of an alternative with respect to a *criterion* by that *criterion's* priority with respect to the final goal.
2. Perform step 1 for all criteria.
3. Add the results from each of the preceding two steps to yield the overall priority of the alternative in consideration.
4. Repeat steps 1 through 3 for all alternatives to determine overall priorities for all the alternatives.

Ranking

The following is the procedure for ranking the alternatives by calculating their overall numerical priorities:

1. Add each column of the decison N × N priority matrix A to render column sums S1, S2, ..., Sn.
2. Normalize the column elements of matrix A by dividing each element by the sum of the column in which that element resides. This yields N × N matrix B.
3. Calculate the average for each row of matrix B. This yields N × 1 matrix X, which is called a priority Eigen vector, which contains the overall priorities for each alternative.

Figure 6.2 illustrates this procedure.

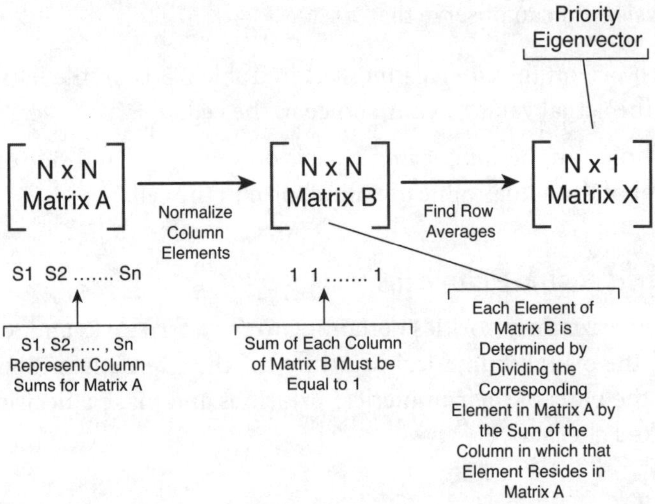

Figure 6.2 Calculating Overall Priority and Ranking for Alternatives

These steps can be applied to our hypothetical vacation selection scenario as shown in the matrixes in Table 6.6.

Table 6.6 Vacation Destination Reciprocal Matrix

Matrix A					
Hawai	1	7	7	7/	
Florida	1/7	1	1/5	1/5	
Las Vegas	1/7	5	1	1/7	→
Lake Tahoe	1/7	5	7	1	
Column Sums	1,4286	18	15.2	8.3428	

Matrix B						Priority Eigen Vector
Hawai	0.7000[3]	0.3889	0.4605	0.8390		0.5971
Florida	0.1000	0.0556	0.0132	0.0240		0.0482
Las Vegas	0.1000	0.2778	0.0658	0.0171	→	0.1152
Lake Tahoe	0.1000	0.2778	0.4605	0.1199		0.2396
Column Sums	1	1	1	1		

[3] 1/1.4286

Now let's check for the consistency of the above matrix.

According to Saaty (2008), for a reciprocal matrix to be consistent,[4] the largest Eigen vector value is equal to the number of criteria, that is, $\lambda_{max} = n$.

$\lambda_{max} = (0.5971)(1.4286)+(0.0482)(18)+(0.1152)(15.2)+(0.2396)((8.3428) = 5.47$

Consistency Index, CI $= (\lambda_{max} - n)/(n - 1) = (5.47 - 4)/(4 - 1) = 0.49$

Consistency Ratio, CR = CI/RI, where RI is the Random Consistency Index obtained from Table 6.7.

Saaty (2008) suggested the values in Table 6.7 for random consistency indices (RI) corresponding to each value of number of criteria (up to 10).

Table 6.7 Saaty's Random Consistency Indices Table

n	1	2	3	4	5	6	7	8	9	10
RI	0	0.16	0.58	0.9	1.12	1.24	1.32	1.41	1.45	1.49

According to Saaty (2008), a matrix is consistent if its CR is less than 10% (< 0.1).[5]

In our case, CR = 0.49/0.9 = 0.54 = 5.4% < 10%.

Because our CR is less than 10%, our matrix is consistent.

Make a Decision

The Eigen vector can be sorted in the descending order to render the sorted matrix in Table 6.8.

Table 6.8 Sorted Vacation Destination Matrix

Hawaii	0.5971
Lake Tahoe	0.2396
Las Vegas	0.1152
Florida	0.0482

---

[4] A comparison matrix A is said to be consistent if $a_{ij}.a_{jk} = a_{ik}$ for all $i, j,$ and k.

[5] If CR $\leq$ 10%, the inconsistency is acceptable; however, if it is > 10%, the subjective judgment needs to be revised.

At this point decision-makers can make their decision by choosing the highest ranked alternative, which in this case is Hawaii.

AHP Pros and Cons

Although there are a few cons (disadvantages) of the AHP approach, overall its pros (advantages) outweigh them and therefore this approach is very useful in complex decision-making in group and multi-criteria environments. Some of its many applications include project selection, project planning, prediction, resource acquisition and allocation, conflict resolution, and project risk management.

The pros of the AHP approach include the following:

- It allows complex decision-making involving multiple criteria.
- It allows both qualitative (subjective) and quantitative (objective) evaluation criteria.
- It involves decision hierarchy and pairwise comparisons for the alternatives and the evaluation criteria, which make it easy to understand.
- The pairwise comparisons only focus on two entities at a time, which makes the comparison process easier.
- It allows group decision making, which
    - Helps increase the participation of group members
    - Allows leveraging the knowledge and experiences of the group members
    - Minimizes the dominance of the decision-making process by one individual

The following are some cons of the AHP:

- It is hard to use when the number of factors in the evaluation criteria are more than seven because of increased pairwise comparison complexity.[6]
- The development of its subjective scale is based on expert judgment, which makes the scale susceptible to human errors and biases.
- Adding or removing an alternative or a criterion is difficult.

---

[6] Depending on the complexity of the decision, AHP tools may include manual (by hand) calculations, an Excel spreadsheet, or sophisticated software. An example of professional commercial AHP software is *Expert Choice* developed by Expert Choice, Inc.

Summary

The mind map in Figure 6.3 summarizes the AHP.

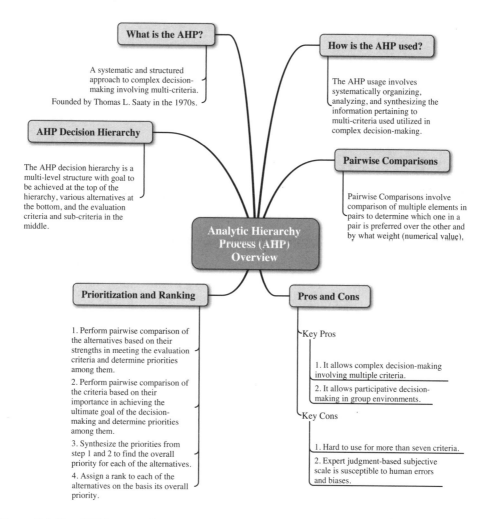

Figure 6.3 The AHP Overview Summary

Key Terms

AHP

Decision Hierarchy

Eigen Value

Eigen Vector

Evaluation Criteria

Intensity of Importance

Pairwise Comparison

Priority

Ranking

Relative Weight

Saaty Scale

Synthesis

Case Study: Topa Technologies Uses the AHP to Select the Project Manager

Topa Technologies, a leading construction company in Nevada, USA, earned a multi-million-dollar contract to build a state-of-the-art shopping mall in the suburbs of Carson City. Before embarking on this journey to a successful project, Topa faced a challenge to select the most suitable project manager for the project. Several outstanding candidates applied for the advertised position but the company wanted to perform a thorough screening using 360-degree evaluation criteria due to criticality of this key position. To accomplish its goal, the company decided to use the AHP as the selection vehicle for this position. This approach was in line with the company's goal of adopting the data-driven decision-making philosophy rather than to continue using the same old highly subjective "seat of the pants" legacy style.

Determine the Evaluation Criteria

The goal was to select the best candidate out of the top four contenders—Steve, Nate, Rick, and Cindy. The evaluation criteria included the following factors:

- Experience
- Academic Qualifications
- PMP Credentials
- Soft Skills

Table 6.9 outlines the credentials of these four candidates against the evaluation criteria.

Table 6.9 Candidates' Credentials

	Candidates			
	Steve	Nate	Rick	Cindy
Experience	Ex-Marine retrained as Project Manager; 10 years of solid experience in managing commercial construction projects.	26 years in construction industry managing mid- to mega-size commercial as well as non-commercial construction projects.	10 years of teaching experience in a junior college; 11 years of experience in managing various small to medium-size non-commercial construction projects.	Has owned her own consulting company for the past 15 years and manages primarily non-commercial construction projects.
Academic Qualifications	Marketing MBA from California State University, Sacramento.	MBA in Project Management from Keller Graduate School of Management, DeVry University.	MS in Civil Engineering from San Jose State University; Certificate in Project Management from University of California, Davis Extension.	BS in Economics from University of Puerto Rico, Mayaguez (UPRM).
PMP Credentials	Yes	Yes	Yes	No
Soft Skills	Leadership qualities include MBWA and data-driven decision-making; great communicator and easily approachable; big picture oriented.	Leads by example using data-driven approach; possesses excellent inspirational and motivational skills; detail oriented.	Great facilitator; primarily consensus-based decision-maker; delegator; big picture oriented.	Believes in close supervision of the team with results-oriented approach; strong believer of motivating via rewards and punishment; fluent in Spanish.

Develop the Decision Hierarchy

Figure 6.4 shows the AHP decision hierarchy developed for making the recruitment decision for the position of the project manager.

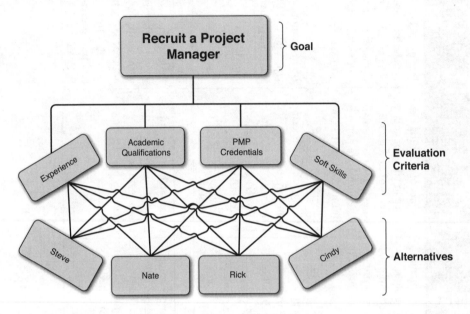

Figure 6.4 The AHP Decision Hierarchy for Project Manager Recruitment

Perform the Analysis

The following was the general approach used in this analysis:

1. Determined *priorities* for the alternatives (relative strength of the candidates) with respect to each factor of the evaluation criteria.

2. Determined *priorities* for each factor of the evaluation criteria based on their importance in achieving the stipulated goal.

3. Combined both types of priorities to determine the holistic priority for each candidate.

4. Compared the candidates on the basis of their individual aggregate priorities. The candidate with the highest aggregate priority was the most suitable candidate.

The priorities were determined on the basis of pairwise comparisons of all interconnected criteria and the alternatives. Each alternative was compared with respect to its contribution to the criterion at the upper level in the hierarchy. The matrix in Table 6.3 captures the outcomes of all comparisons.

The Saaty Scale (refer to Table 6.1) was used to assign weights to the participating nodes in the hierarchy for the sake of comparison and ultimately to determine priority.

The weighted alternatives (candidates) were first compared with respect to their individual strengths in meeting each of the evaluation criteria. Subsequently, the factors of the criteria were compared with respect to their importance to achieving the goal of successfully recruiting the project manager.

Relative Strength of the Candidates with Respect to Each Factor of the Evaluation Criteria

The first step was to determine the relative strength of the candidates with respect to each factor of the evaluation criteria.

Relative Strength of the Candidates with Respect to Experience

The information on each candidate's experience was available as part of the job application; however, it lacked objectivity for measuring the experience. The AHP enabled the recruitment team to develop a scale to measure the relative strengths of the candidates pertaining to experience.

To achieve this, the candidates were compared in pairs on the basis of their experience-related strengths. The weaker in the pair was assigned a weight of 1 and the stronger was assigned the weight according to the Saaty Scale, as shown in Table 6.10.

Table 6.10   Relative Strength of the Candidates with Respect to Experience

Pair #	Candidate 1	Weight	Candidate 2	Weight	Explanation
1	Steve	1	Nate	5	Nate had more and diverse experience.
2	Steve	3	Rick	1	Steve's experience was more relevant to the project requirements.
3	Steve	4	Cindy	1	Steve's experience was more relevant to the project requirements.
4	Nate	5	Rick	1	Nate had more and diverse experience.

Pair #	Candidate 1	Weight	Candidate 2	Weight	Explanation
5	Nate	5	Cindy	1	Nate had more and diverse experience.
6	Rick	1	Cindy	3	Cindy had more experience relevant to the project requirements.

Following the row-column sequence, the relative weights were transferred to the following matrix shown in Table 6.11. The weight for the weaker element of the pair is the reciprocal of the weight of the one that is stronger.

Table 6.11

Experience	Steve	Nate	Rick	Cindy
Steve	1	1/5	3	4
Nate	5	1	5	5
Rick	1/3	1/5	1	1/3
Cindy	1/4	1/5	3	1

The next step was to find the right Eigen vector for this matrix, which was calculated as follows:

1. All column cell values were added up (shown in Table 6.12).

Table 6.12

Experience	Steve	Nate	Rick	Cindy
Steve	1	1/5	3	4
Nate	5	1	5	5
Rick	1/3	1/5	1	1/3
Cindy	1/4	1/5	3	1
Sum of Column Cell Values	6.58	1.6	12	10.33

2. The value of each cell of the columns of the matrix was divided by the sum of the values of the corresponding column (shown in Table 6.13).

Table 6.13

Experience	Steve	Nate	Rick	Cindy
Steve	0.150	0.125	0.250	0.387
Nate	0.760	0.625	0.417	0.484
Rick	0.050	0.125	0.083	0.032
Cindy	0.040	0.125	0.250	0.097

3. The new values of each row of the matrix were averaged (shown in Table 6.14).

Table 6.14

Experience	Steve	Nate	Rick	Cindy	Priority Eigen Vector
Steve	0.150	0.125	0.250	0.387	0.228
Nate	0.760	0.625	0.417	0.484	0.572
Rick	0.050	0.125	0.083	0.032	0.072
Cindy	0.040	0.125	0.250	0.097	0.128

Relative Strength of the Candidates with Respect to Academic Qualifications

Next, the candidates were compared in pairs on the basis of their strengths pertaining to their academic qualifications. The weaker in the pair was assigned a weight of 1 and the stronger was assigned the weight according to the Saaty Scale, as shown in Table 6.15.

Table 6.15 Relative Strength of the Candidates with Respect to Academic Qualifications

Pair #	Candidate 1	Weight	Candidate 2	Weight	Explanation
1	Steve	1	Nate	4	Nate had a master's degree in project management.
2	Steve	1	Rick	3	Rick possessed more academic qualifications. Plus, he had additional project management qualifications.
3	Steve	4	Cindy	1	Steve possessed a higher degree than Cindy.

Pair #	Candidate 1	Weight	Candidate 2	Weight	Explanation
4	Nate	1	Rick	1	Nate had comparable academic qualifications to Rick.
5	Nate	3	Cindy	1	Nate possessed a higher degree than Cindy.
6	Rick	4	Cindy	1	Rick possessed more academic qualifications.

Following the row-column sequence, the relative weights were transferred to the matrix in Table 6.16. The weight for the weaker element of the pair is the reciprocal of the weight of the one that is stronger.

Table 6.16

Academic Qualifications	Steve	Nate	Rick	Cindy
Steve	1	1/4	1/3	4
Nate	4	1	1	3
Rick	3	1	1	4
Cindy	1/4	1/3	1/4	1

The next step was to find the right Eigen vector for this matrix, which was calculated as follows:

1. All column cell values were added up (shown in Table 6.17).

Table 6.17

Academic Qualifications	Steve	Nate	Rick	Cindy
Steve	1	1/4	1/3	4
Nate	4	1	1	3
Rick	3	1	1	4
Cindy	1/4	1/3	1/4	1
Sum of Column Cell Values	8.25	2.58	2.58	12

2. The value of each cell of the columns of the matrix was divided by the sum of the values of the corresponding column (shown in Table 6.18).

Table 6.18

Academic Qualifications	Steve	Nate	Rick	Cindy
Steve	0.121	0.097	0.129	0.333
Nate	0.484	0.388	0.388	0.250
Rick	0.365	0.388	0.388	0.333
Cindy	0.030	0.129	0.097	0.083

3. The new values of each row of the matrix were averaged (shown in Table 6.19).

Table 6.19

Academic Qualifications	Steve	Nate	Rick	Cindy	Priority Eigen Vector
Steve	0.121	0.097	0.129	0.333	0.170
Nate	0.484	0.388	0.388	0.250	0.378
Rick	0.365	0.388	0.388	0.333	0.369
Cindy	0.030	0.129	0.097	0.083	0.085

Relative Strength of the Candidates with Respect to PMP Credentials

Next, the candidates were compared in pairs on the basis of their possession of the PMP credentials. The weaker in the pair was assigned a weight of 1 and the stronger was assigned the weight according to the Saaty Scale as shown in Table 6.20.

Table 6.20   Relative Strength of the Candidates with Respect to PMP Credentials

Pair #	Candidate 1	Weight	Candidate 2	Weight	Explanation
1	Steve	1	Nate	1	Both were PMP credentialed.
2	Steve	1	Rick	1	Both were PMP credentialed.
3	Steve	9	Cindy	1	Cindy did not possess PMP.
4	Nate	1	Rick	1	Both were PMP credentialed.
5	Nate	9	Cindy	1	Cindy did not possess PMP.
6	Rick	9	Cindy	1	Cindy did not possess PMP.

Following the row-column sequence, the relative weights were transferred to the matrix in Table 6.21. The weight for the weaker element of the pair is the reciprocal of the weight of the one that is stronger.

Table 6.21

PMP Credentials	Steve	Nate	Rick	Cindy
Steve	1	1	1	9
Nate	1	1	1	9
Rick	1	1	1	9
Cindy	1/9	1/9	1/9	1

The next step was to find the right Eigen vector for this matrix, which was calculated as follows:

1. All column cell values were added up (shown in Table 6.22).

Table 6.22

PMP Credentials	Steve	Nate	Rick	Cindy
Steve	1	1	1	9
Nate	1	1	1	9
Rick	1	1	1	9
Cindy	1/9	1/9	1/9	1
Sum of Column Cell Values	3.11	3.11	3.11	28

2. The value of each cell of the columns of the matrix was divided by the sum of the values of the corresponding column (shown in Table 6.23).

Table 6.23

PMP Credentials	Steve	Nate	Rick	Cindy
Steve	0.321	0.321	0.321	0.321
Nate	0.321	0.321	0.321	0.321
Rick	0.321	0.321	0.321	0.321
Cindy	0.036	0.036	0.036	0.036

3. The new values of each row of the matrix were averaged (shown in Table 6.24).

Table 6.24

PMP Credentials	Steve	Nate	Rick	Cindy	Priority Eigen Vector
Steve	0.321	0.321	0.321	0.321	0.321
Nate	0.321	0.321	0.321	0.321	0.321
Rick	0.321	0.321	0.321	0.321	0.321
Cindy	0.036	0.036	0.036	0.036	0.036

Relative Strength of the Candidates with Respect to Soft Skills

Next, the candidates were compared in pairs on the basis of their relative strengths in soft skills. The weaker in the pair was assigned a weight of 1 and the stronger was assigned the weight according to the Saaty Scale as shown in Table 6.25.

Table 6.25 Relative Strength of the Candidates with Respect to Soft Skills

Pair #	Candidate 1	Weight	Candidate 2	Weight	Explanation
1	Steve	1	Nate	2	Nate was slightly better than Steve in soft skills.
2	Steve	1	Rick	1	Steve and Rick had comparable soft skills.
3	Steve	4	Cindy	1	Cindy sounded like a micro-manager.
4	Nate	3	Rick	1	Nate was slightly better than Rick in soft skills.
5	Nate	4	Cindy	1	Cindy sounded like a micro-manager.
6	Rick	4	Cindy	1	Cindy sounded like a micro-manager.

Following the row-column sequence, the relative weights were transferred to the matrix in Table 6.26. The weight for the weaker element of the pair is the reciprocal of the weight of the one that is stronger.

Table 6.26

Soft Skills	Steve	Nate	Rick	Cindy
Steve	1	1/2	1	4
Nate	2	1	3	4
Rick	1	1/3	1	4
Cindy	1/4	1/4	1/4	1

The next step was to find the right Eigen vector for this matrix, which was calculated as follows:

1. All column cell values were added up (shown in Table 6.27).

Table 6.27

Soft Skills	Steve	Nate	Rick	Cindy
Steve	1	1/2	1	4
Nate	2	1	3	4
Rick	1	1/3	1	4
Cindy	1/4	1/4	1/4	1
Sum of column cell values	4.25	2.08	5.25	13

2. The value of each cell of the columns of the matrix was divided by the sum of the values of the corresponding column (shown in Table 6.28).

Table 6.28

Soft Skills	Steve	Nate	Rick	Cindy
Steve	0.235	0.240	0.190	0.308
Nate	0.471	0.480	0.571	0.308
Rick	0.235	0.160	0.190	0.308
Cindy	0.059	0.120	0.048	0.077

3. The new values of each row of the matrix were averaged (shown in Table 6.29).

Table 6.29

Soft Skills	Steve	Nate	Rick	Cindy	Priority Eigen Vector
Steve	0.235	0.240	0.190	0.308	0.243
Nate	0.471	0.480	0.571	0.308	0.457
Rick	0.235	0.160	0.190	0.308	0.223
Cindy	0.059	0.120	0.048	0.077	0.076

Criteria versus the Goal

After completing the evaluation of various alternatives in terms of their strengths in meeting the criteria, the recruitment team evaluated the factors of the evaluation criteria in terms of their importance in achieving the ultimate goal of recruiting the project manager.

To perform this evaluation, the recruitment team followed the same evaluation approach that they followed in evaluating various alternatives in the previous section.

Table 6.30 captures the weights used for various pairs of the factors in the evaluation criteria.

Table 6.30   Alternative Evaluation with Respect to the Goal

Pair #	Criterion 1	Weight	Criterion 2	Weight	Explanation
1	Experience	5	Academic Qualifications	1	Experience was considered more important for the size and complexity of the project.
2	Experience	4	PMP Credentials	1	Experience was considered more important for the size and complexity of the project.
3	Experience	6	Soft Skills	1	Experience was considered more important for the size and complexity of the project.
4	Academic Qualifications	1	PMP Credentials	1	Both were considered equally important.

Pair #	Criterion 1	Weight	Criterion 2	Weight	Explanation
5	Academic Qualifications	1	Soft Skills	2	Academic qualifications were important but soft skills were considered more important for that project.
6	PMP Credentials	1	Soft Skills	1	Both were considered equally important.

Again, to prioritize various factors in the evaluation criteria, the same procedure was adopted as was done in the previous section for prioritizing various alternatives.

Following the row-column sequence, the relative weights were transferred to the matrix in Table 6.31. The weight for the weaker element of the pair is the reciprocal of the weight of the one that is stronger.

Table 6.31

Evaluation Criteria	Experience	Academic Qualifications	PMP Credentials	Soft Skills
Experience	1	5	4	6
Academic Qualifications	1/5	1	1	2
PMP Credentials	1/4	1	1	1
Soft Skills	1/6	1/2	1	1

The next step was to find the right Eigen vector for this matrix, which was calculated as follows:

1. All column cell values were added up (shown in Table 6.32).

Table 6.32

Evaluation Criteria	Experience	Academic Qualifications	PMP Credentials	Soft Skills
Experience	1	5	4	6
Academic Qualifications	1/5	1	1	2
PMP Credentials	1/4	1	1	1
Soft Skills	1/6	1/2	1	1
Sum of Column Cell Values	1.62	7.50	7	10

2. The value of each cell of the columns of the matrix was divided by the sum of the values of the corresponding column (shown in Table 6.33).

Table 6.33

Evaluation Criteria	Experience	Academic Qualifications	PMP Credentials	Soft Skills
Experience	0.619	0.667	0.571	0.600
Academic Qualifications	0.124	0.133	0.143	0.200
PMP Credentials	0.155	0.133	0.143	0.100
Soft Skills	0.103	0.067	0.143	0.100

3. The new values of each row of the matrix were averaged (shown in Table 6.34).

Table 6.34

Evaluation Criteria	Experience	Academic Qualifications	PMP Credentials	Soft Skills	Priority Eigen Vector
Experience	0.619	0.667	0.571	0.600	0.614
Academic Qualifications	0.124	0.133	0.143	0.200	0.150
PMP Credentials	0.155	0.133	0.143	0.100	0.133
Soft Skills	0.103	0.067	0.143	0.100	0.103

According to Saaty (2008), for a reciprocal matrix to be consistent, the largest Eigen vector value is equal to the number of criteria, that is, $\lambda_{max} = n$.

$\lambda_{max} = (0.614) (1.62)+(0.150) (7.50)+(0.133) (7)+(0.103) ((10) = 4.08$

Consistency Index, CI $= (\lambda_{max} - n)/(n - 1) = (4.08 - 4)/(4 - 1) = 0.36$

Consistency Ratio, CR = CI/RI, where RI is the Random Consistency Index obtained from Table 6.35.

Saaty (2008) suggested the values in Table 6.25 for random consistency indices (RI) corresponding to each value of number of criteria (up to 10).

Table 6.35   Saaty's Random Consistency Indices Table

n	1	2	3	4	5	6	7	8	9	10
RI	0	0.16	0.58	0.9	1.12	1.24	1.32	1.41	1.45	1.49

According to Saaty (2005), a matrix is consistent if its CR is less than 10% (< 0.1).

In our case, CR = 0.36/0.9 = 0.4 = 4% < 10%.

Because our CR is less than 10%, our matrix is consistent.

Synthesize and Rank Priorities

The recruitment team had determined the following two lists of priorities thus far:

- A list containing priorities of various alternatives (candidates) with respect to the evaluation criteria
- A list of priorities of various factors of the evaluation criteria with respect to the goal

These priorities were further synthesized to determine the priorities of various alternatives with respect to the final goal.

Synthesizing

The following synthesis procedure was used by the team:

1. Multiply the priority of the alternative with respect to *experience* by *experience's* priority with respect to the final goal.

2. Multiply the priority of the alternative with respect to *academic qualifications* by *academic qualifications'* priority with respect to the final goal.

3. Multiply the priority of the alternative with respect to *PMP credentials* by *PMP credentials'* priority with respect to the final goal.

4. Multiply the priority of the alternative with respect to *soft skills* by *soft skills'* priority with respect to the final goal.

5. Add the results from each of the preceding four steps.

Ranking

Table 6.36 contains the calculations for determining the overall priority for each of the four alternatives used for ranking.

Table 6.36 Determining Overall Priorities for the Candidates

Alternative	Criterion	Alternative-Criterion Priority (ACP)	Criterion-Goal Priority (CGP)	Total Priority = ACP x CGP	Overall Priority for the Alternative
Steve	Experience	0.228	0.614	0.140	**0.233**
Steve	Academic Qualifications	0.170	0.150	0.026	
Steve	PMP Credentials	0.321	0.133	0.043	
Steve	Soft Skills	0.243	0.103	0.025	
Nate	Experience	0.572	0.614	0.351	**0.498**
Nate	Academic Qualifications	0.378	0.150	0.057	
Nate	PMP Credentials	0.321	0.133	0.043	
Nate	Soft Skills	0.457	0.103	0.047	
Rick	Experience	0.072	0.614	0.044	**0.165**
Rick	Academic Qualifications	0.369	0.150	0.055	
Rick	PMP Credentials	0.321	0.133	0.043	
Rick	Soft Skills	0.223	0.103	0.023	
Cindy	Experience	0.128	0.614	0.079	**0.104**
Cindy	Academic Qualifications	0.085	0.150	0.013	
Cindy	PMP Credentials	0.036	0.133	0.005	
Cindy	Soft Skills	0.076	0.103	0.008	

Make a Decision

The analysis results in Table 6.36 provided sufficient information to the recruitment team to make a decision on the candidate of choice. The candidate who ranked the highest was the clear choice.

Conclusion

The four alternatives (candidates) were ranked on the basis of their overall priorities as shown in Table 6.37. Obviously, Nate was recruited for the position of project manager based on this ranking.

Table 6.37 Final Ranking of the Candidates Based on Their Overall Priorities

Alternative (Candidate)	Overall Priority	Rank Based on Overall Priority
Steve	0.233	2
Nate	0.498	1
Rick	0.165	3
Cindy	0.104	4

Case Questions

1. List the alternatives, evaluation criteria, and the goal for decision-making in this case.

2. Describe the synthesizing process used in this case.

3. What was the final decision? Did Topa achieve its stipulated goal?

Chapter Review and Discussion Questions

1. Define the AHP. What does it entail?

2. What is a pairwise comparison?

3. What are the three main levels of the AHP decision hierarchy?

4. How do you assign the weights to various nodes or elements of the AHP decision hierarchy?

5. Describe the procedure for synthesizing and ranking the priorities.

6. List the pros and cons of the AHP.

Bibliography

BPMSG. (2010). "Analytic Hierarchy Process AHP - Business Performance Management." Retrieved May 14, 2015, from https://www.youtube.com/watch?v=18GWVtVAAzs

Geopel, K.D. (2013). *AHP Introduction*. Changi Business Park, Singapore.

Geopel, K.D. (2013). *Implementing the Analytic Hierarchy Process as a Standard Method for Multi-Criteria Decision Making in Corporate Enterprises*—A New AHP Excel Template with Multiple Inputs. Changi Business Park, Singapore

Ishizaka, A., & Labib, A. (2009). "Analytic Hierarchy Process and Expert Choice: Benefits and Limitations." Retrieved May 15, 2015, from http://www.palgrave-journals.com/ori/journal/v22/n4/full/ori200910a.html

Liu, Y. (2014). "Analytic Hierarchy Process." Retrieved May 10, 2015, from http://www.wright.edu/~yan.liu/AHP.pdf

Mocenni, C. (2014). "The Analytic Hierarchy Process." Retrieved May 13, 2015, from http://www.dii.unisi.it/~mocenni/Note_AHP.pdf

Saaty, T.L. (2008). "Decision Making with the Analytic Hierarchy Process." *Int. J. Services Sciences*, 1 (1), pp. 83-98.

Saaty, T.L., and Vargas, L.G. (2001). "Models, Methods, Concepts & Applications of the Analytic Hierarchy Process." Boston: Kluwer's Academic Publishers.

7

Lean Six Sigma

Learning Objectives

After reading this chapter, you should be familiar with

- The synergistic blend of Lean and Six Sigma
- Common types and causes of waste
- Lean versus Six Sigma
- DMAIC methodology
- PDSA cycle
- The Model for Improvement
- Lean Six Sigma (LSS) tools

> "Measurement is the first step that leads to control and eventually to improvement. If you can't measure something, you can't understand it. If you can't understand it, you can't control it. If you can't control it, you can't improve it."
>
> —*H. James Harrington, IBM quality expert who wrote the 1987 book* Poor Quality Costs

In a highly competitive contemporary business environment, high quality, lower costs, minimal inventory, on-time delivery, and customer satisfaction constitute a major strategic goal for organizations to gain and sustain competitive advantage. LSS methodology, with its underlying philosophy of continuous improvement, can help streamline business processes within an organization, which can address the following three fundamental questions that are aligned with strategic organizational goals:

1. How to improve quality of business processes, products, and services?
2. How to control costs?
3. How to ensure on-time delivery of products and services?

This chapter discusses the basics of the LSS approach along with the associated tools to show how LSS can improve the business processes and help organizations achieve their strategic goals and objectives.

What Is Lean Six Sigma?

The LSS approach is a synergistic blend of two methodologies—Lean and Six Sigma. Both have a positive impact on business and project processes (the goal of both is to streamline the processes) but applying both together tremendously enhances their synergistic positive impact.

Both Lean and Six Sigma aim at eliminating waste, but with different approaches. Whereas Lean targets elimination of waste by reducing the non-value-added[1] steps from processes, Six Sigma focuses on eliminating defects and reducing variation from processes. Lean and Six Sigma methodologies complement each other—the synergy gained by combining them brings 360-degree benefits to the processes. In fact, in recent history, their combination has proven to be so powerful that it has become a common practice to use Lean and Six Sigma in tandem. According to *goleansixsigma.com*, a LSS training company, "Lean accelerates Six Sigma, delivering greater results than what would typically be achieved by Lean or Six Sigma individually. Combining these two methods gives your improvement team a comprehensive tool set to increase the speed and effectiveness of any process within your organization—resulting in increased revenue, reduced costs and improved collaboration." LSS utilizes Six Sigma's DMAIC[2] strategy for process improvement coupled with Lean strategy for waste elimination to achieve accuracy and speed in delivery of the results (products and services) of the projects and operations of the organization to the end users.

---

[1] A non-value-added step or activity in a process is the one that consumes time and resources but does not add any value to the outcome of the process and does not contribute to the value perceived by the end-user (customer).

[2] The acronym DMAIC (pronounced as *dee-maik*) stands for five phases (**D**efine, **M**easure, **A**nalyze, **I**mprove/**I**mplement, and **C**ontrol) of Six Sigma's structured, standardized, and systematic process for problem resolution and defect elimination. According to the American Society for Quality (ASQ), "DMAIC is a data-driven quality strategy used to improve processes. It is an integral part of a Six Sigma initiative, but in general can be implemented as a standalone quality improvement procedure or as part of other process improvement initiatives such as lean."

Lean

Longo (2012) defines Lean as "An integrated approach to utilizing Capital, Materials, and Human resources to produce just what is needed, when it is needed, in the amount needed with minimum Materials, Equipment, Labor and Space."

The Lean concept originally came from the Japanese Toyota production system's primary goal to minimize the waste. This methodology streamlines business and manufacturing processes by identifying and eliminating unnecessary, redundant, and wasteful steps and keeping only the ones that add value. Because Lean eliminates waste, it enhances the true value received by the organizations by enabling them to do more with less. It also enhances the value in the eyes of the customers of the organizations (improves customer satisfaction) by enabling them to receive high-quality products and services on time.

For Lean to be effective end-to-end application must occur across all business or project processes; otherwise its full benefits will not be realized due to pockets of bottlenecks.

Waste

The following are some common types of wastes that are addressed by Lean:

- *Transportation:* Unnecessary movement and handling; Delays caused by long distance between source and destination of the raw materials or finished products; Avoidable people travel

- *Slow speed or pace:* Slow approval processes; Red Tape; Slow procurement; Slow decision-making

- *Inventory:* Delays and nuisance caused by idle/surplus inventory

- *Wait:* Wait for approvals and decisions; Workers wait caused by unplanned process downtime; Wait time caused by inefficient processes; Wait caused by long setup and lead time; Wait caused by unnecessary lag in project schedule activities and by unreasonable sequential relationship among activities

- *Overproduction:* Producing more than the market demand; High work-in-progress; High stock of finished products; High stock of raw materials

- *Overpadded estimates:* Unnecessary lags in project activity duration estimates; Overestimation of project resources

- *Redundancy:* Duplicate non-value-add processes or project activities

- *Rework:* Waste of time and money because rework caused by poor quality of raw materials, processes, products, services, or workmanship; Returns; Dissatisfied customers

- *Inspection:* Unnecessary verification steps; Cost outweighing benefits
- *Non–value-adding steps:* Process steps or activities that contribute nothing to the value perceived by the customer

Common Causes of Waste

The following list summarizes some common causes of waste:

- Unnecessary reviews
- Unreasonably long review processes
- Unnecessary approvals
- Unreasonably long approval processes
- Lack of conformance to the established quality standards
- Lack of coordination among people handling materials
- Long setup and lead time
- Poor maintenance and control
- Lack of training
- Poor project and process management skills
- Poor planning
- Poor scheduling
- Unorganized workplace
- Poor supplier quality and reliability
- Lack of automation

Six Sigma

Motorola was the first American company to implement the Six Sigma concept in the form of a total quality management system. It adopted this concept to be able to compete with the high-quality Japanese products.

The primary goal of Six Sigma methodology is to achieve continuous process improvement by reducing the number of defects in the process. It involves continuous improvements in quality and efficiency by streamlining and improving of business processes. It also provides a business or project real and measurable results for better decision-making.

Six Sigma–level quality is highly sought after in today's business landscape. As illustrated in Figure 7.1, a process based on the Six Sigma concept is 99.99966% defect-free (or

99.99966% accurate), which implies that it only has 3.4 defects per million opportunities (DPMO). This process is considered to be highly predictable, consistent, and reliable due to very few defects and low variability.

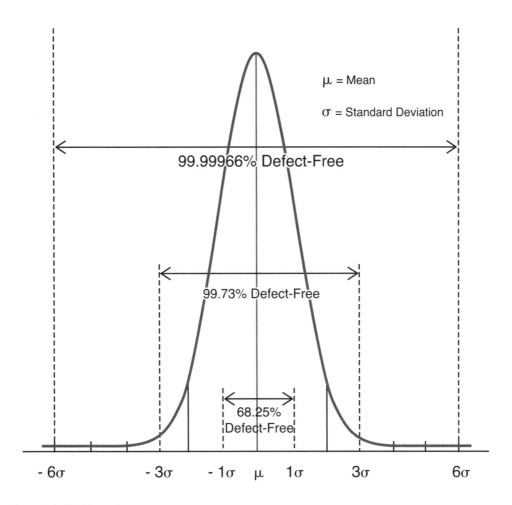

Figure 7.1 Six Sigma Accuracy

Example:

According to a survey, the mean annual salary of a PMP credentialed project manager in the United States is $96,000, with a standard deviation of $1975. The data set from the survey results has a bell-shaped distribution. Approximately what percentage of PMP credentialed project managers are there for annual salaries between $85,000 and $107,000. How accurate is this analysis?

Solution:

In this example,

Mean μ = 96000

Standard deviation σ = 1975

Upper (Right) Control Limit (UCL) of the bell curve,

  $\mu + N\sigma$ = 107000, where N = Number of standard deviations = 1,2,3,....,6

  or $N = (107000 - \mu)/\sigma = (107000 - 96000)/1975$ = 5.6 (Approximately)

Lower (Left) Control Limit (LCL) of the bell curve,

  $\mu - N\sigma$ = 85000, where N = Number of standard deviations = 1,2,3,....,6

  or $N = (85000 - \mu)/\sigma = (85000 - 96000)/1975$ = – 5.6 (Approximately)

This analysis reflects Six Sigma level of accuracy and implies that 99.99966% PMP credentialed project managers fall between the given annual salary range. In other words, there are 99.99966% chances to find a PMP credentialed project manager within the annual salary range of $85,000 to $107,000.

Lean versus Six Sigma: Side-by-Side Comparison

Table 7.1 outlines the comparison between Lean and Six Sigma based on key criteria.

Table 7.1   Lean versus Six Sigma

Criterion	Lean	Six Sigma
Process Improvement	Eliminate/minimize waste	Eliminate/minimize variation
Business Justification	Speed	Six Sigma level of accuracy
Cost Reduction	Targets reduction of operating costs	Targets reduction of cost of poor quality
Complexity of Undertaking	Intermediate	High
Customer Satisfaction Focus	Yes	Yes
People Empowerment	Yes	Yes
Improvement Culture Promoted	Culture of continuous improvement	Culture of continuous improvement
Key Tools	Value Stream Map (VSM), Kanban, Teamwork, Problem Solving, etc.	Brainstorming, Cause-and-Effect Diagrams, 5 Whys, Pareto Analysis, etc.

How LSS Can Improve the Status Quo

LSS utilizes the DMAIC process based on underlying best practices and tools from Lean and Six Sigma to help improve the status quo in terms of the following:

- Eliminate/minimize defects to reduce returns, rework, scrap, waste, and customer dissatisfaction
- Reduce lead and cycle time
- Achieve consistency through standardized processes
- Reduce process variation
- Reduce non-value-added inventory
- Streamline supply chain

DMAIC

DMAIC is LSS's process improvement engine that provides well-structured phases of the improvement cycle from defining the problem to implementing the improvement. The key activities in a DMAIC cycle include defining (understanding) the problem, understanding the processes, collecting process data, analyzing the collected data, identifying possible causes via root cause analysis (RCA), determining appropriate corrective actions, evaluating various corrective actions to select the best one, implementing the solution or corrective action, validating the solution, and monitoring and controlling the improved processes to sustain improvement.

DMAIC has gained tremendous global popularity as a model of choice for process improvement because of its following two key advantages:

- It facilitates rapid delivery of the improvement results.
- It enables project teams to start performing more efficiently and effectively.

Figure 7.2 illustrates the DMAIC methodology.

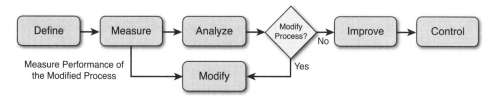

Figure 7.2 DMAIC Methodology for Process Improvement

Define

During the define phase of DMAIC, the improvement project is officially launched. Perform the following steps in this phase:

1. Define the problem and the improvement opportunity.

2. Define the objectives and scope for the improvement project.

3. Define key improvement metrics and success criteria.

Measure

DMAIC's measure phase is used for understanding the current situation as well as for measuring the performance of the modified process. Perform the following steps in this phase:

1. Develop a baseline by assessing the current performance.

2. Understand all possible factors that could have contributed to the current situation.

3. Measure the performance of the modified process, if applicable.

Analyze

As its name implies, during the analyze phase you analyze the factors identified to be possible contributors to the problem or current situation and converge only on a few key contributors by eliminating insignificant or non-important factors. Perform the following steps in this phase:

1. Utilize analytical tools and techniques to evaluate the possible contributing factors.

2. Find the root cause(s).

3. Decide whether the existing process needs modification or whether an improvement (new enhancement) needs to be implemented.

Improve

During DMAIC's improve phase, you develop and implement a solution to improve the status quo. Perform the following steps in this phase:

1. Develop a feasible solution and action plan that can lead to an improvement.

2. Implement the solution.

Control

The control phase ensures that any improvements are sustainable. Perform the following steps in this phase:

1. Validate the improvement results against the success-measuring criteria.

2. Utilize appropriate tools and techniques to ensure that the improvements are sustainable.

The PDSA Cycle

The PDSA (<u>P</u>lan, <u>D</u>o, <u>S</u>tudy, <u>A</u>ct) or PDCA (<u>P</u>lan, <u>D</u>o, <u>C</u>heck, <u>A</u>ct) Cycle, as shown in Figure 7.3, is also called the Deming cycle after this concept's originator, Edward Deming (1900–1993). This iterative cycle embedded into the DMAIC phases provides a framework for improvement and is the focal point of the LSS process or system improvement efforts.

The PDSA cycles, according to Langley, et al., the authors of *The Improvement Guide* (2009), "can be used throughout the project, in any activity of the project, including any phase and activity within the DMAIC model project framework, to facilitate learning." PDSA is used within the DMAIC phases to test various hypotheses.

Example: The Model for Improvement

According to Langley, et al., the Model for Improvement can be defined as the combination of rapid PDSA (or PDCA) cycles and the following three questions:

- What are we trying to accomplish?

- How will we know a change is an improvement?

- What changes can we make that will result in an improvement?

You ask these three questions repeatedly as part of running a trial through PDSA cycle(s), learning from the results of the trial, and taking further actions based on the learning as explained next:

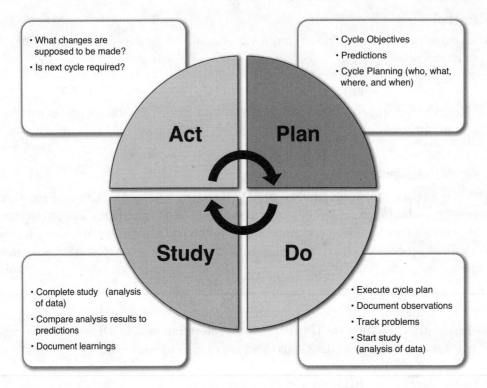

Act
- What changes are supposed to be made?
- Is next cycle required?

Plan
- Cycle Objectives
- Predictions
- Cycle Planning (who, what, where, and when)

Study
- Complete study (analysis of data)
- Compare analysis results to predictions
- Document learnings

Do
- Execute cycle plan
- Document observations
- Track problems
- Start study (analysis of data)

Figure 7.3 The PDSA Cycle

<u>Plan:</u> The first PDSA cycle segment involves planning for the cycle itself. You perform the following steps in this segment:

1. Identify the opportunity.
2. Define the objectives of the PDSA cycle.
3. Develop predictions.[3]
4. Make the plan for the PDSA cycle—that is, who will do what, where, and when during the cycle?

---

[3] "The PDSA cycle is a learning cycle based on experiments. When using the PDSA cycle predictions of the results are important. This is important for several reasons but most notably due to an understanding of the theory of knowledge. We will learn much more if we write down our prediction. Otherwise we often just think (after the fact); yeah that is pretty much what I expected (even if it wasn't). Also we often fail to think specifically enough at the start to even have a prediction. Forcing yourself to make a prediction gets you to think more carefully up front and can help you set better experiments." Hunter, J. (2012), *Curious Cat Management Improvement Blog: Keys to the Effective Use of the PDSA Improvement Cycle.*

Do: The second segment includes the execution of the plan from the first segment (implementing the change on a small scale[4]). You perform the following steps in this segment:

1. Collect and document observations during the execution of the PDSA plan.

2. Conduct a post-execution debrief.

3. Collect and document post-execution reflection notes from the improvement team.

4. Compile the results from various surveys, if applicable.

5. Organize the collected data for analysis in the next segment of the PDSA cycle.

Study: The third segment includes analyzing the data collected in the second segment. You perform the following steps in this segment:

1. Analyze (study) the data collected from executing the PDSA plan.

2. Draw inferences from the data analysis.

3. Compare inferences to the predictions from the first segment.

4. Document the findings:

    a. Do inferences match the predictions?

    b. Are there any new findings that did not match the predictions?

Inferences—Predictions Comparison During the Study Segment of the PDSA Cycle

Julie, a patient with symptoms of stomach pain, goes to her primary care physician, who predicts that the patient's stomach pain is due to acid reflux; he then orders an endoscopy test for Julie and expects one of the following two possible outcomes based on the test results:

Scenario 1: Julie indeed has been suffering from acid reflux. In this scenario, the inferences match the predictions and the doctor prescribes a treatment plan to combat the acid reflux.

Scenario 2: Julie does not have any complications related to the acid reflux; rather, a new finding indicates that she has a kidney stone. In this scenario, the inferences do not match the predictions and the doctor prescribes a treatment plan in line with the new findings.

---

[4] Much like testing the hair die on a small skin patch first to ensure there is no adverse reaction before applying on the entire scalp.

Act: The fourth segment includes deciding next steps based on the results. You perform the following steps in this segment:

1. Discuss the comprehensive cycle evaluation report with the improvement team.
2. Decide whether the current model needs any modifications or adjustments.
3. Decide what changes need to be made to the process or the system.
4. Decide whether another PDSA cycle is required.
   a. If the change was successful, implement it on a larger scale.
   b. If the change was not successful, begin another PDSA cycle.

Thus, the PDSA technique can prove to be very helpful within the LSS DMAIC phases to test any hypothesis quickly for various product and/or process improvement projects.

Lean Six Sigma Tools

LSS methodology uses a multitude of qualitative as well as quantitative tools in pursuit of process improvement. Not all organizations use all the tools. LSS experts including but not limited to LSS Black Belts,[5] Green Belts,[6] and project managers in an organization decide what tools can be used in a particular project. Because every process improvement project involves change, organizational support is needed to sustain the process improvement efforts and implement the desired changes. The roles that provide the organizational support include Champions[7] and Executives.

This section focuses on the most commonly used tools in each LSS DMAIC phase.

Define Phase

The key tools used during the define phase include a project charter; stakeholder analysis; matrix diagram, supplier, input, process, output, customer (SIPOC) diagram; strengths, weaknesses, opportunities, threats (SWOT) analysis; VSM; and voice of the customer (VOC), as discussed in the upcoming sections.

---

[5] LSS Black Belt professionals lead the process improvement projects as well as train and coach the project teams.

[6] LSS Green Belt professionals perform data collection and analysis for the process improvement projects led by Black Belts.

[7] According to ASQ (http://asq.org/), Champions "translate the company's vision, mission, goals and metrics to create an organizational deployment plan, identify individual projects, identify resources, and remove roadblocks" and Executives "provide overall alignment by establishing the strategic focus of the Six Sigma program within the context of the organization's culture and vision."

Project Charter

The project charter is a statement used to accomplish the following key milestones:

- Formal authorization of the project
- Business justification of the project
- High-level definition of scope and direction of the project
- An agreement between the project team and the sponsor about the project expectations
- Assignment of the project manager

Stakeholder Analysis

You do a stakeholder analysis to

- Identify diverse stakeholders (individuals or groups who have a vested interest in how a process performs); analyze their level of interest, influence, and power; figure out whether they are supporters or resisters; and then formulate a strategy to bring everyone onboard with the process changes.
- Understand how and when to approach stakeholders and communicate with them to get their buy-in.

Matrix Diagram

A matrix diagram can help you identify, analyze, and evaluate the existence and strength of relationships between two or more sets of information, as shown in Table 7.2.

SIPOC

SIPOC stands for Supplier, Input (from supplier to process), Process, Output (from process to customer), Customer.

A SIPOC diagram helps you understand a process within its contextual environment, which includes its upstream links with the customers and downstream links with the suppliers. This information is critical in pinpointing where the bottlenecks can be in the process and its associated environment.

Figure 7.4 outlines the SIPOC diagram for a typical integrated circuit (IC) design validation process.

Table 7.2 Matrix Diagram

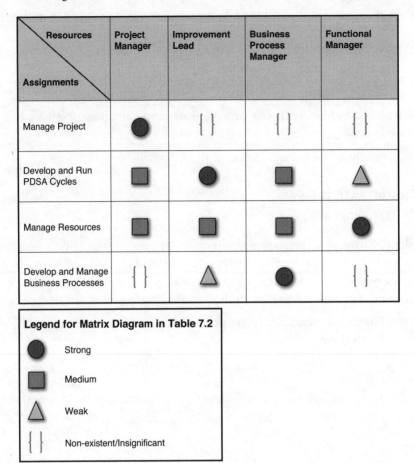

Resources / Assignments	Project Manager	Improvement Lead	Business Process Manager	Functional Manager
Manage Project	●	{ }	{ }	{ }
Develop and Run PDSA Cycles	■	●	■	△
Manage Resources	■	■	■	●
Develop and Manage Business Processes	{ }	△	●	{ }

Legend for Matrix Diagram in Table 7.2

● Strong

■ Medium

△ Weak

{ } Non-existent/Insignificant

Supplier	Input	Process	Output	Customer
Define Department	Raw Design	Validation Process	Validated Design	Fabrication Unit
S	I	P	O	C

Figure 7.4 A Typical SIPOC Diagram

SWOT Analysis

As shown in Figure 7.5, a SWOT analysis looks at the **S**trengths, **W**eaknesses, **O**pportunities, and **T**hreats of an organization in the context of its internal and external environments. The strengths and weaknesses factors are associated with the organization's internal environment, whereas opportunities and threats are associated with the external environment. These factors have tremendous impact on the strategic planning processes of the organization and hence they must be analyzed.

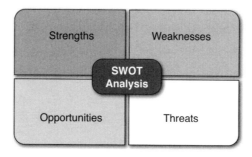

Figure 7.5 SWOT Analysis

A SWOT analysis provides an organization answers to the following questions:

- How do we capitalize on strengths?
- How do we minimize the impact of threats?
- How do we take advantage of opportunities?
- How do we handle threats, if identified?

Value Stream Map (VSM)

A value stream map (VSM) is a Lean tool that provides a comprehensive overview of an entire process analyzing what is required to meet customer needs. It is used to perform end-to-end analysis of the current state of a process and determine its target state. It uses graphics or icons to provide a visual map of the process, which helps all project stakeholders to understand how value is created and where the waste can be.

For example, assume you want to capture the current and target states, respectively, of a built-to-order computer manufacturing process. For this process:

Total process cycle time = Value-added time + Non-value-added time

Overall Process efficiency = Total value-added time / Total process cycle time

Current State　In the current state of the process, orders received from the customers are manually processed by marketing. It takes 30 minutes per order for marketing to interpret and download the order and send it to the assembly unit in Excel spreadsheet format. Assembly technicians pull the parts from the inventory to build the order, which takes about 45 minutes per order. The parts are transported on pushcarts and stocked near the assembly stations. The parts are then sorted for the order at-hand. This whole process takes about 90 minutes. A yellow triangle represents surplus inventory near the assembly stations. The assembled computer is then pushed on a cart to the testing station. If the unit fails during the test, it is pulled out for repairs and retested. Computers tested successfully are packed and shipped to the customer.

Figure 7.6 shows the end-to-end process and the time taken by each step of the process, both value-added and non-value-added.

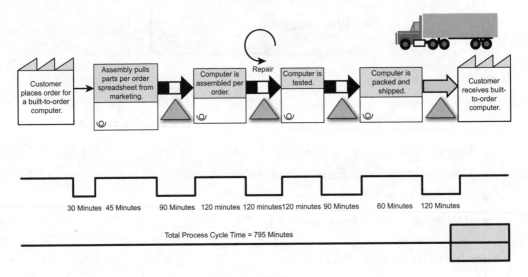

Figure 7.6 Current State of the Process

Total cycle time for the current state of the process

 = Value-add time + Non-value-add time

 = 345 + 450

 = 795 Minutes

Overall efficiency of the current process

 = Total value-added time / Total process cycle time

 = 345 / 795

 = 43.4%

Target State   The target state includes measures taken to reduce the wasteful (non-value-added) time from the process:

- Replace the spreadsheet-based manual order processing with an integrated Enterprise Resource Planning (ERP) solution where orders placed by a customer appear almost instantaneously at the workstation on the assembly line.
- Replace the pushcart way of transportation with automatic conveyor belts.
- Eliminate surplus inventory by adopting the just-in-time inventory system.
- Improve quality and minimize repairs.

Figure 7.7 shows the modified (target) end-to-end process and the time taken by each step of the process, both value-added and non-value-added.

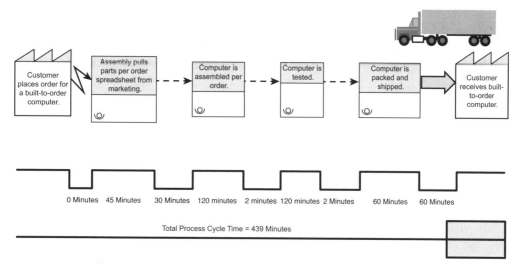

Figure 7.7   Target State of the Process

Total cycle time for the target state of the process

> = Value-added time + Non-value-added time
> = 345 + 94
> = 439 Minutes

Overall Process efficiency

> = Total value-add time / Total process cycle time
> = 345 / 439
> = 78.6%

Clearly, the target state is 35.2% (78.6 – 43.4) more efficient than the current state.

Voice of the Customer (VOC)

The voice of the customer VOC process is to capture and understand feedback or requirements from current and future customers (internal as well as external) about what satisfies or dissatisfies them and what their tastes and preferences are, and then customizing the offerings to fulfill customers' needs to their satisfaction.

According to *www.isixsigma.com*, the VOC is "the term used to describe the stated and unstated needs or requirements of the customer. The voice of the customer can be captured in a variety of ways: Direct discussion or interviews, surveys, focus groups, customer specifications, observation, warranty data, field reports, complaint logs, etc."

Measure Phase

The *Measure* phase of the DMAIC process includes the LSS tools that help measure the process performance. The list of key tools used in this phase includes, but is not limited to, process map or flowchart, capacity analysis, brainstorming, affinity diagram, nominal group technique, check sheet, histogram, trend analysis, and Pareto chart.

Process Map/Process Flowchart

A process map provides a pictorial representation of the sequence of steps that comprise a process. It provides visual illustration of what gets performed in the process, where the holdups are, and where the improvements can be made.

Figure 7.8 illustrates a process map for the development of a project management plan along with potential process holdups.

Capability Analysis

You use the capability analysis statistical tool to assess the ability of a process to meet specifications and performance standards required by the customer. It compares actual process performance standards with the required performance standards.

The process capacity is analyzed by calculating the mean μ and standard deviation σ of the performance distribution of a process and comparing it to the established specification limits (SL) as shown in Figure 7.9. The specification limit on the left-hand side of the mean is called the Lower Specification Limit (LSL) and the one on the right-hand side is called the Upper Specification Limit (USL).

The mean of the performance distribution represents the central tendency of the performance distribution, and its standard deviation represents the magnitude of variation in the performance.

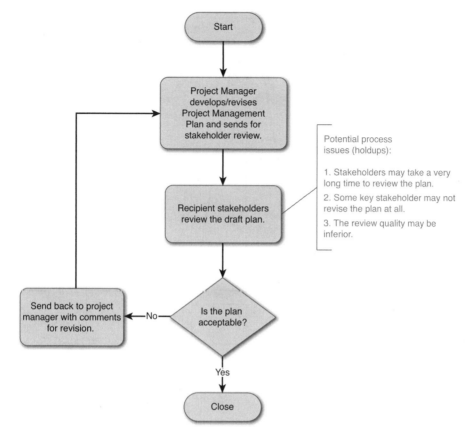

Figure 7.8 Process Map for Development of Project Management Plan

The performance variation can also be calculated mathematically using the formula:

$$PV = |\,SL - \mu\,|\,/\,\sigma$$

where PV stands for *performance variation*, and SL stands for *specification limit* (upper or lower).

Brainstorming

Brainstorming is a simple and effective tool to creatively and effectively elicit a large number of ideas from participants. The basic characteristic of brainstorming is that all ideas are welcome without any judgment or criticism.

It facilitates participation by all team members and prevents domination of the decision-making process by only a few people.

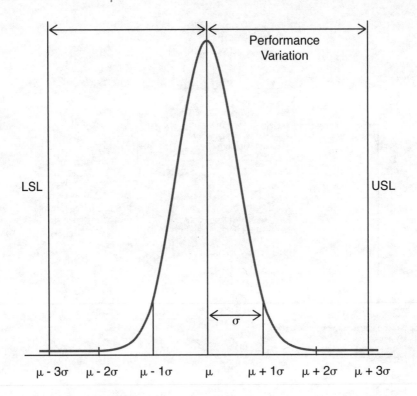

Figure 7.9 Process Capability Measurements

You can use an *affinity diagram* to gather the ideas generated via brainstorming and group them into different categories based on their type and characteristics.

For example, brainstorming about the causes of a computer failure might generate ideas pointing to memory, processor, disk drives, operating system, application software, connectivity, virus, file system, user accounts, operation, and so on, which you can then group into the following categories:

- Hardware
- Software
- Networking
- Users
- Administration

Nominal Group Technique (NGT)

Nominal group technique is an enhanced version of brainstorming because it includes an additional voting process to rank the ideas generated via the brainstorming process. Nominal group technique (NGT) facilitates quicker decision-making by helping team members focus on the relative importance of the issues or solutions being discussed. For example,

1. Have each participant write down as many ideas as possible within a specified time limit.

2. Collect all ideas from the participants and write them on a white board or flipchart.

3. Discuss each idea with the participants and make additions, deletions, or alterations by unanimous team consensus as needed.

4. Vote, rank, and prioritize ideas.

For example, a nominal group technique approach can be used for evaluating and ranking the ideas generated via brainstorming. The following steps outline a typical voting process:

1. All participants write down their individual votes.

2. All votes are consolidated for a group discussion.

3. All participants discuss the consolidated votes to create and validate the final idea ranking.

Check Sheet

A check sheet is a structured form for recording and compiling historical data or real-time observational data to identify trends and patterns in the data.

This tool is useful for collecting data from repeated operations either by the same person or at the same place. It is also used to capture data on frequency and patterns of occurrence pertaining to defects, issues, or events.

Table 7.3 shows the check sheet used for collecting data on the causes of failures for a computer being tested in computer manufacturing operations.

Table 7.3 Check Sheet

Cause of Failure	Week 1	Week 2	Week 3	Week 4	Week 5	Week 6	Total
Assembly Errors	ЖЖ I I I	ЖЖ	I I	I I I	I I	I	20
Test Operator Error	ЖЖ I I I	I I I I	I	I	I I	ЖЖ I I	22
Unit Hardware Defects	I I	I	I I I I	I I I	ЖЖ I I I	I	18
Test Infrastructure Issues	ЖЖ I I I	I I	I	ЖЖ	I I I	I I I	21
Total	23	12	8	12	14	12	81

Histogram

A histogram is a frequency distribution bar chart that shows how often different values in a data set occur. It is also a stepping stone to development of a Pareto chart (discussed in the next subsection).

Figure 7.10 shows an example histogram for the frequency of occurrence of process defects over a period of 10 weeks.

Trend Analysis

A run chart (Figure 7.11), a complementary chart to a histogram, is used to perform trend analysis in the *Measure* phase of the DMAIC process. It is important for you to understand the difference between a histogram and a run chart. A histogram is used to show the frequency of occurrence of data and the shape of the frequency distribution is used to analyze the defects or variations in the process. On the other hand, a run chart is based on the same data that histogram is based on but it displays data in a chronological order which can be used to analyze the defects or variations in the process over time.

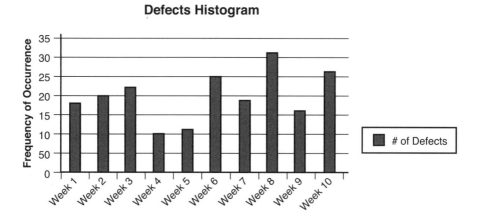

Figure 7.10 Histogram for Frequency of Occurrence of Process Defects

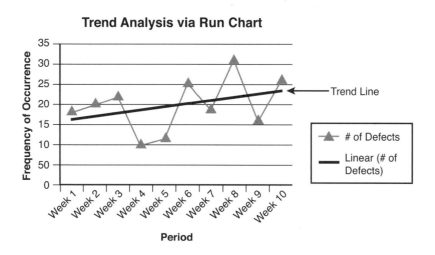

Figure 7.11 Trend Analysis for Process Defects

Pareto Chart

A Pareto chart, also known as a Pareto diagram or Pareto analysis, is a bar graph used to analyze the frequency of problems. It is basically a sorted histogram showing the relative frequency of occurrence of problems or defects in descending order. Nonetheless, a histogram finds application in its own right; for example, a resource histogram is commonly used for planning resources for a project over the project timeline. For the success of a project, the project manager must proactively know what type of and how many resources will be needed during each month or week of the project timeline.

Figure 7.12 shows a Pareto chart based on the histogram in Figure 7.10.

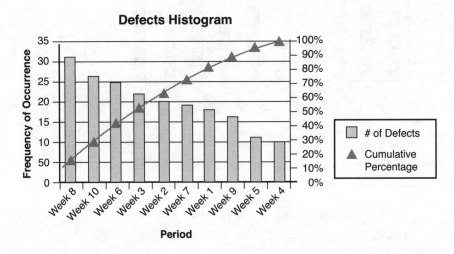

Figure 7.12 Pareto Chart for Frequency of Occurrence of Process Defects

Analyze Phase

The LSS tools in the *Analyze* phase of the DMAIC process are used to determine the root causes of variation and poor process performance. The key analysis tools include, but are not limited to, brainstorming and affinity diagrams (see the earlier "Measure Phase" for more on these), fishbone and scatter diagrams, root cause analysis, and failure modes and effects analysis (FMEA).

Fishbone Diagram

Also called cause-and-effect diagram or Ishikawa diagram (after Kaoru Ishikawa who introduced this diagram for use), a fishbone diagram is a powerful and useful way of collecting brainstorming ideas for finding all possible causes for an effect (or defect, issue, or problem).

As you can guess, it is called a fishbone diagram due to its shape. Its bones or branches represent main categories of the causes being captured. Figure 7.13 shows a fishbone diagram for analyzing issues in a restaurant business.

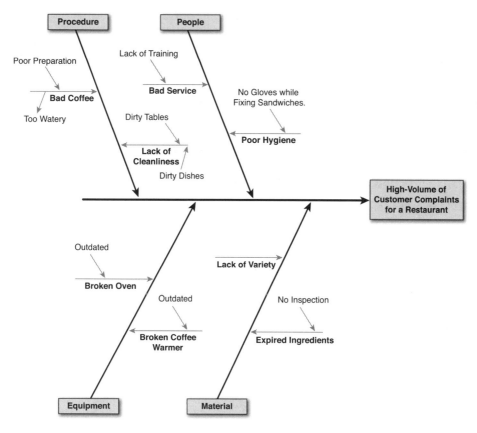

Figure 7.13 Fishbone Diagram for a Restaurant Service Issue

Scatter Diagram

Within the *Analyze* phase of the DMAIC process, scatter diagrams are used to study how one variable (independent) affects the other variable (dependent) and this relationship between the two is known as *correlation* between them.

See the "Correlation" section in Chapter 5, "Statistics Fundamentals II," for more on scatter diagrams.

Root Cause Analysis (RCA)

According to Andersen and Fagerhaug (asq.org, 2006), a root cause is "a factor that caused a nonconformance and should be permanently eliminated through process improvement." A root cause analysis (RCA) helps you find the root cause (also called the highest-level cause) of a problem. It is geared toward finding the cure rather than just treating the symptoms so that the same problem does not occur again.

5 Whys: A Simple Technique to Determine the Root Cause

The 5 Whys is a simple technique used in the *Analyze* phase of the DMAIC process.

Asking "Why" five times (a rule of thumb), you are most likely able to reach the root cause of the problem or you can at least pave the way for a quicker discovery of the root cause.

Steps to Using the 5 Whys Technique

1. Write the problem in a descriptive form.
2. Ask first "Why" and write down the answer.
3. If answer to the first "Why" did not determine the root cause, ask second "Why" and record the answer.
4. Continue asking "Why" up to five times or until the root cause is found.

Example Problem:

You are a project manager for a time-sensitive project. Recently, your project management analyst lead (a key resource) quit, triggering a project risk for potential schedule delays.

Root Cause Analysis Using 5 Whys:

First Why: Why did the project management analyst lead suddenly quit?

Answer: Because she was not happy in her current position.

Second Why: Why was she not happy in her current position?

Answer: Because she was living with uncertainty.

Third Why: Why was she living with uncertainty?

Answer: Because she might not be able to continue to work in her current position.

Fourth Why: Why might she not be able to continue to work in her current position?

Answer: Because her current position was a limited term.

Fifth Why: Not needed

Answer: N/A

You can clearly observe in this example that the fourth "Why" leads you to the root cause for which you can develop an appropriate corrective action (e.g., making the position permanent) to eliminate it.

Failure Modes and Effects Analysis (FMEA)

Failure modes and effects analysis (FMEA) is a step-by-step approach for identifying possible product, service, and process failures and for analyzing the potential effects of these failures.

Failure modes represent the specific ways in which a failure may occur. Effects analysis refers to analyzing the effects or consequences of the failure.

To perform FMEA:

1. Prioritize the possible failures based on the following criteria:

   - Level of severity or seriousness

   - Frequency of occurrence

   - Ease of detection

2. Take appropriate measures to eliminate or reduce failures, targeting the highest-priority failures first.

Table 7.4 depicts a typical FMEA example.

Table 7.4   Failure Modes and Effect Analysis (FMEA) Example

Failure Mode	Potential Effect of Failure	Potential Cause	Severity Level (S)[8]	Frequency of Occurrence (F)[9]	Ease of Detection (D)[10]	Priority Ranking (S×F×D)	Corrective Action	Owner	Estimated Completion Date
Coffee served was cold	Customer dissatisfaction	Coffee warmer broken	5	3	5	75	Replace coffee warmer	Jeff Brown	December 22, 2015
Poor service	Customer dissatisfaction	Lack of training	3	3	3	27	Arrange employee training	Patricia Sanchez	December 15, 2015

---

[8] High = 5, Medium = 3, Low = 1

[9] High = 5, Medium = 3, Low = 1

[10] High = 5, Medium = 3, Low = 1

Improve Phase

The LSS tools used in the *Improve* phase of the DMAIC process include, but are not limited to design of experiments and Kaizen. These tools are used to improve the performance of a process by addressing and eliminating/minimizing the root causes.

Design of Experiments (DOE)

When multiple factors contribute to a problem or influence the outcome of a complex process or system, understanding the contribution or influence of each individual factor becomes difficult. Often, the contribution or influence of one-factor-at-a-time (or OFAT) is studied while holding all other factors or variables constant, but this method is very inefficient.

Design of Experiments (DOE) is a statistical and systematic method of studying the contribution or influence of a mix of multiple factors without having to use the inefficient OFAT approach. It involves trial and error; thus, it is performed iteratively until an optimal mix of multiple factors is found to produce the desired result.

A food recipe preparation is a good example of the application of DOE, which involves multiple factors (ingredients, heat, and cooking time). Recipe ingredients are mixed and processed and the resulting dish is tested for quality and taste. This trial-and-error-based experiment is repeated iteratively until an optimal mix is found to render the desired quality and taste.

Kaizen

Kaizen is a Japanese word that means "continuous improvement." This LSS method is based on the notion that subtle but continuous improvements gradually over time will have a tremendous positive impact.

Sometimes, making some small improvements quickly is necessary. Such quick improvement efforts are called *Kaizen events*.

Both Kaizen and Kaizen events have similarities in terms of the cost of improvements (low in both cases) and the stakeholder buy-in (high in both cases). The magnitude of improvements, however, is different for both; for Kaizen, it is subtle but increases gradually over time and for Kaizen events, it is large but followed by quick improvements over a period of 3 to 5 days.

Control Phase

In the *Control* phase of the DMAIC process, you use the control chart, special causes of variation, the 5Ss (visual management), GANNT charts, and VSM tools to keep an improved process at its current level (sustain the improvement).

Control Chart

Also referred to as *statistical process control*, you use a control chart to monitor, control, and improve the performance of a process or system over time, analyzing special causes of variation.

Figure 7.14 shows a control chart. It has an upper control limit (UCL) above the mean line and a lower control limit below the mean line. The dots represent performance data values observed over time and are plotted in time order. The location of these data points on the control chart plot indicates whether the process is in control (consistent variation) or out of control (unpredictable and inconsistent due to special causes of variation).

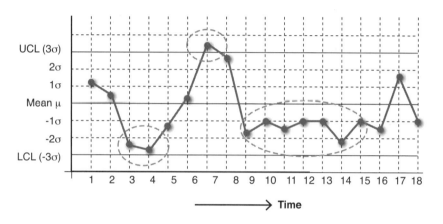

Figure 7.14 Control Chart Showing Special Causes of Variation in a Process

Common and Special Causes of Variation

Common causes of variation are the result of *predictable* errors. The usual morning and afternoon work-related rush-hour traffic on weekdays is an example of a common cause.

Special causes of variation are the result of *unpredictable* errors. An unusual traffic jam on Sunday morning due to an accident is an example of a special cause.

The following are some observations that indicate special causes of variation in Figure 7.14:

- A point outside the control limits UCL and LCL (point 7)
- Two out of three consecutive data points are on the same side of the mean and farther than 2σ from it (points 3 and 4)

In addition, a cluster of seven or more points above or below mean (points 9 through 15) or any consistent patterns in the data plot indicate special causes of variation (something unusual).

5Ss (Visual Management)

The 5Ss method (or visual management) is used to create visual controls for an improved process. This method is referred to as visual management because it enables you to know the status of any process by visually looking at it. The focus of this method is to create a quality work environment so that just by glancing at it, you can assess the process performance in terms of its operating within the control limits, problem-solving effectiveness, and continuing to meet the performance expectations.

A poor quality (unorganized) work environment can push a process into an unstable and out-of-control state. When parts, supplies, and information cannot be accessed within a reasonable time frame, unnecessary wait can result in lost productivity, delayed schedule, and hence lost revenue.

Figure 7.15 depicts the essence of the 5Ss method.

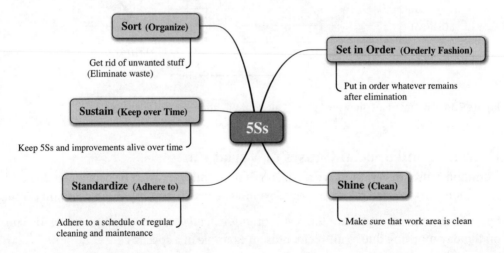

Figure 7.15 5Ss (Visual Management)

The 5Ss method provides a multitude of benefits including the following:

- Reduced number of defects
- Enhanced safety
- Improved reliability

- Higher availability of systems and services
- Reduced cost
- Improved quality
- Improved productivity
- Improved workplace morale
- Improved asset utilization
- Improved employee satisfaction
- Reduced turnover

GANTT Chart

The LSS process improvement projects need to be managed like any other project. A GANTT chart, also called a bar chart, is a graphical form of managing and controlling the project schedule. Figure 7.16 shows a sample GANTT chart.

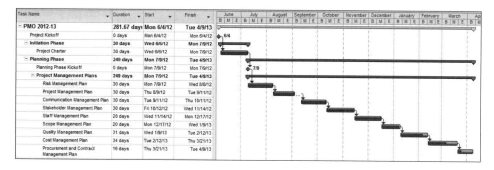

Figure 7.16 A Sample GANTT Chart

The word "GANTT" is not an acronym; rather it is named after Henry Gantt, the designer of this chart. The horizontal bars area on the right-hand side of Figure 7.16 represents a GANTT chart. The length of each bar represents the duration of the corresponding project activity on the left-hand side. The solid black line superimposing some bars show the task progress in terms of percent complete.

Value Stream Map (VSM)

VSM was discussed earlier in the "Define Phase" section as well. It helps identify waste in a process in terms of non-value-added steps or activities. It is used in the *Control* phase of DMAIC to ensure that the improved process continues to operate waste-free.

Summary

Figure 7.17 summarizes the LSS approach.

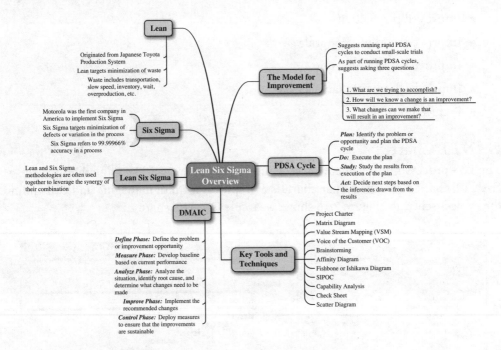

Figure 7.17 Lean Six Sigma Summary

Key Terms

5Ss

Affinity Diagram

Brainstorming

Capability Analysis

Check Sheet

Control Chart

Design of Experiments (DOE)

DMAIC

Failure Modes and Effect Analysis (FMEA)

Fishbone Diagram

GANTT Chart

Histogram

Kaizen

Kaizen Events

Lean

Matrix Diagram

Model for Improvement	SIPOC
Nominal Group Technique (NGT)	Six Sigma
Pareto Chart	Stakeholder Analysis
PDSA	SWOT Analysis
Process Map	Value Stream Map (VSM)
Project Charter	Voice of the Customer (VOC)
Root Cause Analysis (RCA)	
Scatter Diagram	

Case Study: Ropar Business Computers (RBC) Implements a Lean Six Sigma Project to Improve Its Server Test Process

Ropar Business Computers (RBC) is located in the heart of the California state capital city Sacramento, providing computing solutions and services to various state government agencies as well as some private organizations. To eliminate waste, boost performance of its internal manufacturing operations, and improve its customer satisfaction, RBC engaged independent LSS consultant Larry Lumbar to audit its server test process. Based on the recommendations of the consultant, RBC decided to undertake an LSS project to identify the process bottlenecks and wasteful process steps and improve the status quo.

As a project manager and LSS expert Larry initiated the improvement project. He formulated his improvement strategy based on the following three questions:

1. What are we trying to accomplish?
2. Will we know a change is an improvement?
3. What changes can we make that will result in improvement?

Define Project and Identify Project Team Members

The following helps to answer the question "What are we trying to accomplish?"

Project Description (What/How): Improve the server test process quality by reducing defects in the test process and by implementing an effective root cause analysis process.

Project Scope: To identify the top two test process areas of improvement and create and implement the improvement plan to reduce test downtime, reduce support escalations, and increase customer satisfaction.

Project Team Members: Larry Lumbar (Project Manager and LSS Expert), Nick Larsen (Test Manager), Glen Thomas (Process Support Engineer)

Define Improvement Objectives

To answer the question "How will we know a change is an improvement?" Larry and his team developed a set of objectives and measures, as follows:

Objective 1: Reduce test process downtime by more than 50% average per month per target test area.

Measure: Review the test process downtime reported by the test operators.

Objective 2: Reduce number of support escalations by more than 50% average per month per target test area.

Measure: Escalations records from the database.

Objective 3: Improve customer satisfaction from below average to above average.

Measure: Customers' responses via surveys/interviews.

Table 7.5 captures the success-measuring criteria.

Table 7.5 Baseline Performance and Success-Measuring Criteria

Performance Metric	Baseline Performance	Target Performance
Process downtime	Average 3–10 hours per month	Average 2–6 hours per month
Number of support escalations	Average 4 per month	Average 2 per month
Customer satisfaction	Below average	Above average

PDSA Cycles

Table 7.6 outlines the PDSA cycles that the project/improvement team used to accomplish the target goals and answer the question "What changes can we make that will result in improvement?"

Table 7.6 PDSA Cycles

PDSA Cycle	Description	Tools Used	Results/Observations
Define Phase: DSA cycles : 1, 2	Define the problem and set goals. Determine stakeholders and key requirements of the project.	Project charter SIPOC Stakeholder analysis	The goals must be realistic, measurable, and clearly defined. Baseline needs to be determined. Stakeholder analysis brings everyone on the same page and helps effectively serve the stakeholder needs.
Measure Phase: PDSA cycles : 3	Collect data, measure current performance, and determine areas of improvement.	Pareto analysis Trend analysis Capability analysis	The top two areas of the test process that needed improvement were Testview[11] and Diagnostics Servers because these two areas ranked the highest based on the average number of defects per month
Analyze Phase: PDSA cycles : 4, 5	Identify defects in target test areas of improvement and perform root cause analysis.	Process map (flowchart) Cause-and-effect (fishbone) diagram	The defects associated with target area 1 (Testview) fell under the following defect categories: • Stability • Efficiency • Reliability • Supportability The defects associated with target area 2 (Diagnostics Servers) fell under the following defect categories: • Hard disk space Analysis revealed the following: • The root causes for Testview defects included remote client file system, too many configuration files, inadequate automation, and inefficient directory structure. • The root causes for Diagnostic Servers defects included large amount of obsolete data accumulated and lack of file system monitoring system.

PDSA Cycle	Description	Tools Used	Results/Observations
Improve Phase: PDSA cycle : 6, 7	Develop and implement the process improvement solutions; continue monitoring defects to ensure the positive impact of the improvements.	Design of Experiments Process map (flowchart) Trend analysis Surveys	The improvement team redesigned Testview and changed the status quo of Diagnostics Servers test area with a goal to achieve significant and sustainable improvements in the test process. The defects trend analysis reflected significant reduction in Testview and Diagnostics Servers–related defects and customer survey results reflected above average satisfaction level.
Control Phase: PDSA cycles : 8	Deploy measures to ensure that the improvements are sustainable.	Control chart Surveys	The cohesive efforts put in this project by the improvement team yielded great results. Constant monitoring and control were necessary to sustain the improvement results.

[11] Automated software suite used by RBC to test its server products

Select PDSA Cycles Explained

This section elaborates on PDSA cycles 5 and 7, randomly selected for the sake of illustration. PDSA 5 entails the RCA and PDSA 7 covers the validation of the effectiveness of the implemented improvement solution.

PDSA 5: Root Cause Analysis (RCA)

Figure 7.18 explains the steps that Larry and his improvement team undertook in PDSA cycle 5 to determine the root causes for the test process issues.

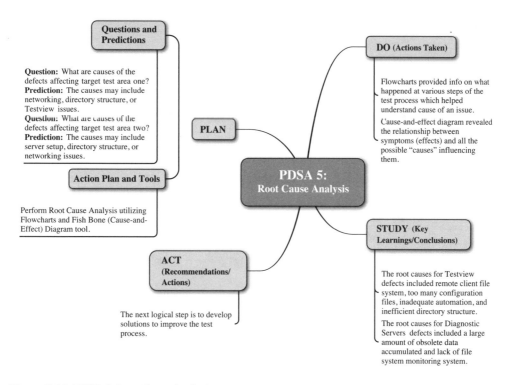

Figure 7.18 PDSA 5: Root Cause Analysis

Current Process Flow of Defect Tracking, Reporting, and Resolving (PDSA 5)

Figure 7.19 shows the current (pre-improvement) process flow for tracking, reporting, and resolving the test process defects. The defects identified are shown in red color.

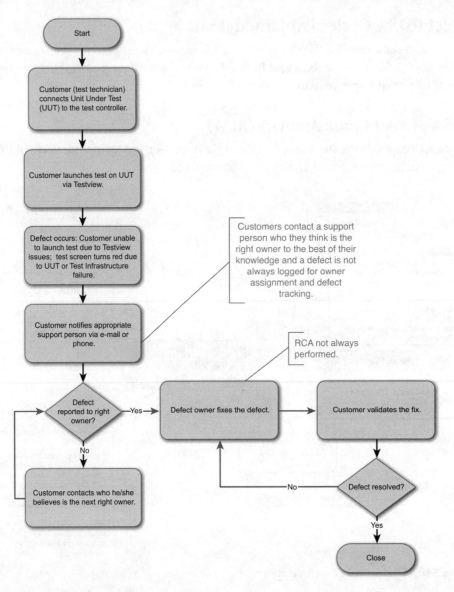

Figure 7.19 Current Process Flow

RCA for Diagnostics Server Issues (PDSA 5)

Larry facilitated a brainstorming session with his team, subject matter experts, and a few other key stakeholders to collect possible causes for the space issues pertaining to the diagnostic servers. He used the cause-and-effect diagram (shown in Figure 7.20) to collect, organize, and analyze data to determine the root cause.

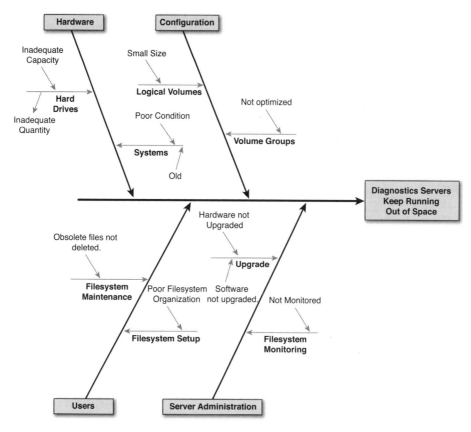

Figure 7.20 The Cause-and-Effect Diagram for Diagnostics Server Issues

RCA for Testview Issues (PDSA 5)

Larry utilized brainstorming and the cause-and-effect diagram to perform RCA for issues with Testview as well. Figure 7.21 shows the cause-and-effect diagram that Larry and his team used for determining the root causes for Testview issues.

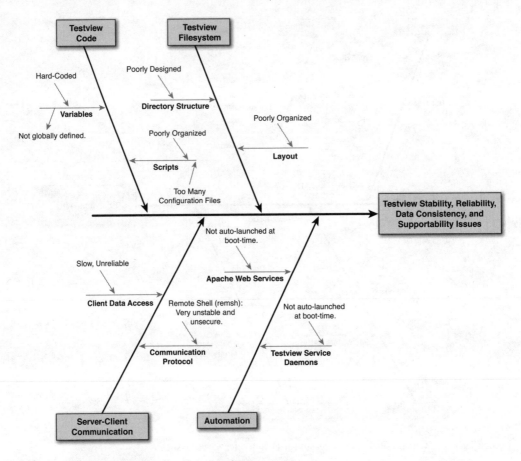

Figure 7.21 The Cause-and-Effect Diagram for Testview Issues

PDSA 7: *Validating the Improvement Solution Effectiveness*

Figure 7.22 explains the steps that Larry and his improvement team undertook in PDSA cycle 7 to make sure that the implemented improvement solution was effective as expected.

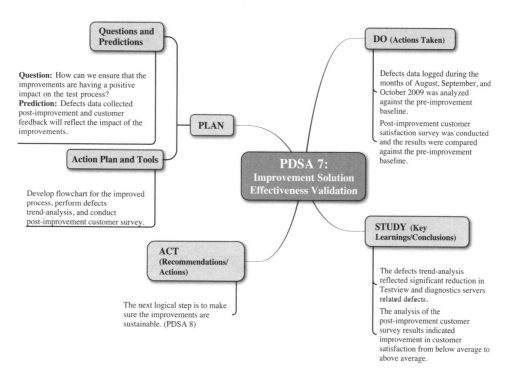

Figure 7.22 PDSA 7: Validating the Improvement Solution Effectiveness

Improved Process Flow of Defect Tracking, Reporting, and Resolving (PDSA 7)

Figure 7.23 shows the flowchart of the improved (target) process. The side notes in this figure reflect the improvements and their effect.

Actual Results Realized

Larry led the successful process improvement project for RBC by using the structured and systematic LSS methodology. He started by understanding the existing process, establishing the baseline process performance, and establishing performance metrics. Thereafter, he determined the target performance goals and performed gap analysis (gap = target performance – baseline performance) to define the scope of the improvements needed to fill that gap. Finally, he documented the actual results achieved as shown in Table 7.7.

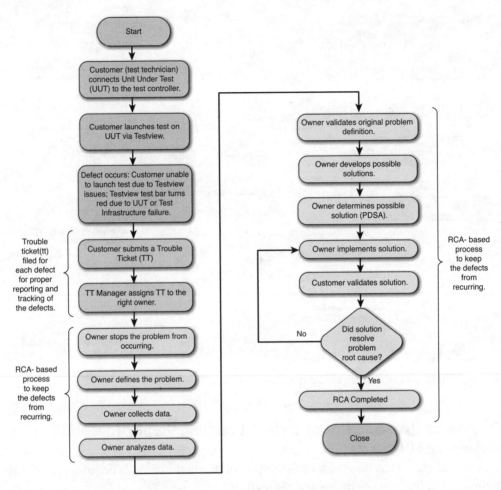

Figure 7.23 Improved (Target) Process Flow

Table 7.7 Post-Improvement Results Realized

Performance Metric	Baseline Performance	Target Performance	Actual Results Realized
Process downtime	Average 3–10 hours per month	Average 2–6 hours per month	Average 0–2 hours per month
Number of support escalations	Average 4 per month	Average 2 per month	Average 0 per month
Customer satisfaction	Below average	Above average	Above average

Conclusion

RBC was able to realize more than 50% improvement in its server test process by implementing the LSS process improvement project. This improvement resulted in an annual cost savings of $785,000. The improvement team received kudos from the senior management and changes from the improved server test process were leveraged across all global factories and subcontractors of RBC.

Case Questions

1. What were the success-measuring criteria for the improvement project discussed in this case? Were they met?
2. What is the difference between baseline and target performance?
3. What LSS tools were used in PDSA 3?
4. What process defects were discovered during the analyze phase of DMAIC?

Chapter Review and Discussion Questions

1. What is the difference between Lean and Six Sigma?
2. What are some common types of waste?
3. How accurate is the Six Sigma process?
4. What do DMAIC and PDSA stand for?
5. Describe the Model for Improvement.
6. What is a PDSA cycle? What are its advantages?
7. You have just completed a PDSA cycle. How will you determine whether another PDSA cycle is needed?
8. What is the advantage of SWOT analysis in LSS?
9. How do you calculate the efficiency of a process?
10. Calculate the performance variation of a process where the mean (μ) is 0.5, standard deviation (σ) is 1.2, and the upper specification limit (USL) is 1.5.
11. What is the difference between a histogram and a Pareto chart?
12. Why gives the fishbone diagram its name?
13. What is the difference between a common and a special cause?

Bibliography

asq.org. (2006). "Root Cause Analysis." Retrieved September 18, 2015, from http://asq.org/quality-press/display-item/index.html?item=H1287&xvl=76BK_H1287

asq.org. (2014). "Six Sigma Belts, Executives and Champions – What Does It All Mean?" Retrieved June 24, 2015, from http://asq.org/learn-about-quality/six-sigma/overview/belts-executives-champions.html

asq.org. (2014). "The Define Measure Analyze Improve Control (DMAIC) Process." Retrieved June 22, 2015, from http://asq.org/learn-about-quality/six-sigma/overview/dmaic.html

asq.org. (2015). "Integrating Lean and Six Sigma." Retrieved May 18, 2015, from http://asq.org/learn-about-quality/six-sigma/lean.html

Bonacorsi, S. (2015). "Six Sigma and Lean Resources - SWOT Analysis." Retrieved June 18, 2015, from http://6sixsigma.com/index.php/Six-Sigma-Articles/SWOT-Analysis.html

Business Dictionary. (2015). "What Is Synergistic Effect? Definition and Meaning." Retrieved September 19, 2015, from http://www.businessdictionary.com/definition/synergistic-effect.html

GoLeanSixSigma. (2015). "What Is Lean Six Sigma?" Retrieved May 22, 2015, from https://goleansixsigma.com/what-is-lean-six-sigma/

Gygi, C. et al. (2012). *Six Sigma for Dummies*, 2nd ed. Hoboken, New Jersey: John Wiley & Sons, Inc.

Hunter, J. (2012). "Keys to the Effective Use of the PDSA Improvement Cycle » Curious Cat Management Improvement Blog." Retrieved May 20, 2015, from http://management.curiouscatblog.net/2012/03/06/keys-to-the-effective-use-of-the-pdsa-improvement-cycle/

iSixSigma. (2014). "Voice Of the Customer (VOC)." Retrieved June 10, 2015, from http://www.isixsigma.com/dictionary/voice-of-the-customer-voc/

Kubiak, T. M. and Benlow, D. W. (2009). *The Certified Six Sigma Black Belt Handbook*, 2nd ed. ASQ Quality Press.

Langley, G.L. et al. (2009). *The Improvement Guide: A Practical Approach to Enhancing Organizational Performance*, 2nd ed. San Francisco, California, USA: Jossey-Bass Publishers.

Levinson, W.A. and Rerick, R.A. (2002). *Lean Enterprise: A Synergistic Approach to Minimizing Waste*. ASQ Quality Press.

Longo, E. (2012). Principles of Lean Six Sigma. Retrieved June 19, 2015, from http://academic.uprm.edu/ispeprsc/media/(2012.04.28)_Principles_of_Lean_Six_Sigma_2012.pdf

Microsoft. (2015). "Create a Value Stream Map." Retrieved May 22, 2015, from https://support.office.com/en-ie/article/Create-a-value-stream-map-35a09801-999e-4beb-ad4a-3235b3f0eaa3

ProcessFix Limited. (2014). "Run Chart and Histogram." Retrieved June 22, 2015, from http://www.gcu.ac.uk/media/gcalwebv2/theuniversity/supportservices/pace/documents/Run Chart & Histogram - Control Tool.pdf

Singh, H. (2014). *Mastering Project Human Resource Management*, 1st ed. Upper Saddle River, New Jersey: Pearson FT Press.

Swan, E. (2015). "Stakeholder Analysis." Retrieved June 23, 2015, from https://goleansixsigma.com/stakeholder-analysis/

Tague, N. R. (2004). *The Quality Toolbox*, 2nd ed. ASQ Quality Press.

Villanova University. (2014). "Body of Knowledge for Lean Six Sigma Black Belt." Retrieved May 23, 2015, from http://www.villanovau.com/media/10501706/lean-six-sigma-black-belt-bok.pdf

8

Statistical Applications in Project Management

Learning Objectives

After reading this chapter, you should be familiar with the applications of the following items specific to project management:

- Probability theory
- Probability distributions
- Critical Path method
- Critical Chain method
- Program Evaluation and Review Technique
- Graphical Evaluation and Review Technique
- Beta distribution
- Triangular distribution
- Normal distribution
- Correlation and covariance
- Prediction analytics—linear regression
- Earned Value Management
- Confidence intervals
- Hypothesis testing

> "The greatest moments are those when you see the result pop up in a graph or in your statistics analysis—that moment you realize you know something no one else does and you get the pleasure of thinking about how to tell them."
>
> —*Emily Oster, Ph.D. (Harvard University), American economist*

We discussed statistical fundamentals in Chapters 4, "Statistical Fundamentals I: Basics and Probability Distributions" and 5, "Statistical Fundamentals II: Hypothesis, Correlation, and Linear Regression." In this chapter you learn how to apply the statistical theory and principles in real-life projects.

As you learned in Chapter 4, uncertainty is embedded in all types of projects. We cannot know the outcome of a random project event with certainty but we can forecast the pattern of its behavior using various statistical methods. Proper forecasting is necessary to achieve a reasonable level of accuracy in estimation throughout the project life cycle. The quality of project planning depends on the level of accuracy of the estimation. Also, on-time and under-budget completion is the prerequisite for a project to be called a "successful project," which depends on the reliability of the prediction of project costs and schedule, as wrote Walt Lipke, PMI[1] —Oklahoma City Chapter, "An objective of project management is to have the capability to reliably predict cost and schedule outcomes." In general, project management is primarily about the effective management of the triple constraints (budget, schedule, and scope). The purpose of this chapter is to arm project managers with the essential statistical tools and techniques for effective project management.

Statistical Tools and Techniques for Project Management

A single-point or deterministic estimate cannot reveal the outcomes of random project events with certainty. The knowledge of statistics can be applied to forecast a reasonable range of possibilities; this is called the *probabilistic estimation*. The key statistical concepts, tools, and techniques that can be applied for forecasting the project behavior include the following:

- Probability theory
- Probability distributions
- Central Limit Theorem
- Critical Path method (CPM)
- Critical Chain method (CCM)
- Program Evaluation and Review Technique (PERT)
- Graphical Evaluation and Review Technique (GERT)
- Correlation and covariance

---

[1] Project Management Institute

- Predictive analytics: linear regression
- Prediction using Earned Value Management (EVM) coupled with confidence intervals and hypothesis testing

The following sections give an overview of these items.

Probability Theory

The use of probability theory in an uncertain project environment can go a long way toward helping project managers make informed and rational decisions. For instance:

- Different probabilities are associated with various possibilities for the outcome of a single project event. These probabilities pertaining to a single event must fall in the range from 0 to 1. This condition is in line with the probability theory because the minimum probability of an event happening is 0% and the maximum probability of an event happening is 100%.

- The concept of relative frequency in probability theory helps forecast a specific outcome. For example, saying, "There is one chance in three[2] that a project change request will be approved by the CCB," refers to a specific outcome. On the other hand, saying, "There is a 30% chance that the change request will be approved by the CCB," refers to a "confidence" of the outcome to be within a range.

- Some project events are not mutually exclusive (not independent of each other). This interdependency diminishes the probability of either of the events happening as planned.

It is important for a project manager to have at least basic understanding of probability theory because all projects involve uncertainty. The knowledge of probability theory comes in handy in making the best possible judgment in the project environment full of uncertainty.

Probability Distributions

The most commonly used probability distributions in project management include the following:

---

[2] When a change request is reviewed by the project Change Control Board (CCB), there are the following three possibilities for the outcome:

1. The change request is approved, 2. The change request is rejected, or 3. The change request is sent back to the requester for more information.

- **Normal** distribution finds common application in summary results.

- **BETA** and **Triangular** distributions are used at the work package level in the work breakdown structure for estimating activity duration and activity cost during the project planning stage.

- **Uniform** distribution determines a two-point estimate of the highest (maximum) and lowest (minimum) limits of a random variable. It is useful in project risk management.

- **Poisson** distribution describes discrete occurrences of a defined interval; for example, "Number of change requests submitted per month."

- **Binomial** distribution is a discrete distribution involving only two outcomes per trial. The Go / No Go decision at a project stage gate review is an example.

Chapters 1 and 4 discuss these distributions in detail.

Central Limit Theorem

Chapter 4 covers the central limit theorem. According to this theorem, if the sample size "n" becomes large ($\geq$ 30, n approaches infinity), the distribution of the means of the independent sample elements will be approximately equal to a normal distribution.

The Central Limit Theorem validates the fact that the sum of means of the durations of all project activities on the critical path is equal to the mean time of the entire project and the sum of the variances pertaining to all activities on the critical path is equal to the variance of the project.

Critical Path Method (CPM)

A project network diagram includes the following:

- Project activity list
- Duration of each project activity
- Relationships (dependencies) among project activities

The CPM technique is used with a project network diagram to determine the critical path in the network of interconnected project activities.

The *critical path* is the longest path in the project network diagram. This means that any activity on the critical path, if delayed, can delay the project. Thus, a critical path also gives the shortest time possible to complete the project. Having more than one critical path on a project is possible.

The CPM technique also determines the slack or float for the project network activities. The activities with zero float are on the critical path where the activities that have slack associated with them can be delayed without elongating the total duration of the project.

Take a look at the project network diagram in Figure 8.1, drawn using the Activity on Node (AON) diagramming method, also known as the Precedence Diagramming Method (PDM).

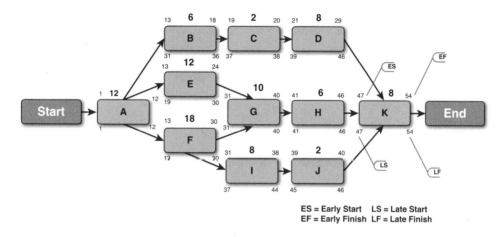

Figure 8.1 Project Activity Network Diagram Using AON

This diagram shows the following four paths from start to end:

Path 1: Start → A → B → C → D → K → End

Path 2: Start → A → E → G → H → K → End

Path 3: Start → A → F → G → H → K → End

Path 4: Start → A → F → I → J → K → End

The duration of each path can be found by adding the durations of individual activities that constitute that path.

Path 1: 12 + 6 + 2 + 8 + 8 = 36

Path 2: 12 + 12 + 10 + 6 + 8 = 48

Path 3: 12 + 18 + 10 + 6 + 8 = **54**

Path 4: 12 + 18 + 8 + 2 + 8 = 48

Obviously, activities on Path 3 constitute the critical path, because

- Path 3 is the longest path in the network
- Float for each activity on Path 3 is 0

These are the conditions for a critical path.

Calculating Float for an Activity

The *float* of an activity is the duration by which that activity can be delayed without impacting the critical path.

Consider activity K from the network diagram in Figure 8.1. Assume the unit of time is day.

Activity K has the following characteristics:

> Duration = 8 days
>
> ES (Early Start) = 47th day
>
> EF (Early Finish) = 54th day
>
> LS (Late Start) = 47th day
>
> LF (Late Finish) = 54th day

You determine ES and EF for each activity by performing the forward pass (from start to end), and determine LS and LF by performing the backward pass (from end to start).

Forward Pass

The first activity always starts at the beginning of day 1. Thus, ES for activity A = 1. EF for activity A = 12 because it finishes at the end of day 12. Based on this logic, activity B will start at the beginning of day 13 and will conclude at the end of day 18 because the duration of activity B is 6 days. The forward pass is completed by repeating this process for the rest of the network activities till End is reached. Figure 8.1 shows the values of ES and EF for all the activities.

Backward Pass

If you take a look at the network diagram in Figure 8.1, you will notice that activity K is the last activity before End is reached. This last activity finishes at the end of day 54. Thus, LF for activity K = 54. LS for activity K = 47 because it starts at the beginning of day 47. Based on this logic, activity H will complete at the end of day 46 and will start at the beginning of day 41 because the duration of activity H is 6 days. The backward pass is completed by repeating this process for the rest of the network activities until Start is reached. Figure 8.1 shows the values of LS and LF for all the activities.

To determine the float or slack for an activity, you use the following equation:

LS – ES = LF – EF

The float for activity K in Figure 8.1 = 47 – 47 = 54 – 54 = 0, which signifies that activity K is on the critical path.

Shortening the Critical Path

The CPM analysis can provide very useful information to project managers to decide what they can do to mitigate the critical paths to avoid project schedule delays and reduce the schedule as much as possible. Project managers can decide to pursue one or both of the following techniques to shorten the critical path:

- **Fast-tracking:** The process of minimizing lag and maximizing lead for the project network activities. In other words, the fast-tracking process involves performing as many activities in parallel as possible.

- **Crashing:** This depends on the notion that more resources can complete the work quicker than fewer resources. Thus, crashing involves adding more resources to shorten the duration of the activities on the critical path.

The preceding CPM analysis assumes that the durations of all the activities in the network are precisely known or *deterministic*, but this is not always the case. You see how to statistically estimate the activity durations when they are *not deterministic*, in the forthcoming section titled "Program Evaluation and Review Technique (PERT)."

Critical Chain Method (CCM)

The CPM discussion showed that the critical path analysis uses forward and backward passes to Early Start, Late Start, Early Finish, and Late Finish for the project network activities but it does not take resource limitation into consideration. The project schedule is developed based on interactivity dependencies, and the task owners pad their activities with safety margins or buffers as the contingency plan for uncertainties. This padding may be based on the rough order of magnitude estimate, which may result in a waste of time because not all activities need the extra time. In that case, the extra time would cause the dead-wait, meaning the successor activities would wait until the total duration time for the predecessor activities (activity duration + buffer) expires.

In 1997, Dr. Eliyahu M. Goldratt developed CCM, which takes into consideration the following:

- Task dependencies
- Limited resources
- Buffers

You can perform the following steps to develop a CCM-based project schedule:

1. Identify activities that result in the longest path to project completion. These activities are called *critical chains*. The non-critical chain activities converge to the critical chain as feeders.

2. Optimize buffer management to reduce the activity duration estimates and in turn reduce the overall project schedule. Streamline the project schedule by mitigating uncertainties and waste due to overestimation of activity durations and the buffers.

You optimize buffer management by stripping the individual activities of their buffers and summing up the individual buffers as the comprehensive project buffer (PB), as shown in Figure 8.2. The project buffer is shared by all activities as needed. CCM uses the 50% probability time estimates to calculate the project activity durations rather than using the traditional 95% probability.

The various buffers in Figure 8.2 are as follows:

- **Project buffer:** This buffer pools all activity-specific buffers in a non-critical chain and makes them available at the end of the chain for all activities to share. It is the difference between original and new schedule estimates.

- **Feeding buffer:** This buffer serves the same purpose as the project buffer but it is added where the activity path feeds into the critical chain path.

- **Resource buffer:** This buffer gives the critical resources[3] a heads-up about an upcoming critical chain activity that they are part of so that they can prepare to work on tasks on the critical chain on a priority basis. The resource buffer does not consume any resources, time, or money.

---

[3] Resources used in the critical chain activities

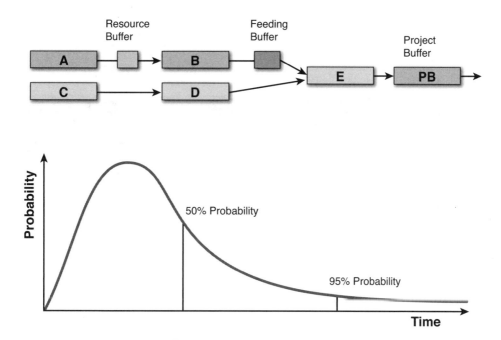

Figure 8.2 CCM Buffers

Program Evaluation and Review Technique (PERT)

The earlier "Critical Path Method" discussed how the durations of the project activities are not always *deterministic*. Often the activities have a range of possible durations. In this *probabilistic* scenario, we would need to determine the probability of the project completing by certain time period. We can find this probability by first estimating the mean and standard deviation of the duration for each activity and subsequently calculating the mean and standard deviation of the project as a whole. The PERT estimation is also known as Three-Point Estimation. As an example, let

- The shortest (optimistic) time to complete an activity be O *(best case scenario)*
- The most likely (realistic) time to complete an activity be R *(normal case scenario)*
- The longest (pessimistic) time to complete an activity be P *(worst case scenario)*

Using this information:

- The estimated activity duration = **(P + 4R + O) / 6**
- The standard deviation for this estimate is $\sigma = $ **(P – O) / 6**
- The variance for this estimate is $\sigma^2 = $ **[(P – O) / 6]²**

Table 8.1 shows the estimation of the duration of various activities in a project network diagram using the PERT technique.

Table 8.1 Project Network Activity Duration Estimation Using PERT

Activity	Predecessor	Pessimistic (P)	Realistic (R)	Optimistic (O)	Estimated Duration (P+4R+O)/6	Standard Deviation $\sigma =$ (P – R)/6	Variance σ^2
A	—	9	5	2	5	1.17	1.36
B	A	10	6	3	6	1.17	1.36
C	B	7	4	2	4	0.83	0.69
D	B	8	6	4	6	0.67	0.44
E	C	7	5	2	5	0.83	0.69
F	D	8	4	3	5	0.83	0.69
G	E, F	9	6	3	6	1.00	1.00

For "N" activities on a network path, the sum of the estimated durations of all the activities gives us the estimated duration of the complete path.

Mathematically, the estimated duration of the network path = $\Sigma[(P_N + 4R_N + O_N) / 6]$

Where, N = 1, 2, 3, ..., N

Similarly, to find the estimated variance for the total path as well, add the variances of individual activities on the path.

Using the duration mean and standard deviation of the path, you can determine the probability of the completion of the path by certain time.

Based on the central limit theorem (discussed in Chapter 4), you can assume that the project completion time will be normally distributed.

The z statistic in this scenario can be calculated as follows:

z = (Target Time – Path Mean) / Standard Deviation of the Path

You can now find the probability of the completion of the activity path by a certain target time by using either the z-table (cumulative normal distribution table) or the Excel NORMDIST function.

You can find the probabilities of completion of other independent[4] activity paths in the project activity network in a similar fashion. You can then multiply the probabilities for all the paths to determine the joint probability of completion of all the paths by certain target time. This gives us the probability of completion of the entire project by the specified target time.

Graphical Evaluation and Review Technique (GERT)

PERT and CPM are very useful techniques for modeling the project activity networks but they lack the capability of modeling the networks where the level of complexity is high. The GERT technique addresses this limitation of PERT and CPM.

Introduced by Dr. Alan B. Pritsker of Purdue University in 1966, GERT is a technique that can be used to model and analyze highly complex networks. Unlike PERT and CPM, GERT possesses features such as probabilistic branching, network looping, multiple outcomes, and multiple node realization. This method is primarily used for the activities that are either partially performed or repeatedly performed (loop).

For example, in a data center setup project, software is installed on each computer as soon as its hardware installation is complete instead of waiting for completion of the installation of hardware for all computer systems in the data center. Because the software installation activity will be performed repeatedly until all computers are completed, GERT can be used to calculate the total duration of the installation project.

Figure 8.3 presents the GERT modeling for the data center installation project. As you can see in this figure, the GERT modeling has two types of nodes: deterministic and probabilistic. All the nodes in this figure except nodes C, F, and G are deterministic. The probabilistic nodes have multiple possible outcomes each associated with a probability of occurrence. However, the sum of these all individual probabilities for the activities originating from a probabilistic node must be 1.00.

The activity emanating from node C and looping back to node B would cause activity B-C to be repeated. Similarly, the activity emanating from node F and looping back to node E would cause activity E-F to be repeated. The activity labeled "Terminate" would cause the network flow to the "sink" node labeled H. Successful installation takes the network to node I where the project can come to an end. The activities labeled "Reinstall" would cause all activities on the network to be repeated. Table 8.2 depicts the analysis of this network.

---

[4] Two paths are independent when they do not share the same resources.

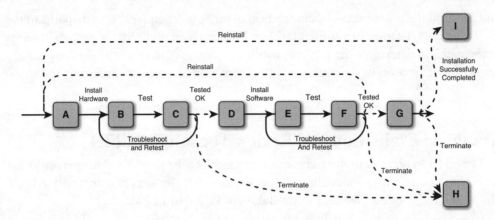

Figure 8.3 Using GERT to Calculate Estimated Duration for a Data Center Installation Project

Table 8.2 Project Network Activity Path Duration Estimation Using GERT

Source Node	Terminal Node	Probability	Distribution Type of Activity Duration	Minimum Duration MID	Maximum Duration MAD	Expected Value (Estimated Duration) $\mu = (MID + MAD)/2$	Standard Deviation for Normal Distribution $\sigma = (MAD - \mu)/3$ (3 sigma on each side of mean μ with 100% probability)
A	B	100%	Normal	1	3	2	0.3
B	C	100%	Normal	3	7	5	0.7
C	D	70%	N/A (Dummy)	N/A	N/A	0	N/A
C	B	20%	Triangular	2	5	N/A	N/A
C	H	10%	N/A (Dummy)	N/A	N/A	0	N/A
D	E	100%	Normal	1	3	2	0.3
E	F	100%	Normal	4	8	6	0.7
F	G	60%	N/A (Dummy)	N/A	N/A	0	N/A
F	A	10%	N/A (Dummy)	N/A	N/A	0	N/A
F	E	20%	Triangular	3	5	N/A	N/A
F	H	10%	N/A (Dummy)	N/A	N/A	0	N/A

Source Node	Terminal Node	Probability	Distribution Type of Activity Duration	Minimum Duration MID	Maximum Duration MAD	Expected Value (Estimated Duration) $\mu = (MID+MAD)/2$	Standard Deviation for Normal Distribution $\sigma = (MAD - \mu)/3$ (3 sigma on each side of mean μ with 100% probability)
G	A	10%	N/A (Dummy)	N/A	N/A	0	N/A
G	H	10%	N/A (Dummy)	N/A	N/A	0	N/A
G	I	80%	N/A (Dummy)	N/A	N/A	0	N/A

GERT is a useful technique but it is not without its drawbacks:

- It requires a complex program such as Monte Carlo simulation for modeling.
- It is considered to be less accurate than PERT and CPM.

That is why the use of GERT is rare. It is primarily used in systems with high complexity, such as a research and development project.

Correlation and Covariance

Chapter 5 of this book covers correlation, which, if you remember, is the relationship between two variables—one dependent and the other independent. This correlation can be positive, negative, or none at all. The coefficient of correlation dictates the type and level of correlation. This coefficient varies between –1 (strong negative correlation) and +1 (strong positive correlation).

Let us discuss how the concept of correlation can be used in making effective project management decisions.

Table 8.3 shows the historical data pertaining to the training budget and average per month late deliverables for seven similar projects. You can analyze how these two variables *x* and *y* are correlated.

Table 8.3 Project Training Budget versus % of Late Deliverables Historical Data

Project #	Training Budget (% of Total Project Budget) X	% of Late Deliverables (average per month) Y
1	10	5
2	2	44
3	7	10
4	15	2
5	0	58
6	4	34
7	1	47

Plotting the dependent variable x (percent of late deliverables) along the x-axis and the independent variable y (training budget) renders the scatter plot shown in Figure 8.4, which shows correlation between the two variables.

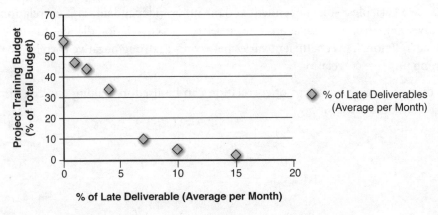

Figure 8.4 Correlation Between Project Training Budget and % of Late Deliverables

The scatter plot in Figure 8.4 depicts a strong negative correlation between training budget and percent of late deliverables. From this we can forecast that the investment in project staff training is directly proportional to the percentage of project deliverables delivered on time.

The sample correlation coefficient is $r = COV(x, y) / \sqrt{V_x^2 \times V_y^2}$

where $COV(x, y)$ represents the covariance of variables x and y and is calculated by the following formula:

$COV(x, y) = \Sigma(X - \bar{X})(Y - \bar{Y}) / n - 1$

The covariance measures the variability of the (x, y) coordinates (represented by the dots in the scatter plot) around the means of independent variable x and dependent variable y, respectively (considered simultaneously).

V_x^2 is the sample variance of x, defined as $V_x^2 = \Sigma(X - \bar{X})^2 / n - 1$

It is the measure of the variability of the x score ($\bar{X}$) around its sample mean.

Similarly,

V_y^2 is the sample variance of y, defined as $V_y^2 = \Sigma(Y - \bar{Y})^2 / n - 1$

It is the measure of the variability of the y score ($\bar{Y}$) around its sample mean.

To determine these variances, we first need to find out ΣX, $\bar{X}$, $\Sigma(X - \bar{X})^2$, ΣY, $\bar{Y}$, and $\Sigma(Y - \bar{Y})^2$.

ΣX = sum of all values of $x = X_1 + X_2 + ... + X_7$

$= 10 + 2 + 7 + 15 + 0 + 4 + 1$

$= 39$

The mean training budget, $\bar{X} = \Sigma(X / n)$

$= 39 / 7$

$= 5.6$

ΣY = sum of all values of $y = Y_1 + Y_2 + ... + Y_7$

$= 5 + 44 + 10 + 2 + 58 + 34 + 17$

$= 170$

The mean percentage of late deliverables, $\bar{Y} = \Sigma(Y / n)$

$= 170 / 7$

$= 24.3$

All these values are shown in Table 8.4.

Table 8.4 Table to Calculate $\Sigma(X - \bar{X})^2$ and $\Sigma(Y - \bar{Y})^2$

Project #	Training Budget (% of Total Project Budget) $x = X_1, X_2, ..., X_n$	$(X - \bar{X})$	$(X - \bar{X})^2$	% of Late Deliverables (average per month) $y = Y_1, Y_2, ..., Y_n$	$(Y - \bar{Y})$	$(Y - \bar{Y})^2$
1	10	10 – 5.6 = 4.4	19.36	5	5 – 24.3 = –19.3	372.49
2	2	2 – 5.6 = –3.6	12.96	44	44 – 24.3 = 19.7	388.09
3	7	7 – 5.6 = 1.4	1.96	10	10 – 24.3 = –14.3	204.49
4	15	15 – 5.6 = 9.4	88.36	2	2 – 24.3 = –22.3	497.29
5	0	0 – 5.6 = –5.6	31.36	58	58 – 24.3 = 33.7	1135.69
6	4	4 – 5.6 = –1.6	2.56	34	34 – 24.3 = 9.7	94.09
7	1	1 – 5.6 = –4.6	21.16	47	47 – 24.3 = 22.7	515.29
	$\Sigma X = 39$	$\Sigma(X - \bar{X}) = -0.2$	$\Sigma(X - \bar{X})^2 = 177.7$	$\Sigma Y = 170$	$\Sigma(Y - \bar{Y}) = 29.9$	$\Sigma(Y - \bar{Y})^2 = 3207.43$

Using the results from Table 8.4, we can now calculate variances.

The variance of training budget, $V_x^2 = \Sigma(X - \bar{X})^2 / n - 1$

$= 177.7 / 6$

$= 29.6$

The variance of percent of late deliverables, $V_y^2 = \Sigma(Y - \bar{Y})^2 / n - 1$

$= 3207.43 / 6$

$= 534.6$

Now let's calculate the covariance and the sample correlation coefficient.

$COV(x, y) = \Sigma(X - \bar{X}) (Y - \bar{Y}) / n - 1$

Table 8.5 shows the calculations for $\Sigma(X - \bar{X}) (Y - \bar{Y})$.

Table 8.5 Table to Calculate $\Sigma(X - \bar{X})(Y - \bar{Y})$

Project #	$(X - \bar{X})$	$(Y - \bar{Y})$	$(X - \bar{X})(Y - \bar{Y})$
1	4.4	−19.3	−84.92
2	−3.6	19.7	−70.92
3	1.4	−14.3	−20.02
4	9.4	−22.3	−209.62
5	−5.6	33.7	−188.72
6	−1.6	9.7	−15.52
7	−4.6	22.7	−104.42
			$\Sigma(X - \bar{X})(Y - \bar{Y}) = -694.14$

$COV(x, y) = 694.14 / 6$

$= 115.69$

The sample correlation coefficient, $r = COV(x, y) / \sqrt{V_x^2 \times V_y^2}$

$= -115.69 / \sqrt{(29.6 \times 534.6)}$

$= -115.69 / 125.79$

$= -0.92$

The very close proximity of this correlation coefficient to −1 indicates that a strong negative correlation exists between the percentage of the project budget allocated for training and the monthly average percentage of the late deliverables. In other words, more training leads to increased percentage of deliverables that are delivered on time.

Predictive Analysis: Linear Regression

Predictive analytics include a variety of statistical techniques that are used to analyze current and historical factual information to make predictions about the future uncertainties.

Regression analysis is one of the key statistical techniques of predictive analytics, which is used for studying relationships among variables (a dependent variable and one or more independent variables; also known as predictors). It involves establishing a mathematical equation as a model to represent the interactions between the participating variables.

As discussed in Chapter 5 of this book, linear regression is an extension of correlation where we can analyze the correlation between two sets of variables to make better decisions.

The linear regression model portrays the correlation between one dependent variable and one or more independent variables. The dependent or response variable is a linear function of the independent variable(s). The following relationship represents the equation for multiple linear regression where the dependent variable $\hat{y}$ is a function of multiple independent variables $x_1, x_2, ..., x_k$.

$$\hat{y} = b + m_1 x_1 + m_2 x_2 + ... + m_k x_k$$

where $\hat{y}$ is the expected or predicted value of the dependent variable, $x_1, x_2, ..., x_k$ are independent or predictor variables, $m_1, m_2, ..., m_k$ are the estimated regression coefficients, and b is the y-intercept (the value of y when all independent variables are equal to zero).

Let us discuss how multiple linear regression can be used in making effective project management decisions.

Keeping the triple constraints of project management in mind (time, cost, and scope), consider a scenario where a project manager wants to know how a 10% increase in the project scope and six weeks increase in the project schedule with respect to the baseline would impact the project costs based on the historical data given in Table 8.6.

Table 8.6 Multiple Linear Regression Historical Data

Scenario	Change in Project Costs with Respect to Cost Baseline (Budget) Y	Percent Change in Project Scope with Respect to Scope Baseline X_1	Change in Project Schedule (in weeks) with Respect to Baseline Schedule X_2
1	$44,434	8	2
2	$16,282	2	0
3	$42,132	6	4
4	$54,484	12	5
5	$43,401	7	2
6	$36,234	4	4
7	$42,431	7	1

Scenario	Change in Project Costs with Respect to Cost Baseline (Budget) Y	Percent Change in Project Scope with Respect to Scope Baseline X_1	Change in Project Schedule (in weeks) with Respect to Baseline Schedule X_2
8	$68,444	13	10
9	$48,934	9	3
10	$70,114	15	4
11	$11,332	1	0
12	$47,430	5	7

The first step is to express this problem in the form of multiple linear regression equation. The expected or predicted value of the project costs, $\hat{y} = b + m_1 x_1 + m_2 x_2$ where

   x_1 is the percent change in project scope

   x_2 is the change in the project schedule in terms of weeks

   m_1 is the estimated regression coefficient that quantifies the relationship between the change in project scope and the outcome y

   m_2 is the estimated regression coefficient that quantifies the relationship between the change in project schedule and the outcome y

Substituting the values of x_1 and x_2, the equation becomes, $\hat{y} = b + m_1{}^*10 + m_2{}^*6$

Now use Microsoft Excel to find the y-intercept and the correlation coefficients needed in the regression equation.

When you launch Excel, first make sure that the Data Analysis option exists on the ribbon under Data. If not, follow these steps to add and activate the Data Analysis toolset:

1. Choose File, Options. The Excel Options window appears.
2. Click the Add-Ins tab and then select Analysis ToolPak, as shown Figure 8.5.
3. In the same window, click Go as shown in Figure 8.6.

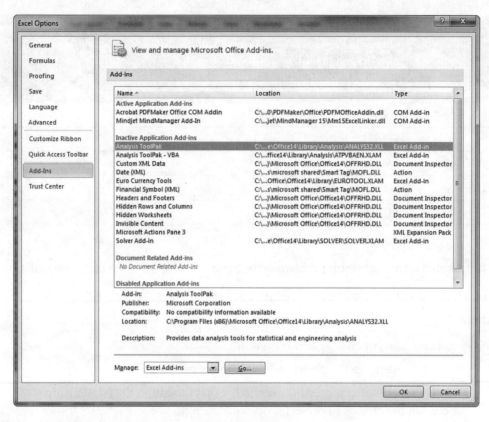

Figure 8.5 Enabling Data Analysis Option in Excel—Exhibit 1

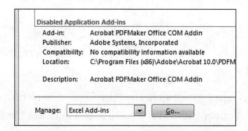

Figure 8.6 Enabling Data Analysis Option in Excel—Exhibit 2

4. Select the Analysis ToolPak check box in the Add-Ins dialog box, shown in Figure 8.7, and click OK.

5. Verify that the Data Analysis option is available under the Tools tab, as shown in Figure 8.8.

Figure 8.7 Enabling Data Analysis Option in Excel—Exhibit 3

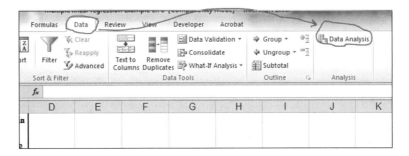

Figure 8.8 Enabling Data Analysis Option in Excel—Exhibit 4

6. Click on Data Analysis, select Regression from the Analysis Tools menu, and click OK as shown in Figure 8.9.

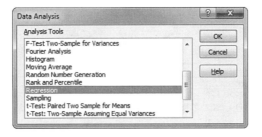

Figure 8.9 Running Regression Using Data Analysis—Exhibit 1

7. In the Regression window that appears (see Figure 8.10), select the Labels check box and select the range for X and Y values from the table. Also select the Output Option where you want the analysis report to show up.

Figure 8.10 Running Regression Using Data Analysis—Exhibit 2

8. Click OK to complete the regression analysis. The results appear as shown in Figure 8.11.

SUMMARY OUTPUT

Regression Statistics	
Multiple R	0.971806
R Square	0.944407
Adjusted R	0.930509
Standard E	4808.216
Observatio	11

ANOVA

	df	SS	MS	F	ignificance F
Regressior	2	3.14E+09	1.57E+09	67.95131	9.55E-06
Residual	8	1.85E+08	23118943		
Total	10	3.33E+09			

	Coefficients	tandard Err	t Stat	P-value	Lower 95%	Upper 95%	.ower 95.0%	Upper 95.0%
Intercept	14254.91	2920.128	4.881604	0.001222	7521.08	20988.73	7521.08	20988.73
8	3102.136	414.4902	7.484219	7.03E-05	2146.319	4057.952	2146.319	4057.952
2	1828.526	619.9293	2.949572	0.018438	398.9665	3258.086	398.9665	3258.086

m_1
m_2

Figure 8.11 Running Regression Using Data Analysis—Exhibit 3

The values of interest to us in these results are as follows:

Y-intercept, b = 14254.91

Correlation Coefficient for x_1, m_1 = 3102.136

Correlation Coefficient for x_2, m_2 = 1828.526

Substituting these values in question $\hat{y} = b + m_1{}^*10 + m_2{}^*6$

The expected or predicted value of the project costs, $\hat{y}$ = 14254.91 + 3102.136*10 + 1828.526*6 = \$56,247.43

Thus, based on the historical trend, a 10% increase in the project scope and a six-week increase in the project schedule will cause a \$56,247.43 increase in the project costs with respect to the baseline.

Confidence Intervals: Prediction Using Earned Value Management (EVM) Coupled with Confidence Intervals

Chapter 4 of this book covers confidence intervals and the next section (shaded area) provides a detailed review of the Earned Value Management (EVM) for your reference.

The following sections cover predicting (forecasting) the project cost and time outcomes at any time during the project life cycle.

Cost (Budget) Performance Measurement

This section measures how the project is doing with respect to the cost management at the time of measurement. In other words, it measures the cost efficiency (rate of spending) of the project at the time of measurement and also gives a snapshot of the budget status at that time (overspending, underspending, or spending as budgeted or planned).

Estimated Cost at Completion, ECC = BAC / CPI

where

BAC = Budget at Completion = Total Project Budget (as planned)

CPI = Cost Performance Index (cost efficiency[5]) = EV_c / AC

---

[5] Indicates actual (measured) value in terms of money for spending of each unit of money

where

EV_C[6] = Earned Value (the worth of actual progress made till the time of measurement), and

AC = Actual Cost (actual cost incurred till the time of measurement)

Time (Schedule) Performance Measurement

This section measures how the project is doing with respect to the time or schedule management at the time of measurement. In other words, it measures the schedule efficiency (rate of progress) of the project at the time of measurement and also gives a snapshot of the schedule status at that time (ahead of schedule, behind schedule, or on schedule as planned).

Estimated Duration at Completion, EDC = PDC / SPI

where

PDC = Planned Duration at Completion = Total Project Budget (as planned)

SPI = Schedule Performance Index (schedule efficiency[7]) = EV_S / PV

where

EV_S = Earned Value (the worth [in terms of money] of actual percent of work completed at the time of measurement)

= Actual percent of work completed at the time of measurement * BAC

PV = Planned Value (the worth [in terms of money] of work that was planned to have been completed at the time of measurement)

= Actual duration completed at the time of measurement / Total duration) * BAC

Cost and Schedule Forecasting with Statistics

Both CPI and SPI are normally distributed around the mean. Thus, we can use statistical tools and techniques for forecasting.

As defined in Chapter 4, a confidence interval is an interval estimate with a range of values specifying probability or confidence that the value of a parameter of interest lies within it.

The upper and lower limits of a confidence interval are called confidence limits (CL).

---

[6] Subscript c denotes the value is cumulative till the time of measurement

[7] Indicates actual (measured) rate of progress with respect to the planned rate of progress

Mathematically $CL = \bar{x} \pm z_c^* \sigma / \sqrt{n}$

where

$\bar{x}$ = Sample mean (Point estimate of population mean μ)

$z_c^* \sigma / \sqrt{n}$ = Margin of error in estimating

z_c[8] = Value related to area under the normal distribution curve with level of confidence typically 90% or 95%

σ = Sample standard deviation

n = Sample size

For normal distribution, $z = 1.6449$ for Confidence Level = 90% and 1.9600 for Confidence Level = 95%.

The values of upper and lower confidence limits based on a specified level of confidence provide significant forecasting information for project managers to make informed decisions.

However, there is a little challenge. The statistical tools and techniques are based on the assumption that the normal distribution of the population under consideration is infinite, but projects by definition are finite (they have a definite start and end). Thus, both cost and schedule distribution warrant adjustments for the finite nature of the projects. As the project progresses, the adjusted upper and lower confidence limits approach each other and eventually conclude at the mean.

The following are the adjustment factors for cost and schedule:

$AF_C = \sqrt{((BAC - EV_C) / (BAC - (EV_C/n)))}$

$AF_S = \sqrt{((PDC - EV_S) / (PDC - (EV_S/n)))}$

where AF stands for adjustment factor and n denotes the sample size.

Because CPI and SPI are normally distributed, the mean is the logarithm of the cumulative value of CPI or SPI.

Standard Deviation $\sigma = \sqrt{(\Sigma(\ln{}^9 \text{ period CPI or SPI} - \ln \text{ cumulative CPI or SPI})^2 / ('n - 1))}$

---

[8] Use t_c (t-distribution) if sample size n < 30

[9] "ln" stands for *Natural Logarithm*

In relationship $e^y = x$, base e logarithm of x, $ln(x) = log_e(x) = y$

Where e is a constant or Euler's number ≈ 2.71828183

Source: http://www.rapidtables.com/math/algebra/Ln.htm

And

CL (CL_C for cost and CL_S for schedule) = ln cumulative CPI or SPI $\pm z_c * (\sigma/\sqrt{n}) * AF$

Thus, forecast for Lower CL (LCL) for cost, $EAC_L = BAC / e^{(CL_C^{(-)})}$

And, forecast for Upper CL (UCL) for cost = $BAC / e^{(CL_C^{(+)})}$

Similarly, forecast for LCL for schedule, $EAC_S = PDC / e^{(CL_S^{(-)})}$

And, forecast for UCL for schedule = $PDC / e^{(CL_S^{(+)})}$

where "e" is natural logarithmic number = 2.718

These LCLs and UCLs are further tested using the statistical hypothesis test at 0.05 significance,

where

H_a = The hypothesis testing result for each CL when the test statistic is in the critical region (0.05 with 95% Confidence Level), and

H_0 = The hypothesis testing result for each CL when the test statistic is not in the critical region.

Binomial distribution can be used to further compute the probability of obtaining reliable results (denoted by H_a).

Earned Value Management (EVM)

Earned Value Management (EVM) is an objective technique to measure the project performance. The underpinning notion is that any amount of completed project work creates value (worth) in the project. For example, procurement of $10,000 worth of raw materials would create an equivalent of $10,000 value in the project, which is called Earned Value (EV). Thus, the EVM quantifies the project performance in terms of dollars.

Using EVM, the current project performance is measured by comparing the EV against the baseline or Planned Value (PV). The current performance measurement via the EV mechanism would indicate whether the project is ahead of the planned schedule, on schedule, or behind schedule. From a cost performance point of view, the EV measurement would indicate the project is under budget, on budget, or over budget. EVM is used to forecast future project schedules and cost performance based on the current performance measured using the EV. The forecasting is based on the assumption that the measured rate of performance will prevail until the end of the project. It is also helpful in making appropriate corrective action decisions if the project performance is not within the planned limits.

Example EVM Problem

The estimated cost rate to build a 12,000 yard paved road in a new subdivision development is $20 per linear foot. The total duration of the project is planned to be 12 weeks. The project manager uses EVM to measure the project performance on a monthly basis. At the end of 4 months after the project is started, the project team recorded that 3,300 yards of the road have been completed, incurring a cost of $44,000. How can you use the EVM to measure the current performance and forecast the future performance?

We will first measure and analyze the schedule performance and then the cost performance.

Schedule Performance

1. **Calculate Budget at Completion (BAC).**

    Based on the given data, the total budget to complete the project can be computed, which is called the BAC.

    Thus, BAC = 10,000 yards of the road × $20 per linear yard = $200,000

2. **Calculate PV.**[10]

    PV = the quantified value of the work that was planned to have been completed at the end of 4 months

    = Percentage of the total work planned to have been completed × BAC

    = (4/12) × $200,000

    = $66,667 (rounded)

3. **Calculate EV.**[11]

    EV signifies how much worth of project work (quantitatively) was actually done at the end of 4 months.

    Thus, EV = Actual percentage of the work completed × BAC

    = (3,300 / 10,000) × $200,000

    = $66,000

---

[10] Note: The PV here is also known as Budgeted Cost of Work Scheduled (BCWS)

[11] Also known as Budgeted Cost of Work Performed (BCWP)

---

4. **Calculate Schedule Variance (SV).**

   SV = EV – PV

   = \$66,000 – \$66,667

   = **–\$667** (*This indicates that the project is behind the schedule.*)

   The sign and magnitude of the SV signify how the project is progressing with the schedule.

   SV = 0 implies the project is on schedule (good).

   SV > 0 implies the project is ahead of schedule (good).

   SV < 0 implies the project is behind schedule (bad).

   The absolute value of the magnitude of SV determines how much the project is ahead or behind the schedule.

   Let us convert the monetized SV into actual time.

   SV (time) = SV (monetized) × (Planned Project Schedule / BAC)

   = (–\$667) × (12 weeks / \$200,000)

   = –0.04 weeks

   = –0.04 × 5 working days[12]

   = –0.2 working days

   Thus, the project is behind schedule by 0.2 working days.

5. **Calculate Schedule Performance Index (SPI).**

   SPI gives the schedule efficiency of the project.

   SPI = EV / PV

   = \$66,000 / \$66,667

   = 0.99

   This signifies that the project's schedule efficiency is 99% of the planned efficiency.

   We can use this information to forecast the final schedule for the project as follows:

   Final schedule forecast = Planned Project Schedule / SPI

   = 12 weeks / 0.99

   = 12.13 weeks

---

[12] Assuming five working days in a week

This means that if the project continues to maintain the schedule efficiency of 99%, it will take total 12.13 weeks to complete.

Cost Performance

1. **Calculate BAC.**

   From step 1 of the "Schedule Performance," BAC = $200,000.

2. **Determine Actual Cost (AC).**[13]

   Amount spent so far = AC = $44,000 (given)

3. **Calculate EV.**

   The EV here determines how much should have been spent to complete 3,300 yards of the road.

   Thus, EV = Amount of work completed × Budgeted rate per unit of work completed

   = 3,300 yards × 20 weeks

   = $66,000

4. **Calculate Cost Variance (CV).**

   CV = EV – AC

   = $66,000 – $44,000

   = **$22,000** (*This indicates that the project is under budget.*)

   The sign and magnitude of the CV signify how the project is spending the money.

   CV = 0 implies the project is on budget (good).

   CV > 0 implies the project is under budget (good).

   CV < 0 implies the project is over budget (bad).

   The absolute value of the magnitude of CV determines how much the project is over budget or under budget.

   In this case, the project is under budget by $22,000.

---

[13] Also known as Actual Cost of Work Performed (ACWP)

5. **Calculate Cost Performance Index (CPI).**

   CPI gives the cost efficiency or the spending efficiency.

   CPI = EV / AC

   = $66,000 / $44,000

   = 1.5

   This signifies that the project's spending efficiency is 105%, which means that the project is receiving the value worth $1.5 for each dollar spent on the project.

   We can use this information to forecast the final cost for the project, which is given by Estimate At Complete (EAC):

   EAC = BAC / Cumulative CPI

   = $200,000 / 1.5

   = $133,333

   This means that if the project continues to maintain the cost efficiency of 105%, its revised final budget will be $133,333 (a savings of $200,000 – $133,333 = $66,667 over the life of the project).

Summary

The mind map in Figure 8.12 summarizes the key aspects of this chapter.

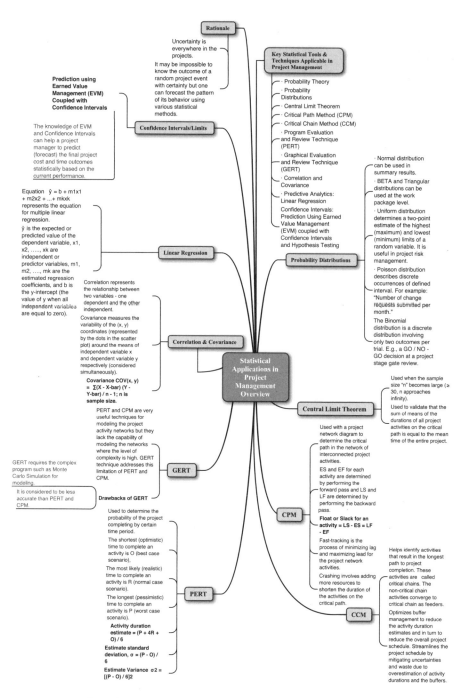

Rationale

Uncertainty is everywhere in the projects.

It may be impossible to know the outcome of a random project event with certainty but one can forecast the pattern of its behavior using various statistical methods.

Key Statistical Tools & Techniques Applicable in Project Management

· Probability Theory
· Probability Distributions
· Central Limit Theorem
· Critical Path Method (CPM)
· Critical Chain Method (CCM)
· Program Evaluation and Review Technique (PERT)
· Graphical Evaluation and Review Technique (GERT)
· Correlation and Covariance
· Predictive Analytics: Linear Regression
Confidence Intervals: Prediction Using Earned Value Management (EVM) coupled with Confidence Intervals and Hypothesis Testing

Prediction using Earned Value Management (EVM) Coupled with Confidence Intervals

The knowledge of EVM and Confidence Intervals can help a project manager to predict (forecast) the final project cost and time outcomes statistically based on the current performance.

Confidence Intervals/Limits

Equation $\hat{y} = b + m_1x_1 + m_2x_2 + ...+ m_kx_k$ represents the equation for multiple linear regression.

$\hat{y}$ is the expected or predicted value of the dependent variable, x_1, x_2, ..., x_k are independent or predictor variables, m_1, m_2, ..., m_k are the estimated regression coefficients, and b is the y-intercept (the value of y when all independent variables are equal to zero).

Linear Regression

Correlation represents the relationship between two variables - one dependent and the other independent.

Covariance measures the variability of the (x, y) coordinates (represented by the dots in the scatter plot) around the means of independent variable x and dependent variable y respectively (considered simultaneously).

Covariance $COV(x, y) = \Sigma(X - X\text{-bar}) (Y - Y\text{-bar}) / n - 1$; n is sample size.

Correlation & Covariance

PERT and CPM are very useful techniques for modeling the project activity networks but they lack the capability of modeling the networks where the level of complexity is high. GERT technique addresses this limitation of PERT and CPM.

GERT requires the complex program such as Monte Carlo Simulation for modeling.

It is considered to be less accurate than PERT and CPM.

Drawbacks of GERT

GERT

Statistical Applications in Project Management Overview

· Normal distribution can be used in summary results.

· BETA and Triangular distributions can be used at the work package level.

· Uniform distribution determines a two-point estimate of the highest (maximum) and lowest (minimum) limits of a random variable. It is useful in project risk management.

· Poisson distribution describes discrete occurrences of defined interval. For example: "Number of change requests submitted per month."

The Binomial distribution is a discrete distribution involving only two outcomes per trial. E.g., a GO / NO - GO decision at a project stage gate review.

Probability Distributions

Used when the sample size "n" becomes large (≥ 30, n approaches infinity).

Used to validate that the sum of means of the durations of all project activities on the critical path is equal to the mean time of the entire project.

Central Limit Theorem

Used with a project network diagram to determine the critical path in the network of interconnected project activities.

ES and EF for each activity are determined by performing the forward pass and LS and LF are determined by performing the backward pass.

Float or Slack for an activity = LS - ES = LF - EF

Fast-tracking is the process of minimizing lag and maximizing lead for the project network activities.

Crashing involves adding more resources to shorten the duration of the activities on the critical path.

CPM

Helps identify activities that result in the longest path to project completion. These activities are called critical chains. The non-critical chain activities converge to critical chain as feeders.

Optimizes buffer management to reduce the activity duration estimates and in turn to reduce the overall project schedule. Streamlines the project schedule by mitigating uncertainties and waste due to overestimation of activity durations and the buffers.

CCM

Used to determine the probability of the project completing by certain time period.

The shortest (optimistic) time to complete an activity is O (best case scenario).

The most likely (realistic) time to complete an activity is R (normal case scenario).

The longest (pessimistic) time to complete an activity is P (worst case scenario).

Activity duration estimate = (P + 4R + O) / 6

Estimate standard deviation, σ = (P - O) / 6

Estimate Variance σ2 = [(P - O) / 6]2

PERT

Figure 8.12 Statistical Applications in Project Management Summary

Key Terms

Activity on Node (AON)

Backward Pass

Beta Distribution

Binomial Distribution

Central Limit Theorem

Change Control Board (CCB)

Confidence Interval

Correlation

Correlation Coefficient

Cost Performance Index (CPI)

Covariance

Crashing

Critical Chain Method (CCM)

Critical Path Method (CPM)

Deterministic

Earned Value (EV)

Earned Value Management (EVM)

Expected Value

Fast Tracking

Feeding Buffer

Float

Forward Pass

Graphical Evaluation and Review Technique (GERT)

Hypothesis Testing

Linear Regression

Lower Control Limit (LCL)

Normal Distribution

Planned Value (PV)

Poisson Distribution

Precedence Diagramming Method (PDM)

Predictive Analytics

Probabilistic

Program Evaluation and Review Technique (PERT)

Project Buffer

Resource Buffer

Schedule Performance Index (SPI)

Standard Deviation

Triangular Distribution

Uniform Distribution

Upper Control Limit (UCL)

Chapter Review and Discussion Questions

1. What is the definition of a successful project?

2. According to statistical theory what are the minimum and maximum limits for the probability of a random event?

3. Discuss one key application of binomial distribution in project management.

4. What role can central limit theorem play in helping a project manager make project decisions?

5. Describe the Model for Improvement. The following are the attributes of a project activity labeled M:

   ES = 12, EF = 25, and LF = 34

   Calculate the activity duration.

6. What is the difference between crashing and fast tracking?

7. How is CCM different from CPM?

8. What is a project buffer in CCM?

9. Calculate estimated duration and standard deviation for a project activity with the following data:

   Pessimistic time = 24 weeks

   Optimistic time = 12 weeks

   Realistic time = 17 weeks

10. How is GERT different from PERT? What are its benefits and drawbacks?

11. Define covariance. Calculate covariance using the following data:

Project #	X	Y
1	6	1
2	2	14
3	7	12
4	15	3

12. The Project Management Office (PMO) of an organization studied the impact of the project manager skills and the level of quality of the project on the project outcome (success or failure) for 10 projects and calculated the following data. Using multiple linear regression, estimate the project outcome for a project when the project manager skill level is rated at 6 and the level of quality implemented is 6 Sigma.

Project #	Outcome Success = 1 Failure = 0	Project Manager Skills (On a scale 1 to 10; 10 being the best)	Level of Quality (# of Sigmas)
1	0	6	1
2	0	3	3
3	1	7	6
4	0	4	3
5	1	7	3
6	0	10	1
7	1	9	6
8	0	2	6
9	1	5	3
10	1	5	6

13. The estimated installation cost rate to install 100 computers in a data center is $10 per computer. The total duration of the project is planned to be 8 weeks. At the end of 3 months after the project is started, the project team noted that 30 of the 100 computers have been installed incurring a cost of $36,282. Using your knowledge of EVM and confidence intervals, forecast the final schedule and cost for the project at the current rate of performance.

Bibliography

Ahuja, H.N. et al. (1994). *Project Management: Techniques in Planning and Controlling Construction Projects,* 2nd ed. Hoboken, New Jersey: John Wiley & Sons, Inc.

Baker, S. (2004). "Critical Path Method (CPM)." Retrieved August 2, 2015, from http://hspm.sph.sc.edu/COURSES/J716/CPM/CPM.html

Barnes, R. et al. (2003). "A Critical Look at Critical Chain Project Management," *Project Management Journal*, 32(2) pp. 24-32.

Bernard, W. T. (1978). "Project Management Using GERT Analysis." Retrieved August 2, 2015, from http://www.pmi.org/learning/gert-graphical-evaluation-review-technique-5716?id=5716

Boston University School of Public Health. (2013). "Introduction to Correlation and Regression Analysis." Retrieved September 26, 2015, from http://sphweb.bumc.bu.edu/otlt/MPH-Modules/BS/BS704_Multivariable/BS704_Multivariable5.html

Bozarth, C. (2011). "Single Regression: Approaches to Forecasting: A Tutorial." Retrieved July 26, 2015, from http://scm.ncsu.edu/scm-articles/article/single-regression-approaches-to-forecasting-a-tutorial

Econometrics Laboratory (EML). (2015). "Regression Analysis." Retrieved July 25, 2015, from http://eml.berkeley.edu/sst/regression.html

Goodpasture, J.C. (2004). *Quantitative Methods in Project Management.* J. Ross Publishing. pp. 173–178.

Goodpasture, J.C. (2013). "Probability Distributions for Project Managers." Retrieved July 22, 2015, from http://flylib.com/books/en/2.573.1.14/1/

Het Project. (2013). "Critical Chain Method." Retrieved August 2, 2015, from http://www.hetproject.com/Francois_Retief_paper_Overview_of_Critical_Chain.pdf

Kapur, G.K. (2005). *Project Management for Information, Technology, Business, and Certification,* 1st ed. Upper Saddle River, New Jersey: Pearson Education.

Lambert, L.R. et al. (2000). *Project Management: The CommonSense Approach,* 3rd ed. Columbus, Ohio: Lee R Lambert & Assoc.

Lotffy, E. (2014). "CPM, PERT, and GERT." Retrieved August 2, 2015, from https://www.linkedin.com/pulse/20140618054203-58881633-cpm-pert-and-gert-retrieved-from-web

Marshall, R. (2007). The Contribution of Earned Value Management to Project Success of Contracted Efforts. *Journal of Contract Management,* pp. 21–33.

Neumann, K. and Steinhardt, U. (1979). *GERT Networks and the Time-Oriented Evaluation of Projects,* 1st ed. Heidelberg, Berlin: Springer-Verlag.

Oster, E. (2014). "Brainy Statistics Quotes." Retrieved August 1, 2015, from http://www.brainyquote.com/quotes/keywords/statistics.html

Pentico, D. (1985). "Estimating Project Costs with Regression and Risk Analysis." Retrieved July 26, 2015, from http://www.pmi.org/learning/estimating-project-costs-risk-analysis-5221

Project Management Institute (2014). *A Guide to the Project Management Body of Knowledge (PMBOK Guide),* 5th ed. Newtown Square, Pennsylvania: Project Management Institute.

Rapid Tables. (2015). "Natural Logarithm - ln(x)." Retrieved July 19, 2015, from http://www.rapidtables.com/math/algebra/Ln.htm

Sampson, S. (2012). "Project Scheduling Analysis: The Critical Path Method (CPM)." Retrieved August 1, 2015, from http://services.byu.edu/t/quant/proj.html

Weber, B. (2015). "Statistics: Session 1." Retrieved August 1, 2015, from http://www.kellogg.northwestern.edu/faculty/weber/emp/_session_1/_session_1.htm

9

Project Decision-Making with the Analytic Hierarchy Process (AHP)

Learning Objectives

After reading this chapter, you should be familiar with

- Applications of the AHP in project management
- Evaluation criteria and sub-criteria
- Net Present Value (NPV)
- Payback period
- Return on Investment (ROI)
- Decision hierarchy
- Comparison matrix
- Pairwise comparison
- Consistency Ratio (CR)
- Consistency Index (CI)
- Eigen (Priority) Vectors
- Synthesis and ranking in the AHP

> "Statistics are like bikinis. What they reveal is suggestive, but what they conceal is vital."
> —*Aaron Levenstein, Business Professor at Baruch College*

Chapter 6, "Analytic Hierarchy Process," provided an overview of the AHP, a technique that was developed by Thomas L. Saaty in the '70s. This technique is extremely useful in making complex decisions involving multiple criteria.

This chapter covers the various applications of the AHP technique in multi-criteria decision-making pertaining to project management.

Project success has strong positive correlation with rational and effective decision-making. Effective stakeholder engagement is also very crucial to the project success. Thus, as Bhushan and Rai (2004) said, if factors like human perceptions and judgments are not given proper consideration in group decision-making in a complex project environment, the chances of the project success will diminish.

As discussed in Chapter 6, the AHP-based decision-making not only takes into consideration quantitative criteria but also considers the qualitative factors such as human perceptions and judgments. It is, in fact, a 360-degree decision-making technique that considers a multitude of criteria by giving each criterion its due weight.

For more on the general AHP approach, refer to Chapter 6. This chapter focuses on how to use this mathematical technique specifically for making complex project management decisions to maximize the chances of the project success.

The AHP can be used for decision-making in many areas of project management, including the following:

- Project evaluation and selection
- Project cost estimation
- Project complexity estimation
- Project risk management
- Change requests prioritization
- Request for Proposal (RFP) bids evaluation for government projects
- Vendor evaluation and selection

NOTE

Covering the AHP-based complete analysis and evaluation of the multiple criteria for all these areas of project management is beyond the scope of this book. However, this chapter does discuss the first area on the preceding list—project evaluation and selection—completely from end-to-end so that you can clearly understand the application of the AHP in project management. For the remaining areas on the list, I identify the evaluation criteria for each area and you can complete the analysis and evaluation on your own by following the worked-out example of the project evaluation and selection area, which follows.

Project Evaluation and Selection

The use of the AHP approach involves systematically organizing, analyzing, and synthesizing the information pertaining to multi-criteria used in complex decision-making.

Organizations are constantly striving to use their finite resources as optimally as possible by investing them in a project that has been selected after very careful evaluation based an objective and mathematical criteria that take into consideration both tangible and intangible factors.

Let's discuss how the organizations can achieve their objective of making a rational decision on project selection by utilizing AHP's multi-criteria-based evaluation technique.

The AHP is a step-by-step methodological process involving the following high-level steps:

1. Determine evaluation criteria.
2. Develop the decision hierarchy.
3. Perform the analysis.
4. Synthesize and rank priorities.
5. Make the decision.

1. Determine Evaluation Criteria

To use the AHP for decision-making, the first step is to identify the evaluation criteria. The following is the list of the main criteria and the sub-criteria for each element or factor of the main criterion (or criteria).

1. Strategic alignment
   a. Achieve long-term goals
   b. Achieve short-term goals
2. Cost
   a. Human resources cost
   b. Raw materials cost
   c. Equipment cost
3. Financial
   a. NPV
   b. Payback Period
   c. ROI

4. General

   a Complexity

   b Time to market

Figure 9.1 provides a graphical illustration of these criteria and sub-criteria.

NOTE

NPV can be defined as the difference between the present values of the incoming cash flows and the outgoing cash flows over a period of time.

Payback period is the time required to recuperate all the original investments.

ROI is used to measure the efficiency of an investment.

ROI = (Gain from Investment – Cost of Investment) / Cost of Investment

---

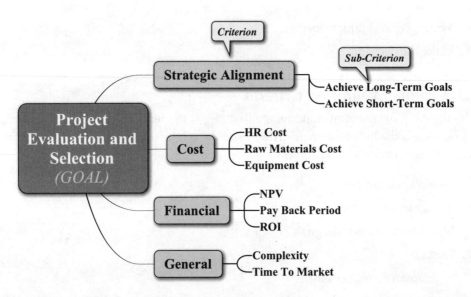

Figure 9.1 Multi-Criteria Mind Map

2. Develop the Decision Hierarchy

Developing and understanding the decision hierarchy is fundamental to using the AHP for decision-making. Figure 9.2 shows the decision hierarchy for our case with the goal

---

to be achieved at the top of the hierarchy, various alternatives at the bottom, and the evaluation criteria and sub-criteria in the middle.

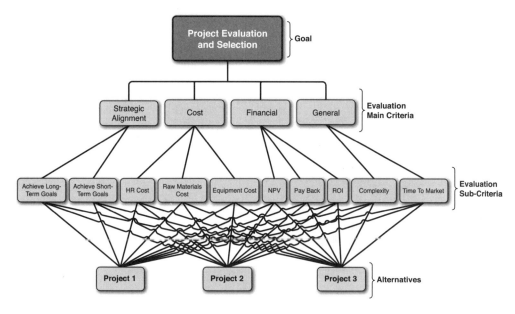

Figure 9.2 The AHP Decision Hierarchy

3. Perform the Analysis

After the hierarchy is developed, the next step is to analyze and evaluate various alternatives in terms of their respective strengths with respect to all factors in the evaluation criteria or sub-criteria. Subsequently, the factors in the evaluation criteria are evaluated in terms of their importance in achieving the stipulated goal. This analysis is necessary to determine relative weights for each level of criteria. It involves the following steps:

1. Determine the comparison matrix.

2. Normalize the comparison matrix.

3. Calculate the Eigen (priority) vector.

4. Determine the CR.

We will apply these four steps to analyze and evaluate the following levels of the decision hierarchy:

- Goal versus criteria
- Criteria versus sub-criteria
- Sub-criteria versus alternatives

Goal versus Criteria

Figure 9.3 illustrates the relationship between the goal and the criteria.

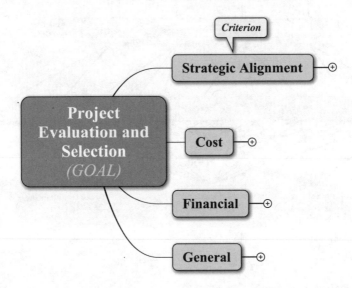

Figure 9.3 Goal versus Criteria Mind Map

The nodes or elements of this mind map (elements or factors of the main criteria) are assigned weights using the weighting scale called the *Saaty Scale,* discussed in Chapter 6. The weight assignment process uses expert judgment.

The weight assignment allows the pairwise comparison of the factors of the evaluation criteria and determines numerical priorities among them.

Step 1: Determine the Comparison Matrix

Table 9.1 captures the weights used for various pairs of the factors in the evaluation criteria. The weight for the weaker element of the pair is the reciprocal of the weight of the one that is stronger.

Table 9.1   Comparison Matrix Based on Relative Weights

Evaluation Criteria	Strategic Alignment	Cost	Financial	General
Strategic Alignment	1	5	4	6
Cost	⅕	1	1	2
Financial	¼	1	1	1
General	⅙	½	1	1

Step 2: Normalize the Comparison Matrix

Normalizing the comparison matrix is a two-step process:

1. Add up cell values for each column (see Table 9.2).

Table 9.2   Comparison Matrix Normalization Step 1

Evaluation Criteria	Strategic Alignment	Cost	Financial	General
Strategic Alignment	1	5	4	6
Cost	⅕	1	1	2
Financial	¼	1	1	1
General	⅙	½	1	1
Sum of column cell values	1.62	7.50	7	10

2. Divide each cell value of a column by the sum of the values of that column (see Table 9.3).

Table 9.3   Comparison Matrix Normalization Step 2

Evaluation Criteria	Strategic Alignment	Cost	Financial	General
Strategic Alignment	1/1.62 = 0.6173	5/7.5 = 0.6667	4/7 = 0.5714	6/10 = 0.6000
Cost	0.2/1.62 = 0.1235	1/7.5 = 0.1333	1/7 = 0.1429	2/10 = 0.2000
Financial	0.25/1.62 = 0.1543	1/7.5 = 0.1333	1/7 = 0.1429	1/10 = 0.1000
General	0.17/1.62 = 0.1049	0.5/7.5 = 0.0667	1/7 = 0.1429	1/10 = 0.1000

Step 3: Calculate the Eigen (Priority) Vector

The next step is to find the right Eigen Vector for this matrix, which was calculated by averaging the new values of each row of the matrix, as shown in Table 9.4.

Table 9.4   Eigen or Priority Vectors

Evaluation Criteria	Strategic Alignment (SA)	Cost (C)	Financial (F)	General (G)	Eigen (Priority) Vector [(SA+C+F+G)/4]
Strategic Alignment	0.6173	0.6667	0.5714	0.6000	0.6139
Cost	0.1235	0.1333	0.1429	0.2000	0.1499
Financial	0.1543	0.1333	0.1429	0.1000	0.1326
General	0.1029	0.0667	0.1429	0.1000	0.1031

Step 4: Determine the CR

The next step is to find the right Eigen Vector for this matrix, calculated as shown in Table 9.5.

Table 9.5   Eigen Value Calculation

Eigen Vector	0.6139	0.1499	0.1326	0.1031
Sum of column cell values	1.62	7.50	7	10
Maximum Eigen Value (λ_m)				

Maximum Eigen Value (λ_m)	$[(0.6139 \times 1.62) + (0.1499 \times 7.50) + (0.1326 \times 7) + (0.1031 \times 10)] = 4.08$

$$CI = (\lambda_m - n) / n - 1$$

where n is number of criteria.

$$CI = (4.08 - 4) / 4 - 1 = 0.0267$$

Saaty (2008) suggested the values shown in Table 9.6 for random consistency indices (RI) corresponding to each value of number of criteria (up to 10).

Table 9.6   Saaty's Random Consistency Indices Table

N	1	2	3	4	5	6	7	8	9	10
RI	0	0.16	0.58	0.9	1.12	1.24	1.32	1.41	1.45	1.49

According to Saaty (2008), a matrix is consistent if its CR is less than 10% (< 0.1), where CR = CI / RI.

In our case, CR = 0.0267/0.9 = 0.0296 = 2.96%

Because our CR is less than 10%, our matrix is consistent.

Criteria versus Sub-Criteria

To complete the next stage of analysis, you have to evaluate sub-criteria (the third level of the decision hierarchy, illustrated in the mind map shown in Figure 9.4) with respect to the main criteria.

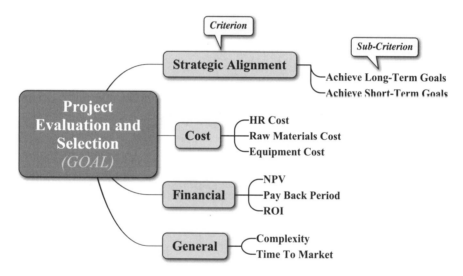

Figure 9.4 Criteria versus Sub-Criteria Mind Map

The steps to complete this evaluation are the same as those for evaluating goal versus criteria. After you complete all steps of the evaluation process, you will achieve the Eigen Vectors you need for ranking the sub-criteria.

The following sections describe the complete end-to-end sub-criteria evaluation process.

Strategic Alignment Criteria

The sub-criteria for Strategic Alignment include Long-Term Goals and Short-Term Goals. Let's perform the step-by-step evaluation for these sub-criteria.

Step 1: Determine the Comparison Matrix

The first step is to determine the pairwise comparison matrix depicting the relative weights of each element of the sub-criteria with respect to the Strategic Alignment factor of the main criteria. The weight for the weaker element of the pair is the reciprocal of the weight of the one that is stronger, as shown in Table 9.7.

Table 9.7   Comparison Matrix

Strategic Alignment	Long-term Goals	Short-term Goals
Long-term Goals	1	3
Short-term Goals	1/3	1

Step 2: Normalize the Comparison Matrix

Normalizing the comparison matrix is a two-step process:

1. Add up cell values for each column as shown in Table 9.8.

Table 9.8   Comparison Matrix Normalization Step 1

Strategic Alignment	Long-term Goals	Short-term Goals
Long-term Goals	1	3
Short-term Goals	1/3	1
Column Total	1.33	4

2. Divide each cell value of a column by the sum of the values of that column as shown in Table 9.9.

Table 9.9   Comparison Matrix Normalization Step 2

Strategic Alignment	Long-term Goals	Short-term Goals
Long-term Goals	1/1.33 = 0.75	3/4 = 0.75
Short-term Goals	0.33/1.33 = 0.25	1/4 = 0.25

Step 3: Calculate the Eigen (Priority) Vector

The next step is to find the right Eigen Vector for this matrix, which is calculated by averaging the new values of each row of the matrix, as shown in Table 9.10.

Table 9.10 Eigen or Priority Vectors

Strategic Alignment	Determination of Eigen Vector		Eigen Vector
Long-term Goals	(0.75+0.75)/2	=	0.75 = 75%
Short-term Goals	(0.25+0.25)/2	=	0.25 = 25%

Step 4: Determine the CR

The next step is to find the right Eigen Vector for this matrix, which is calculated as shown in Table 9.11.

Table 9.11 Eigen Value Calculation

Eigen Vector	0.75	0.25
Sum of column cell values	1.33	4
Maximum Eigen Value (λ_m)	$[(0.75 \times 1.33) + (0.25 \times 4)] = 2$ (rounded)	

$$CI = (\lambda_m - n) / n - 1$$

where n is number of criteria.

$$CI = (2 - 2) / 2 - 1 = 0$$

Saaty (2008) suggested the values shown in Table 9.12 for random consistency indices (RI) corresponding to each value of number of criteria (up to 10).

Table 9.12 Saaty's Random Consistency Indices Table

N	1	2	3	4	5	6	7	8	9	10
RI	0	0.16	0.58	0.9	1.12	1.24	1.32	1.41	1.45	1.49

According to Saaty (2008), a matrix is consistent if its CR is less than 10% (< 0.1), where $CR = CI / RI$.

In our case, CR = 0/0.16 = 0 = 0%.

Because our CR is less than 10%, our matrix is consistent.

The sub-criteria for the remaining factors of the main criteria can be evaluated following the same procedure as for the Strategic Alliance factor of the main criteria.

Tables 9.13 to 9.15 show the Eigen Vectors corresponding to the sub-criteria for the remaining factors of the main criteria.

Table 9.13   Cost Criteria–Based Priority Matrix

Cost	Eigen Vector
Human Resources	0.2585 = 25.85%
Raw Materials	0.5705 = 57.05%
Equipment	0.1710 = 17.10%

Table 9.14   Financial Criteria–Based Priority Matrix

Financial	Eigen Vector
NPV	0.2059 = 20.59%
Payback	0.6411 = 64.11%
ROI	0.1530 = 15.30%

Table 9.15   General Criteria–Based Priority Matrix

General	Eigen Vector
Complexity	0.1667 = 16.67%
Time to Market	0.8333 = 83.33%

Sub-Criteria versus Alternatives (Project Choices)

This analysis involves the lowest two layers of the decision hierarchy. Here, we have to evaluate various alternatives (the lowest level of the decision hierarchy; illustrated in the mind map shown in Figure 9.5) with respect to the sub-criteria.

Again, the steps to complete this stage of evaluation are the same as those we have used so far in this chapter. Tables 9.16 to 9.25 show the Eigen Vectors corresponding to the alternatives with respect to the elements of the sub-criteria.

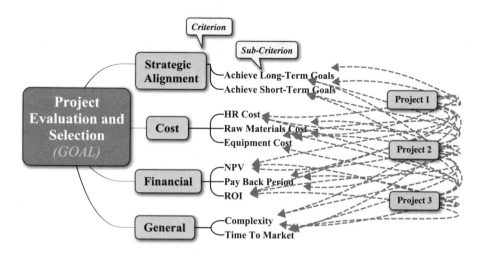

Figure 9.5 Sub-Criteria versus Alternatives Mind Map

Table 9.16 Long-Term Goals Sub-Criteria–Based Priority Matrix

Long-Term goals	Eigen Vector
Project 1	0.6209 = 62.09%
Project 2	0.1195 = 11.95%
Project 3	0.2574 = 25.74%

Table 9.17 Short-Term Goals Sub-Criteria–Based Priority Matrix

Short-Term Goals	Eigen Vector
Project 1	0.3504 = 35.04%
Project 2	0.3640 = 36.40%
Project 3	0.2857 = 28.57%

Table 9.18 Human Resources Sub-Criteria–Based Priority Matrix

Human Resources	Eigen Vector
Project 1	0.7015 = 70.15%
Project 2	0.0620 = 6.20%
Project 3	0.2365 = 23.65%

Table 9.19   Raw Materials Sub-Criteria–Based Priority Matrix

Raw Materials	Eigen Vector
Project 1	0.1710 = 17.10%
Project 2	0.2585 = 25.85%
Project 3	0.5705 = 57.05%

Table 9.20   Equipment Sub-Criteria–Based Priority Matrix

Equipment	Eigen Vector
Project 1	0.4057 = 40.57%
Project 2	0.1145 = 11.45%
Project 3	0.4797 = 47.97%

Table 9.21   NPV Sub-Criteria–Based Priority Matrix

NPV	Eigen Vector
Project 1	0.6845 = 68.45%
Project 2	0.0882 = 8.82%
Project 3	0.2270 = 22.70%

Table 9.22   Payback Sub-Criteria–Based Priority Matrix

Payback	Eigen Vector
Project 1	0.2764 = 27.64%
Project 2	0.3628 = 36.28%
Project 3	0.3608 = 36.08%

Table 9.23 ROI Sub-Criteria–Based Priority Matrix

ROI	Eigen Vector
Project 1	0.3319 = 33.19%
Project 2	0.0805 = 8.05%
Project 3	0.5876 = 58.76%

Table 9.24 Complexity Sub-Criteria–Based Priority Matrix

Complexity	Eigen Vector
Project 1	0.5966 = 59.66%
Project 2	0.3185 = 31.85%
Project 3	0.0849 = 8.49%

Table 9.25 Time to Market Sub-Criteria–Based Priority Matrix

Time to Market	Eigen Vector
Project 1	0.1979 = 19.79%
Project 2	0.1007 = 10.07%
Project 3	0.7014 = 70.14%

4. Synthesize and Rank Priorities

Finally, the priorities pertaining to the alternatives and pertaining to the evaluation criteria and sub-criteria are synthesized to yield the overall numerical priorities for the alternatives. Alternatives are then ranked on the basis of their numerical priorities and the highest ranking alternative is considered in the decision-making.

Synthesis

To synthesize, you need the following two pieces of information with respect to each alternative:

1. Relative priority weights (Eigen Vectors) of the sub-criteria with respect to their respective element of criteria. These refer to the Eigen Vector values contained in Tables 9.10 through 9.15.

2. Relative priority weights (Eigen Vectors) of the alternatives with respect to each element of the sub-criteria. These refer to the Eigen Vector values contained in Tables 9.16 through 9.25.

Now, for each alternative, multiply each value from step 1 by the corresponding value from step 2 and add up all products. Tables 9.26 through 9.28 illustrate these steps for the three alternatives: Project 1, Project 2, and Project 3.

Table 9.26 Final Evaluation Result for Alternative, Project 1

Criteria	Sub-Criteria	Relative Priority Weight (PW)	Relative Alternative Weight (AW)	Product (PW × AW)
Strategic Alignment	Achieving Long-Term Goal	0.7500	0.6209	0.4657
	Achieving Short-Term Goal	0.2500	0.3504	0.0876
Cost	Human Resources Cost	0.2585	0.7015	0.1813
	Raw Materials Cost	0.5705	0.1710	0.0976
	Equipment Cost	0.1710	0.4057	0.0694
Financial	NPV	0.2059	0.6845	0.1409
	Pay Back Period	0.6411	0.2764	0.1772
	ROI	0.1530	0.3319	0.0508
General	Complexity	0.1667	0.5966	0.0995
	Time to Market	0.8333	0.1979	0.1649
Final Evaluation Result for Project 1 (Sum of All Products)				1.5348

Table 9.27 Final Evaluation Result for Alternative, Project 2

Criteria	Sub-Criteria	Relative Priority Weight (PW)	Relative Alternative Weight (AW)	Product (PW × AW)
Strategic Alignment	Achieving Long-Term Goal	0.7500	0.1195	0.0896
	Achieving Short-Term Goal	0.2500	0.3640	0.0910
Cost	Human Resources Cost	0.2585	0.0620	0.0160
	Raw Materials Cost	0.5705	0.2585	0.1475
	Equipment Cost	0.1710	0.1145	0.0196
Financial	NPV	0.2059	0.0882	0.0182
	Pay Back Period	0.6411	0.3628	0.2326
	ROI	0.1530	0.0805	0.0123
General	Complexity	0.1667	0.3185	0.0531
	Time to Market	0.8333	0.1007	0.0839
Final Evaluation Result for Project 2 (Sum of All Products)				0.7638

Table 9.28 Final Evaluation Result for Alternative, Project 3

Criteria	Sub-Criteria	Relative Priority Weight (PW)	Relative Alternative Weight (AW)	Product (PW × AW)
Strategic Alignment	Achieving Long-Term Goal	0.7500	0.2574	0.1931
	Achieving Short-Term Goal	0.2500	0.2857	0.0714
Cost	Human Resources Cost	0.2585	0.2365	0.0611
	Raw Materials Cost	0.5705	0.5705	0.3255
	Equipment Cost	0.1710	0.4797	0.0820

Criteria	Sub-Criteria	Relative Priority Weight (PW)	Relative Alternative Weight (AW)	Product (PW × AW)
Financial	NPV	0.2059	0.227	0.0467
	Pay Back Period	0.6411	0.3608	0.2313
	ROI	0.1530	0.5876	0.0899
General	Complexity	0.1667	0.0849	0.0142
	Time to Market	0.8333	0.7014	0.5845
Final Evaluation Result for Project 3 (Sum of All Products)				1.6997

Ranking

The final values for all the alternatives are then prioritized from highest rank (magnitude) to the lowest rank (magnitude). The alternative with highest rank is selected.

From Tables 9.26, 9.27, and 9.28, respectively:

- Final evaluation result for Project 1 = 1.5348
- Final evaluation result for Project 2 = 0.7638
- Final evaluation result for Project 3 = 1.6997

Rearrange Project Choices by sorting the results in the descending order (result with the highest magnitude on top and the one with lowest magnitude at the bottom).

5. Make the Decision

Table 9.29 lists the projects of the portfolio based on descending order of the ranking based on the final evaluation results. A project manager or a Project Management Office can use this information to make the following decisions:

1. To select the most qualified single project in the portfolio for persual, which in this case will be Project 3 because this is the highest ranking project in the list.

2. To allocate scarce organizational resources including staffing, equipment, and raw materials optimally across the projects in the portfolio. In this case, the highest ranking project (#1) has the highest priority and the lowest ranking project (#2) has the lowest priority to claim the resources.

Table 9.29 Project Ranking Based on Final Evaluation Results

Project Choice	Final Evaluation Result
Project 3	1.6997
Project 1	1.5348
Project 2	0.7638

Thus, the AHP serves as the most effective methodology for enabling the project managers to make the correct project portfolio management decisions.

More Applications of the AHP in Project Management

As we discussed toward the beginning of this chapter, quite a number of project management areas exist where the AHP can be used for decision-making. We have just discussed *Project Evaluation and Selection* using the AHP in the preceding section. Now, we will discuss few more areas briefly.

Project Complexity Estimation

In today's world, the need for innovative project management methodologies and solutions has been growing tremendously largely due to ever-growing complexity of the modern projects. Multiple factors have been contributing to this complexity of the projects and it is of utmost importance to understand the project complexity to develop the appropriate methodologies and solutions to manage these complex projects.

Because multiple factors are responsible for the project complexity, we can use the AHP's multi-criteria analysis to estimate the project complexity. The mind map shown in Figure 9.6 depicts various criteria and sub-criteria that can be analyzed and evaluated via the AHP.

Project Risk Assessment

Project risk assessment involves the following:

- Risk identification
- Risk assessment
- Impact determination
- Control strategy determination

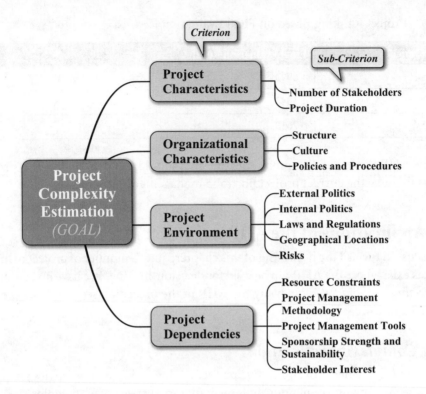

Figure 9.6 Multi-Criteria Mind Map for Project Complexity Estimation

The mind map in Figure 9.7 shows the multi-criteria that you can use in the AHP to assess the project risks.

Project Change Requests Prioritization

Change management is an integral part of the project management. Often the project Change Control Board (CCB) gets overwhelmed with the number of change requests it receives. Thus, there is a need to evaluate and prioritize the incoming change requests using some objective criteria so that the influx of the change requests to the CCB for decision-making can be controlled and managed effectively. This is the perfect scenario where you can use the AHP. Figure 9.8 outlines the multi-criteria for this scenario.

Figure 9.7 Multi-Criteria Mind Map for Project Risk Assessment

Figure 9.8 Multi-Criteria Mind Map for Project Change Requests Prioritization

Summary

The mind map in Figure 9.9 outlines the applications of the AHP in project management.

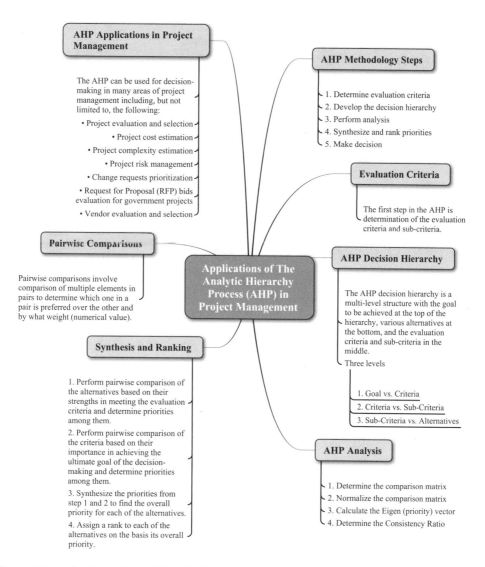

Figure 9.9 Applications of the AHP in Project Management

Key Terms

AHP

CCB

Consistency Ratio

Decision Hierarchy

Eigen Vector

Eigenvalue

Evaluation Criteria/Sub-Criteria

Intensity of Importance

Matrix Normalization

NPV

Pairwise Comparison

Payback

Priority

Ranking

Relative Weight

RFP

ROI

Saaty Scale

Synthesis

Time to Market

Chapter Review and Discussion Questions

1. You are a project manager for a government IT project. Your project is seeking to select a Solution Vendor (also known as a Systems Integrator) for the Design, Development, and Implementation phase via the Request for Proposal (RFP) procurement vehicle. How can you use the AHP to select the best vendor based on certain criteria? Perform all the steps and select the best solution vendor.

2. Your project has been losing lots of quality project and business analysts to attrition. Data collected from the exit interview questionnaire given to those leaving over a period of time has indicated that the root cause of attrition is the staff discontentment due to lack of employee appreciation activities. Better late than never; your project has decided to mitigate the loss by launching an Employee of the Month program to reward and recognize one employee every month for best performance based on some predefined performance criteria. Use the AHP to develop a model to select one best performing employee out of four nominations.

Bibliography

Al-Subhi AL-Harbi, K.M. (2001). "Application of the AHP in Project Management." *International Journal of Project Management*, 19, pp. 19–27.

Bhushan, N., and Rai, K. (2004). *Strategic Decision Making*. London: Springer-Verlag.

BPMSG. (2010). "Analytic Hierarchy Process AHP - Business Performance Management." Retrieved August 16, 2015, from https://www.youtube.com/watch?t=517&v=18GWVtVAAzs

Chankong, V., and Haimes, Y.Y. (1983). *Multiobjective Decision Making*. North-Holland, Amsterdam: Dover Publications.

De Moraes, E.A., and Bernardes, R.C. (2001). *Project Portfolio Management using AHP*. Centro Universitário da FEI São Paulo, SP Brazil.

Dey, P.K. (2002). "Project Risk Management: A Combined Analytic Hierarchy Process and Decision Tree Approach." *Cost Engineering*, 44 (3), pp. 13-26.

Forman, E.H., and Gass, H.I. (2001). "The Analytic Hierarchy Process—An Exposition." *INFORMS Operations Research*, 49 (4), pp. 469–486.

Fu, H. (2009). "Using AHP to Analyze the Priority of Performance Criteria in National Energy Projects." *Proceedings of International Conference on Pacific Rim Management, 19th Annual Meeting*, San Francisco, California.

Geopel, K.D. (2013). *Implementing the Analytic Hierarchy Process as a Standard Method for Multi-Criteria Decision Making in Corporate Enterprises—A New AHP Excel Template with Multiple Inputs*. Changi Business Park, Singapore.

Ho-Leung, R. (2001). "Using Analytic Hierarchy Process (AHP) Method to Prioritise Human Resources in Substitution Problem." *International Journal of The Computer, The Internet and Management*, 9 (1).

Investopedia. (2003). "Return On Investment (ROI) Definition | Investopedia." Retrieved August 15, 2015, from http://www.investopedia.com/terms/r/returnoninvestment.asp

Ishizaka, A., and Labib, A. (2009). "Analytic Hierarchy Process and Expert Choice: Benefits and Limitations." Retrieved August 15, 2015, from http://www.palgrave-journals.com/ori/journal/v22/n4/full/ori200910a.html

Keeney, R.L. and Raiffa, H. (1976.) *Decisions with Multiple Objectives: Preference and Value Tradeoffs*. New York: John Wiley & Sons.

Mustafa, M., and Al-Bahar, J. F. (1991). "Project Risk Assessment Using the Analytic Hierarchy Process." *Engineering Management, IEEE Transactions*, 38(1), 46–52.

Saaty, T.L. (2008). "Decision Making with the Analytic Hierarchy Process." *International Journal of Services Sciences*, 1 (1), pp. 83-98.

Saaty, T.L., and Vargas, L.G. (2001). *Models, Methods, Concepts & Applications of the Analytic Hierarchy Process*. Boston: Kluwer's Academic Publishers.

Vilekar, A. (2014). "10 Hard to Ignore Data Analytics Quotes." Retrieved August 19, 2015, from http://blog.cloudlytics.com/10-hard-ignore-data-analytics-quotes/.

10

Lean Six Sigma Applications in Project Management

Learning Objectives

After reading this chapter, you should be familiar with:

- Synergistic blend of project management and Lean Six Sigma (LSS)
- LSS Remedies for common project management challenges
- Project Management Life Cycle (PMLC) versus LSS DMAIC[1] methodology
- Traditional project charter versus LSS project charter
- Agile project management versus lean methodology
- Role of LSS tools and techniques in PMLC
- Role of LSS tools and techniques in Agile project management
- Role of LSS tools and techniques in improving the Project Management Office (PMO)

> "Measurement is the first step that leads to control and eventually to improvement. If you can't measure something, you can't understand it. If you can't understand it, you can't control it. If you can't control it, you can't improve it."
>
> —*H. James Harrington, IBM Quality Expert*

We discussed the basics of project management and LSS in Chapters 1, "Project Management Analytics" and 7, "Lean Six Sigma," respectively. This chapter presents a hybrid model by integrating the project management and LSS methodologies that entail two scenarios—one with LSS tools and technologies blended into the traditional (Waterfall)

---

[1] DMAIC: **D**efine, **M**easure, **A**nalyze, **I**mprove/Implement, **C**ontrol/Close

project management methodology, and the other involving Agile project management methodology.

All projects face challenges with respect to the triple project constraints of scope, time, and cost as well as to the project quality, but LSS provides the necessary antidote against these challenges. By no means is the LSS methodology a substitute for project management; rather they both complement each other. Their mix creates a unique synergy that facilitates more effective project management in terms of more effective management of these constraints.

The focus of this chapter is to illustrate the mechanism and the benefits of the blended and the Agile approaches, starting with identifying the key project challenges and the LSS remedies for those challenges, followed by a discussion on the integration of the two methodologies.

Common Project Management Challenges and LSS Remedies

We discussed project triple constraints in Chapter 3, "Project Management Framework," which included project scope, schedule, and budget. These triple constraints with project quality embedded within them constitute the focal point of the project management challenges that project managers encounter in their day-to-day job. Poor project selection, poor requirements management, poor staffing acquisition, poor risk and issue management, poor stakeholder management, poor quality management, poor documentation, corner-cutting, lack of adequate success measuring criteria, wasteful and inconsistent processes and procedures, lack of accountability, lack of root cause analysis, lack of governance and oversight, bureaucracy, and lack of data-driven decision-making are some of the key causes of these challenges. Table 10.1 outlines some common challenges encountered by the project managers in the project management environment and corresponding LSS remedies to mitigate them.

Table 10.1 LSS Solutions to Common Project Management Challenges

Common Project Management Challenges	LSS Remedies
Subjective, short-sighted, and poor decision-making	Data-driven, better, and smoother project decision-making
Low stakeholder satisfaction	Improved stakeholder satisfaction
Unstable, inconsistent, and redundant project processes	Reduced process variation
Waste and inefficiencies caused by inconsistency and redundancy	Reduced/eliminated waste caused by inconsistency and redundancy

Common Project Management Challenges	LSS Remedies
Poor quality of project processes and deliverables because of inadequate measurement and control	Improved quality of project processes and deliverables
Cost overruns	Better controlled costs
Schedule slips caused by wasteful non-value-add activities	Shortened schedule due to elimination of non-value-add activities
Daily firefighting	Root cause analysis (RCA); continuous improvement

LSS tools and techniques enable project managers to quantify all decision-making criteria backed by real data and analytics, which make it easier for them to justify their point of view. The bottom line is that incorporation of LSS into project management facilitates quicker decision-making and mitigation of project management challenges.

Project Management with Lean Six Sigma (PMLSS)— A Synergistic Blend

Quality is the life blood of project management. It refers to the degree of correctness in the project processes and deliverables. The projects and project hosting organizations must have quality embedded in their culture, which is only possible if the path of continuous improvement is followed. Integration of LSS tools and techniques with traditional project management methodologies throughout the project life cycle can make continuous improvement a reality.

Both LSS tools and techniques and project management methodologies help with effective management of the project processes in their own right, but the harmonious blend of the complementary attributes of the two can enhance the combined benefits. Project management contributes the process control aspect and LSS contributes the waste and defect-minimizing aspect to the blend, making the blended system stand out with improved consistency, control, and predictability. Implementing the blended system from day one in the project life cycle can help the project:

- Define the problem(s) being addressed better

- Analyze and understand the stakeholder requirements better

- Achieve more accurate estimates in the planning stage of the project life cycle

LSS's DMAIC methodology coupled with iterative PDSA[2] (also known as PDCA[3]) improvement cycles provides a structured approach to finding the root cause(s) of the problem(s) related to project processes and deliverables. The tools and techniques associated with project management methodologies provide a mechanism for execution, control, and completion of the project activities.

PMLC versus LSS DMAIC Stages

As you learned in the beginning of this chapter, project management and LSS are not substitutes for each other; rather, they complement each other. Project management methodology can be leveraged by the LSS DMAIC projects for overarching guidance. Similarly, LSS methodologies and tools can provide additional support to project management for making more efficient and data-driven decisions.

Figure 10.1 depicts the synergistic relationships between PMLC stages and LSS DMAIC stages. The thicker lines represent bilateral relationships and the thinner lines represent the unilateral relationships. The arrows signify the direction of the influence. The bidirectional arrows also signify the commonality between the nodes they are connected to.

Now let's discuss the relationships between the two sides with respect to one PMLC stage at a time.

Initiating

The *Initiating* stage of the PMLC shares some commonality with the *Define* stage of the DMAIC methodology. For instance:

- Both initiatives, one carried out under project management and the other carried out under DMAIC, are projects and need a charter to get authorization to start. The charter is developed in the Initiating stage of the PMLC and in the Define stage of DMAIC. Figures 10.2 and 10.3 outline the key elements of the charters for project management and LSS methodologies, respectively.

- Both require identification and engagement of the project stakeholders to get their buy-in and support for the project.

- Both sides need documented guidelines to guide the projects. However, the level of details for guidelines pertaining to the DMAIC project (see Figure 10.2) is less compared to the guidelines for the project under traditional project management (see Figure 10.3). DMAIC guidelines are contained in the charter itself where

---

[2] PDSA: <u>P</u>lan, <u>D</u>o, <u>S</u>tudy, <u>A</u>ct
[3] PDCA: <u>P</u>lan, <u>D</u>o, <u>C</u>heck, <u>A</u>ct

the project management guidelines are contained in a comprehensive formal project plan.

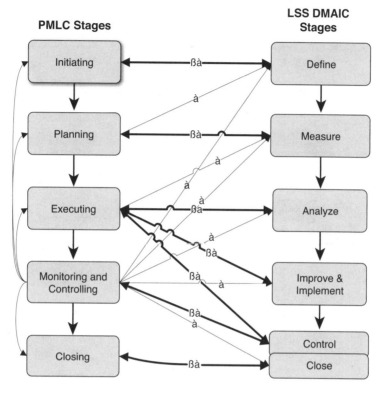

Figure 10.1 Synergistic Relationships between PMLC Stages and LSS DMAIC Stages

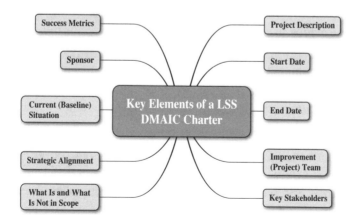

Figure 10.2 Key Elements of an LSS DMAIC Charter

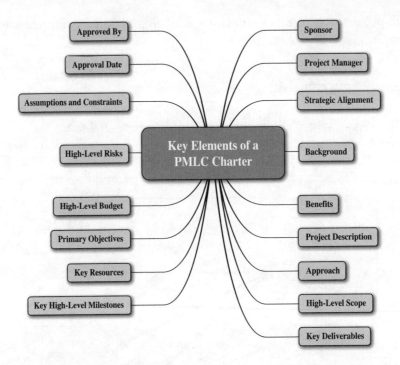

Figure 10.3 Key Elements of a PMLC Charter

Planning

The *Planning* stage of the PMLC shares some commonality with the *Measure* stage of the DMAIC methodology.

- Both deal with assessing the existing state to establish an "as is" baseline. The baseline provides a reference against which the success is measured.

- Both involve planning, developing, and implementing data collection procedures to create a baseline. The PMLC side uses historical project assets, expert judgment, meetings, and analytic techniques to collect data, whereas the LSS DMAIC side uses surveys, interviews, historical performance data (such as logs), and observations to collect data.

Project management *Monitoring and Controlling* processes can cover both sides of data collection and baseline creation. Because the data collection procedure involves planning, assigning roles and responsibilities, and executing the plan, the Monitoring and

Controlling stage of the PMLC can be helpful in monitoring the performance of data collection efforts and making appropriate adjustments as necessary.

Executing

Both sides involve analysis. On the PMLC side, various alternatives are analyzed to find the best solution or the best method. On the LSS DMAIC side, the data collected during the *Measure* stage is analyzed in the *Analyze* stage to understand the status quo ("as is" performance) and perform RCA. Note that LSS methodology focuses on finding the sustainable cure via root cause, not just treating the symptoms.

The key tools used on the LSS side, such as Process Mapping, Value Stream Mapping (VSM), Kaizen, and RCA can also be used on the PMLC side in the *Executing* stage. Similarly, project management guidelines and tools and techniques in the Executing stage and communications as well as stakeholder management knowledge areas can also be applied to provide guidance to the Measure, Analyze, Improve/Implement, and Control stages of LSS DMAIC because these stages involve heavy participation by the improvement team and stakeholders in collecting and analyzing data to understand the "as is" situation, evaluate various alternatives to improve the status quo, roll out the best alternative, and then control the improved state to ensure the sustainability of the improvement. The solution rollout is also a project in its own right and hence the PMLC framework can help provide guidelines to manage that project.

Monitoring and Controlling

PMLC *Monitoring and Controlling* processes span over the entire life cycle of a project—it doesn't matter if the project is a project under traditional project management or it is an LSS project. This is because the tangible work is performed in each phase or stage of the project and the performance must be monitored, measured, and controlled for the success of the project. The control mechanism entails comparing the actual results with the planned or baseline performance and taking appropriate action based on the variance analysis.

Variance = Actual Performance – Baseline Performance

Closing

Commonality exists on both sides with respect to Closing because both sides deal with projects and all projects ultimately come to an end.

How LSS Tools and Techniques Can Help in the PMLC or the PMBOK[4] Process Framework

The PMLC is also referred to as the PMBOK process framework. Project processes in this process framework are categorized into five process groups: Initiating, Planning, Executing, Monitoring and Controlling, and Closing, as shown in Figure 10.4 and discussed in detail in Chapter 1. The preceding section showed how PMLC stages (PMBOK process groups) and LSS DMAIC stages cross-pollinate. In this section, the discussion focuses on learning how various LSS tools and techniques can help project management within the PMLC stages (PMBOK process framework).

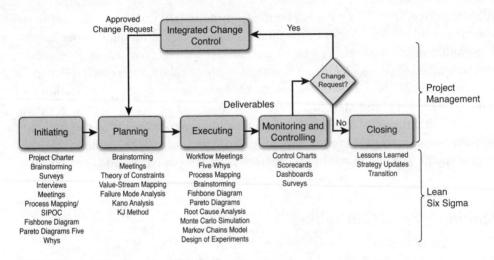

Figure 10.4 Role of LSS Tools and Technologies across PMLC Stages

Initiating

The *Initiating* stage of the PMLC (or the PMBOK *Initiating* process group) includes all the activities necessary for the official launch of the project. The key activities pertaining to this stage include assignment or hiring of the project manager,[5] development

---

4. PMBOK: **P**roject **M**anagement **B**ody **o**f **K**nowledge [Project Management standards and process framework published by the Project Management Institute (PMI)]

5. The project manager is hired or assigned by the project sponsor after the project business case (concept and justification) is approved.

and approval of the project charter,[6] and identification and analysis of the project stakeholders.

Table 10.2 outlines the role of various LSS tools and techniques in the Initiating stage of the PMLC.

Table 10.2   Role of LSS Tools and Techniques in the Initiating Stage of the PMLC

LSS Tool/Technology	Role in Initiating Stage of the PMLC
Project Charter	Authorizes a project to officially start and also authorizes the project manager to use the organizational resources to run the project.
Brainstorming	Can be used in facilitation of the meetings to gather ideas from experts and key stakeholders for development of the project charter and for identification of the stakeholders.
Surveys	Can be used for gathering ideas from experts and key stakeholders for development of the project charter and for identification of the stakeholders.
Interviews	Can be used for gathering ideas from experts and key stakeholders for development of the project charter and for identification of the stakeholders.
Meetings	Can be used for gathering ideas from experts and key stakeholders for development of the project charter and for identification of the stakeholders.
Process Mapping/SIPOC	Can be used for identification of the stakeholders.
Fishbone (cause-and-effect) Diagram	Can be used with brainstorming.

---

[6] The project charter is defined, initiated, and approved by the project sponsor and developed by the project manager. An approved project charter officially authorizes the project manager to undertake the project and use the organizational resources to carry out the project activities. The project manager is obligated to deliver within the terms and conditions specified and agreed upon in the project charter.

LSS Tool/Technology	Role in Initiating Stage of the PMLC
Pareto Diagrams	Can be used to prioritize the identified stakeholders in the order of relative importance based on the chosen criteria so that key stakeholders can be identified. The underlying principle is the 80:20 rule, which means that 20% of the top stakeholders in the priority list have 80% of the impact and influence on the project.
	Can be used in problem resolution if they arise during project charter development or stakeholder identification analysis.
	Can be used with a fishbone diagram to further define and analyze the problem being addressed in the project and to understand the scope of the project better by identifying the problem areas that need the most attention.
Five Whys[7]	Can be used in stakeholder analysis to justify the importance of a particular stakeholder.
	Can be used with a fishbone diagram to perform the RCA.

Brainstorming for Stakeholder Identification

"The project manager can facilitate the stakeholder identification brainstorming session using sticky notes:

- Invite the project team members and other key stakeholders to the brainstorming session.

- Ask the brainstorm session participants to think of any possible stakeholder (individual, group, or organization) names and write those names on the sticky notes.

- Have the participants post the completed sticky notes on a wall.

- Review the sticky notes posted on the wall and remove the ones that are redundant.

- Make a list of the remaining unique stakeholder names."

Source: Singh, H. (2014). Masering Project Human Resource Management. Pearson FT Press

---

[7] Five Whys is a simple LSS technique that involves asking "Why" five times to arrive at the root cause.

Planning

During the planning stage of the PMLC, the key activities include the following:

- Collection, analysis, and documentation of business requirements
- Definition and documentation of the project scope
- Creation of the Work Breakdown Structure (WBS)
- Identification of the staffing needs
- Development and baselining of the project schedule
- Development and baselining of various project management plans such as risk management plan, communications management plan, and so on.

Table 10.3 outlines the role of various LSS tools and techniques in the Planning stage of the PMLC.

Table 10.3   Role of LSS Tools and Techniques in the Planning Stage of the PMLC

LSS Tool/Technology	Role in the Planning Stage of the PMLC
Brainstorming	Can be used in facilitation of the meetings to gather ideas from experts and key stakeholders for project planning.
Meetings	Can be used for gathering ideas from experts and key stakeholders for project planning.

LSS Tool/Technology	Role in the Planning Stage of the PMLC
Theory of Constraints[8] (TOC)[9]	Like common saying "a chain is as strong as its weakest link," any project constraint, if not managed effectively, can keep the project from achieving its objectives. The TOC paradigm can help the project identify that constraint and manage it to mitigate the risk. Because scope, schedule, and cost are the triple constraints of a project per PMBOK, the TOC can help in better planning of project scope, time, and cost management.
Value Stream Mapping (VSM)	VSM can help in project planning in the following ways: ■ In stakeholder management planning by giving more weightage to potentially more value-adding stakeholders. ■ In general by eliminating non-value-add activities from the project processes and saving scarce resources via lean planning.
Failure Modes and Effects Analysis (FMEA)	FMEA can be used in planning for project risk management as follows: ■ Identify potential failure modes and their effects on the project. ■ Assign severity number (SN) ■ Estimate probability of occurrence (PO) ■ Determine likelihood of detection (LD) ■ Risk priority number = SN*PO*LD
Kano Analysis	Created by Japan's Dr. Kano in 1984, Kano Analysis (also known as the Kano Model) can help the project get a better understanding of the business requirements.
KJ Method	Also called the Affinity Diagram, the KJ Method was developed by Jiro Kawakita in the 1960s. This LSS tool can be used in the Planning stage of project management in conjunction with brainstorming. This tool can help organize the ideas collected during the brainstorming session into logical groups based on their natural relationships to make the review and analysis process easier.

---

[8] Originally developed by Dr. Eli Goldratt in 1984; it states, "Every system, no matter how well it performs, has at least one constraint that limits its performance." You use this theory by identifying your constraint and restructuring the way that you work so that you can overcome it.

[9] TOC Steps include the following:

  1. Identify the constraint or the bottleneck that can keep the project from achieving its objectives,

  2. Determine how to manage this bottleneck to mitigate the risk, and

  3. Evaluate performance results and go back to step 2 if the improvement is not as desired.

Executing

During the Executing stage of the PMLC, the project tasks are executed using the guidelines specified in the project management plan. The project manager oversees the work of the project staff and provides guidance and coaching as necessary to keep the staff motivated and productive. The project manager also ensures that project risks, issues, schedule, costs, change requests, deliverables, and so on are diligently managed, problems/conflicts are resolved in a timely manner, and status is reported to the appropriate recipients, in the appropriate format, and at the appropriate time.

Table 10.4 outlines the role of various LSS tools and techniques in the Executing stage of the PMLC.

Table 10.4 Role of LSS Tools and Techniques in the Executing Stage of the PMLC

LSS Tool/Technology	Role in the Executing Stage of the PMLC
Workflow	Project tasks flow through various stages such as development, testing, implementation, acceptance, and so on. This flow of project tasks to various stages is called workflow. Project management can gain the following benefits from a workflow in the executing stage: ■ It provides a repeatable, consistent, and more predictable process. ■ It facilitates more organized work assignments across the project staff. ■ It makes activity duration estimation easier. ■ It promotes better communication among the project staff and other stakeholders by better understanding of the project processes. ■ It makes it easier to spot the bottlenecks in the processes. ■ It helps define the escalation path. ■ It records transition and signoff footprints.
Meetings	Meetings can be used in the executing stage of project management to discuss project risks and issues, conduct brainstorming to seek stakeholders' inputs, exchange information, capture project performance status, and make decisions.
Five Whys	Problems and conflicts are inevitable during the project execution. The RCA process can benefit from the Five Whys.
Process Mapping	Can be used for better understanding of the project processes to find bottlenecks for improvement, perform RCA, improve efficiency, and enhance communications.

LSS Tool/Technology	Role in the Executing Stage of the PMLC
Brainstorming	Can be used in facilitating a meeting to gather ideas from subject matter experts for alternative analysis, RCA, and process improvement.
Fishbone Diagram	Can be used with brainstorming.
Pareto Diagrams	Can be used to prioritize the defects or issues in the project processes from highest frequency of occurrence to lowest frequency of occurrence based on the underlying Pareto principle that 20% of causes are responsible for 80% of the effect. Can be used with a fishbone or cause-and-effect diagram.
RCA	Can be used to find a permanent/sustainable solution to the project issues or conflicts rather than just treating the symptoms.
Monte Carlo Simulation	Discussed in Chapter 2, the Monte Carlo Simulation tool can be used to test "what-if" scenarios for the quantitative risk analysis in project risk management.
Markov Chains	The project decision-making strategy under the Markov Chains Model involves sequential decision problems in which the next strategic action depends on the preceding actions. Thus, predictions for future trials or experiments are influenced by the outcomes from the previous experiments. This type of mathematical form of the decision-making process can be used in qualitative and quantitative analysis of the risks in project risk management.
Design of Experiments	The Executing stage of the project management life cycle involves finding solutions to various project problems and conflicts and making decisions based on multi-criteria factors. Discussed in detail in Chapter 7, the Design of Experiments LSS tool can be used to select the best possible solution based on the optimal mix of the underlying criteria.

Monitoring and Controlling

The *Monitoring and Controlling* activities take place throughout the project life cycle. This process involves analyzing and understanding the variance in actual project performance in terms of project scope, schedule, and cost with respect to the planned or baseline performance and taking appropriate corrective action(s) to achieve the desired performance results if variance is beyond the acceptable limits.

The LSS performance measurement and control tools such as control charts can be used in the Monitoring and Controlling stage of project management. Effective performance measurement with respect to the triple constraints of project management—scope, schedule, and cost—can help the project managers make informed decisions.

Table 10.5 outlines the role of various LSS tools and techniques in the Monitoring and Controlling stage of the PMLC.

Table 10.5   Role of LSS Tools and Techniques in the Monitoring and Controlling Stage of the PMLC

LSS Tool/Technology	Role in the Monitoring and Controlling Stage of the PMLC
Control Charts	Control charts can be used in project management to ensure that project processes are in control and project products (deliverables) are within customer specification limits.
Scorecards	Can be used to ensure that the outcome of the project management activities aligns with the business objectives.
Dashboards	Can be used for project performance reporting in the areas of scope, schedule, budget, and quality, which may include the following: ■ Past performance status ■ Forecast of future trend based on current rate of performance ■ Risks and issues status ■ Tasks completed during the past "N" days ■ Tasks to be completed during the next "N" days ■ Approved change requests during the past "N" days ■ Anything else that needs urgent management attention
Surveys	Can be used for collecting project work performance data, especially when the situation involves ■ Remote and geographically widely spread stakeholders ■ Stakeholder hesitance to identify themselves ■ For fair decision-making (comparing apple to apple) because every subject receives the same set of survey questions.

Closing

The *Closing* stage of the PMLC involves official closure of the project after procurement and contract management activities are closed, product or service is accepted and signed off, lessons learned are captured, all projects artifacts are archived, and project team members are relieved. The project closure can also occur if, for some reason, the project is prematurely terminated.

Table 10.6 outlines the role of various LSS tools and techniques in *Closing* stage of the PMLC.

Table 10.6 Role of LSS Tools and Techniques in the Monitoring and Closing Stage of the PMLC

LSS Tool/Technology	Role in Closing Stage of the PMLC
Lessons Learned	Used to document what went well, what did not go well, what could have been done better so that the future projects can learn to avoid the same pitfalls that the current project faced and to leverage the best practices that the current project benefited from.
Strategy Updates	Can be used to update the go-forward project management strategy based on the lessons learned in the current project.
Transition Criteria	Can be used to successfully transition the final result of the project (product or service) to the post-project stage, such as maintenance and operations.

The Power of LSS Control Charts

"A picture is worth a thousand words." You probably have heard this quote several times. The fact is that this quote represents the reality. Visualization of the data can certainly help you understand the problem better and quicker and also gets your point across more smoothly.

A control chart is a powerful statistical LSS tool that can be used to visualize the observed process data over a period of time to gauge the health of the process and make informed decisions to take appropriate next steps. We have already discussed control charts in detail in Chapter 7, "Lean Six Sigma"; however, a typical control chart is shown in Figure 10.5 for quick reference.

The following are some key benefits of using control charts in project management:

- They depict whether or not the process is predictable and in control with respect to the pre-established and approved control limits and specifications.
- They help monitor stability of the project management processes such as cost-estimating accuracy and schedule variance control.
- They help improve the project management processes and visually show the positive impact of the improvement if it was successful.
- They help the project manager make a data-driven business case to seek the sponsor's approval of more funding for the project.

- They help the project manager to get her point across, get stakeholder buy-in, and negotiate effectively using the visualized data.

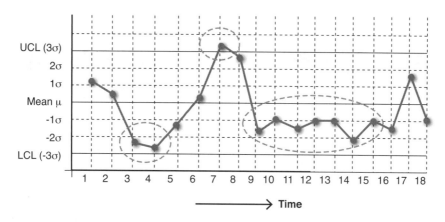

Figure 10.5 Typical Control Chart

Thus, not only does a control chart help with establishing the state of statistical process control, monitoring it, and estimating its capability but it also provides data-based strength to the project manager's arguments during negotiations and while presenting business cases to the sponsor or the senior management for various project approvals and decision-making.

Agile Project Management and Lean Six Sigma

Chapter 7 discusses the fundamentals of the LSS methodology. This section briefly discusses what Agile is and how it is different from Lean before investigating what role LSS methodology can play in Agile project management.

What Is Agile?

The name *Agile* came from the word *agility*, which refers to flexibility and simplicity. That's what the Agile project management methodology is compared to the traditional Waterfall project management methodology. As defined on *http://agilemethodology.org*, Agile project management methodology is "an alternative to traditional project management, typically used in software development. It helps teams respond to unpredictability through incremental, iterative work cadences, known as sprints. Agile methodologies are an alternative to waterfall, or traditional sequential development."

Agile versus Lean

Table 10.7 outlines the contrast between Agile and Lean.

Table 10.7   Agile versus Lean

	Agile	Lean
Approach	Agile approach encompasses specifically the software development industry.	Lean approach is comprehensive, targeting the entire organization or all processes to eliminate waste to achieve the improved efficiency and effectiveness.
Application	Agile is primarily used to manage software development projects.	Lean can be applied to any industry.
Tools	The key Agile tools include Kanban,[10] Quality Function Development (identifying customer value), Design Structure Matrix (DSM), and Visual Control Board.	Wide range of tools including but not limited to Kanban, VSM, Just-In-Time, Kaizen (continuous improvement), PDSA, and RCA.

The bottom line is that Lean places a strong emphasis on "the wholeness" or "the system" approach, and Agile is one of many far-reaching applications of Lean. The key Lean premises include optimizing the whole (system), respecting people, eliminating waste, delivering fast and frequent, building quality within, and creating knowledge. These premises of Lean constitute the driving force behind the Agile approach, which prefers individuals and interactions over processes and tools, working software over comprehensive documentation, customer collaboration over contract negotiation, responding to change over following a plan.

Role of Lean Techniques in Agile Project Management

Agile follows many Lean techniques. That's why Agile project management sometimes is called Lean project management.

---

[10]   Originated in the Japanese auto manufacturing industry, Kanban is an inventory control process in which display cards are used to track or record the movement of the materials through the manufacturing line. It is also associated with the Just-In-Time process, which targets minimizing the standing inventory to zero to eliminate/minimize waste and improve process efficiency.

Table 10.8 summarizes the role of Lean techniques in the Agile project management methodology.

Table 10.8   Role of Lean Techniques in Agile Project Management Methodology

Lean Technique	Role in Agile Project Management Methodology
Specify Value	Specify (understand) value from the customer's point of view to deliver the incremental work product at the end of a sprint that provides the specified value.
Quality at Source	Lean advocates ensuring quality at the source to enable a process to produce a defect-free outcome.
Implement Pull	We should not be telling the customers what they need; rather, we need to hear from them what they need. In other words, development should be driven by the customer requirements (demand).
Empower Team	Agile follows the Lean philosophy of empowering the project team members by allowing them to self-manage themselves and their work. Team members are free to select whatever story from the product backlog they want to work on.
Identify Waste	Following the Lean footsteps, Agile also believes in identifying and removing waste pertaining to the development activities.
Perform Visual Management	Agile follows the Lean way of using visual management to improve development efficiency. Usually, the development team uses a big wall or board to display the burn-down chart that reflects the real-time status of the development activities to all.
Establish Kanban	Agile uses visual methods like Kanban display cards in Lean.
Organize Workplace	Lean promotes an organized workplace for waste-free team communications. Agile follows the lead by requiring the team members to be working at the same location or in close proximity.
Understand Customer Value	According to the Lean philosophy, only a customer can decide what the "value" is for a customer and customer requirements reflect that value. Following the Lean guidelines Agile ensures that the work product produced at the end of a sprint (development cycle) meets the customer requirements.
Amplify Learning	Lean promotes continuous improvement and sustained learning. In Agile, a retrospective at the end of a sprint or development cycle covers the lessons learned; that is, what went well and what can be improved.

Role of Six Sigma Tools and Techniques in the Agile Project Management

We know that Lean focuses on eliminating or reducing the waste and Six Sigma focuses on eliminating or reducing the defects from the processes. Like Lean, Six Sigma also plays a significant role in Agile project management in terms of problem solving. Six Sigma's DMAIC and PDSA tools offer a structured and systematic approach and techniques to define, analyze, and resolve the quality and performance-related problems associated with Agile projects.

The following are the key benefits of Six Sigma tools and techniques in Agile:

- They provide an analytical and systemic way of problem solving.
- They help define the problems better by quantifying their impact.
- They help with finding the root cause rather than just treating the symptoms of the problems.
- They help with establishing performance tracking metrics with associated objective criteria for measuring the improvement progress quantitatively based on numerical data.
- They help with solving the complex problems by breaking them in manageable chunks.
- They help the Agile teams make data-driven informed decisions.
- They promote team participation and continuous improvement.

Lean PMO: Using LSS's DMEDI Methodology to Improve the PMO

The use of DMEDI (**D**efine, **M**easure, **E**xplore, **D**evelop, and **I**mplement) methodology in project management can help eliminate waste due to duplication and undesirable complexities and can make the PMO more customer-focused.

The various stages of DMEDI methodology can be briefly described as follows:

- **Define:** Define project objectives based on customer and business needs and expected financial benefits.

- **Measure:** Capture the Voice of the Customer (VOC) with objective criteria-based performance measurements. QFD can help to accomplish this because it focuses on the critical customer needs and also takes into consideration the customer ratings of competitors.

- **Explore:** Explore various options to find the best possible solution that would most suit the customer needs.

- **Develop:** Develop the PMO by acquiring project resources (staff, facilities, technology, and supplies), by enforcing facts-based governance, and by developing PMO tools and techniques to maximize standardization and consistency across all projects, programs, and portfolios.

- **Implement:** Implement the new PMO model.
  - Use iterative PDSAs to test the new model on a small scale first (may be on a small project) using the objective measurement criteria to measure the success of the new model.
  - Once tested successfully, roll out the model across the board (main PMO, subordinate PMOs, and underlying projects and programs).

WHAT IS QFD?

"Quality Function Deployment (QFD) is a structured approach to defining customer needs or requirements and translating them into specific plans to produce products to meet those needs. The 'voice of the customer' is the term to describe these stated and unstated customer needs or requirements."

Source: Kenneth Crow, DRM Associates

Summary

The mind map in Figure 10.6 summarizes the LSS applications in project management.

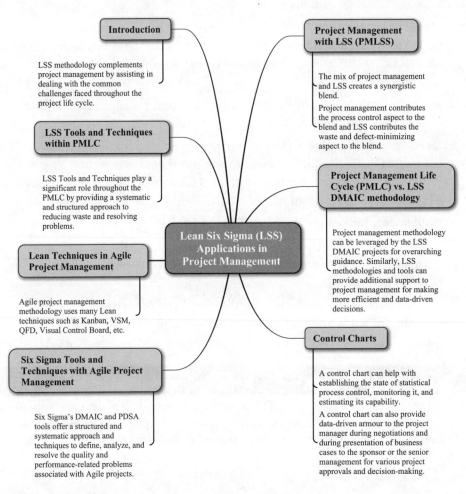

Figure 10.6 Lean Six Sigma Applications in Project Management

Key Terms

Affinity Diagram

Agile

ASQ

Brainstorming

Control Chart

Dashboard

Design of Experiments (DOE)

DMAIC

DMEDI

Failure Modes and Effect Analysis (FMEA)

Fishbone Diagram

Five Whys

Gap Analysis

Kaizen

Kanban

KJ Method

Lean

Markov Chains Model

Pareto Chart

PDSA

PMBOK

PMLSS

PMO

Process Framework

Project Charter

Project Life Cycle

QFD

RCA

Root Cause Analysis (RCA)

Scorecard

SIPOC

Six Sigma

Triple Constraints

Value Stream Mapping (VSM)

Variance

Visual Management

Voice of the Customer (VOC)

Workflow

Case Study: Implementing the Lean PMO

Kavam Corporation is an American multinational computer technology company that has a matrix organizational structure and is headquartered in Rocklin, California. When Kavam hired Jose Avila as its PMO director in March 2012, the company had an entire portfolio of struggling global projects. Jose came with 25 years of solid experience in project and PMO management. In addition, he possessed an MBA, PMP credentials, and Lean Six Sigma (LSS) Master Black Belt from the American Society of Quality (ASQ). Kavam hired him so that he could revamp its sick project management environment.

Jose took the challenge, rolled up his sleeves, put his LSS hat on, and hit the ground running from day one on the job. He used his LSS and project management knowledge, skills, and experience to formulate his strategy, which included the following steps:

1. Define the current state.
2. Determine the target state.
3. Perform the gap analysis.
4. Fill the gap.

Current State

According to Jose's four-step strategy, the first step was to understand and define the current state of Kavam's PMO to establish a baseline with respect to which potential performance could be measured. His findings included the following:

- The PMO stressed more on enforcing process compliance and consistency than delivering customer value
- Waterfall project management methodology
- Waste caused by overheads such as
  - Various subordinate PMOs
  - Process owners
  - Process auditors
  - Budget administration
  - Project coordination within programs
- Too many projects
- Very long duration (multiyear) projects/programs
- Centralized annual planning
- Annual budget
- Lack of performance metrics and objective measurement criteria
- Absence of structured RCA

In addition to defining the current state, Jose also established the performance metrics shown in Table 10.9.

Table 10.9 PMO Performance Metrics Reflecting Current State

Metric	Current State
Project failure rate	63%
Overhead costs	$118M per year
Stakeholder satisfaction	Below 5 (Survey results; on a scale of 1 to 10, with 10 being the highest)

Target State

The second step of the strategy was to determine the target or desired state of the PMO and to develop the metrics for improvement. Jose knew the value of LSS tools and techniques in process improvement. Thus, his vision for the target state was the blend of project management and the LSS methodologies. Following his vision, he defined the target state shown in Table 10.10.

Table 10.10 Target and Current State of PMO Performance

Current State	Target State
More stress on enforcing process compliance and consistency than delivering customer value	More stress on delivering customer value
Waterfall project management methodology	Agile project management methodology
Waste caused by overheads	Waste reduced with reduced overheads
Too many projects	Sprints (development cycles) with small amount of work in progress
Multiyear projects/programs	Projects broken into multiple phases with incremental ramp-up
Centralized annual planning	Decentralized and rolling wave planning
Annual budget	Incremental funding based on the past performance
Lack of performance metrics and objective measurement criteria	Performance metrics and objective measurement criteria
Absence of structured RCA	Structured RCA

Table 10.11 shows the performance metrics reflecting the target and current state and the estimated deadline to achieve the target state.

Table 10.11 PMO Performance Metrics Reflecting Target and Current State

Metric	Current State	Target State (To Be Achieved by December 31, 2013)
Project failure rate	63%	20%
Overhead costs	$118M per year	$60M per year
Stakeholder satisfaction	Below 5 (on a scale of 1 to 10, with 10 being the highest)	6 or more

Gap Analysis

The third step was to perform the gap analysis to figure out what needed to be done to achieve the target state. Jose compared the target state with the current state and found the following gaps between the two:

- Customer value was largely being ignored.
- The existing project management methodology was less effective and efficient.
- The existing environment was plagued with waste related to overheads.
- Too many projects running concurrently were adding complexity to the environment, causing inefficiencies overall, and struggling due to resource constraints.
- Multiyear projects were more prone to sluggishness and failure.
- Long initial planning was eating up too much time.
- Yearly budgets provided less flexibility to changes in funding requirements.
- There was lots of guesswork in decision-making.
- Estimation was poor.
- There was more focus on patchwork (treating the symptoms) than finding the root causes for problems and conflicts.

Filling the Gap

Based on the findings from the gap analysis, step 4 was to formulate a plan to fill the identified gaps and execute that plan with a goal to realize the desired benefits. To achieve this goal, the following objectives needed to be met (based on the established performance metrics):

- Reduce PMO projects' failure rate from 63% to 20% by December 31, 2013
- Reduce PMO overhead costs from $118M per year to $60M per year by December 31, 2013
- Improve stakeholder satisfaction from 4 (below average) to over 6 (on a survey scale from 1 to 10, with 10 being the highest) by December 31, 2013

Jose implemented the following strategic improvement activities to achieve these objectives:

- Replaced the traditional Waterfall project management methodology with the blended (waterfall with embedded LSS tools and techniques) and Agile project management methodologies.
- Incorporated Lean techniques into project management to make the customer value the main driving force behind all project activities.
- Established facts-based project governance rather than just schedule milestones tracking.
- Enforced that all PMOs develop their governance strategies based on performance metrics.
- Enforced performance measurements based on objective criteria. For example,
  - Recommended the use of LSS's DMEDI model as a roadmap for project management
  - Recommended the use of DMAIC, PDSA, and QFD methodologies for process improvement
  - Recommended the use of LSS's Kaizen technique to enforce continuous improvement
- Recommended Lean Six Sigma Green Belt training and certification for all project managers

Conclusion

Jose measured the post-implementation performance data for a period of over one year and analyzed it. The analysis report reflected significant improvement as depicted by Table 10.12.

Table 10.12 Performance Improvement Realized Results

Metric	Baseline (Original) State	Planned Target State	Actual Post-Improvement State
Project failure rate	63%	20%	6%
Overhead costs	$118M per year	$60M per year	$33M per year
Stakeholder satisfaction	Below 5 (on scale of 1 to 10, with 10 being the highest)	6 or more	9

Case Questions

1. What strategy did Jose Avila follow to improve the status quo? Was he successful?
2. What did Jose do the best?
3. What could Jose have done better?
4. What lessons did you learn from this case?

Chapter Review and Discussion Questions

1. What project management challenges have you personally experienced or observed at your workplace?
2. How can LSS tools and techniques help with better estimation during the Planning stage of the PMLC?
3. Can DMAIC replace PMLC?
4. In what sense can Lean and Six Sigma tools and techniques help project management?
5. Describe the commonality between the Initiating stage of the PMLC and the Defining stage of DMAIC.
6. What is the difference between the PMLC and PMBOK process groups?
7. Define *variance* in Monitoring and Controlling.
8. What is the 80:20 rule?
9. Kanban is associated with both Lean and Agile methodologies. How?
10. What steps are involved in using the Theory of Constraints (TOC)?
11. How can DMEDI and QFD help in improving the PMO performance?
12. How can a control chart help a project manager get her point across?

Bibliography

AgileMethodology. (2008). "Understanding Agile Methodology." Retrieved September 24, 2015, from http://agilemethodology.org/

Asq.org. (2009). "Integrating Lean and Six Sigma." Retrieved September 10, 2015, from http://asq.org/learn-about-quality/six-sigma/lean.html

Aveta. (2008). "Effective Project Management With Six Sigma Training." Retrieved September 27, 2015, from http://www.sixsigmaonline.org/six-sigma-training-certification-information/effective-project-management-with-six-sigma-training/

Bower, K. (2015). Learn Statistics with Keith Bower. Retrieved August 30, 2015, from http://www.keithbower.com/

BrightHubPM. (2012). "FMEA: A Fantastic Risk Management Tool Including Worksheet." Retrieved September 10, 2015, from http://www.brighthubpm.com/risk-management/40800-utilizing-fmea-as-a-tool-for-risk-management/#imgn_1

Business Dictionary. (2015). "What is synergistic effect? definition and meaning." Retrieved September 10, 2015, from http://www.businessdictionary.com/definition/synergistic-effect.html

Crow, K. (2014). "Customer-Focused Development with QFD." Retrieved September 27, 2015, from http://www.npd-solutions.com/qfd.html

Dictionary.com. (2015). "Kanban Definition." Retrieved September 20, 2015, from http://dictionary.reference.com/browse/kanban

Fichtner, A. (2012). "Agile Vs. Lean: Yeah Yeah, What's the Difference?" Retrieved September 27, 2015, from http://www.hackerchick.com/2012/01/agile-vs-lean-yeah-yeah-whats-the-difference.html

Gygi, C. et al. (2012). *Six Sigma for Dummies*, 2nd ed. Hoboken, New Jersey: John Wiley & Sons, Inc.

iSixSigma. (2015). "Three Lean Tools for Agile Development Environments." Retrieved September 9, 2015, from http://www.isixsigma.com/methodology/lean-methodology/three-lean-tools-agile-development-environments/

iSixSigma. (2015). "Voice Of the Customer (VOC)." Retrieved September 11, 2015, from http://www.isixsigma.com/dictionary/voice-of-the-customer-voc/

Keyes, J. (2010). "Implementing the Project Management Balanced Scorecard." Retrieved September 2, 2015, from https://www.crcpress.com/Implementing-the-Project-Management-Balanced-Scorecard/Keyes/9781439827185

Kubiak, T.M., and Benlow, D. W. (2009). *The Certified Six Sigma Black Belt Handbook*, 2nd ed. ASQ Quality Press.

Langley, G.L. et al. (2009). *The Improvement Guide: A Practical Approach to Enhancing Organizational Performance*, 2nd ed. San Francisco, California, USA: Jossey-Bass Publishers.

Levinson, W.A., and Rerick, R.A. (2002). *Lean Enterprise: A Synergistic Approach to Minimizing Waste*. ASQ Quality Press.

Lochan, R. (2011). "Lean or Agile? A Comparison of Approach." http://www.process excellencenetwork.com/lean-six-sigma-business-transformation/articles/using-lean-in-agile-software-development-a-compari/

Matthews, P.C., and Philip, A.D. (2011). "Bayesian Project Monitoring." *Proceedings of the 18th International Conference on Engineering Design (ICED 11), Impacting Society through Engineering Design*, Vol. 1: Design Processes, Lyngby/Copenhagen, Denmark, 15.-19.08.2011, pp. 69–78.

Milosevic, D.Z. (2003). *Project Management ToolBox: Tools and Techniques for the Practicing Project Manager*. 1st ed., Hoboken, New Jersey: John Wiley & Sons.

MindTools. (2015). "The Theory of Constraints (TOC)." Retrieved August 27, 2015, from http://www.mindtools.com/pages/article/toc.htm

Mullin, M. (2010). "Value Streams and Project Management - What's The Connection?" Retrieved September 4, 2015, from https://projectmanagementessentials.wordpress.com/2010/02/19/value-streams-and-project-management-whats-the-connection/

Project Management Institute. (2014). *A Guide to the Project Management Body of Knowledge* (PMBOK® Guide), 5th ed. Newton Square, Pennsylvania: Project Management Institute (PMI).

Singh, H. (2014). *Mastering Project Human Resource Management*, 1st ed. Upper Saddle River, New Jersey: Pearson FT Press.

Spool, J. (2004). "User Interface Engineering." Retrieved September 14, 2015, from http://www.uie.com/articles/kj_technique/

Tague, N. R. (2004). *The Quality Toolbox*, 2nd ed. ASQ Quality Press.

TaskTrakz. (2013). "What Is Project Management Workflow?" Retrieved September 12, 2015, from http://www.slideshare.net/MatthewWarton/what-is-project-management-workflow

Verduyn, D. (2014). "The Kano Model - Customer Satisfaction Model." Retrieved September 8, 2015, from http://www.kanomodel.com/

A

z-Distribution

Table A-1 Negative z Scores

z	0.09	0.08	0.07	0.06	0.05	0.04	0.03	0.02	0.01	0.00
-3.4	0.0002	0.0003	0.0003	0.0003	0.0003	0.0003	0.0003	0.0003	0.0003	0.0003
-3.3	0.0003	0.0004	0.0004	0.0004	0.0004	0.0004	0.0004	0.0005	0.0005	0.0005
-3.2	0.0005	0.0005	0.0005	0.0006	0.0006	0.0006	0.0006	0.0006	0.0007	0.0007
-3.1	0.0007	0.0007	0.0008	0.0008	0.0008	0.0008	0.0009	0.0009	0.0009	0.0010
-3.0	0.0010	0.0010	0.0011	0.0011	0.0011	0.0012	0.0012	0.0013	0.0013	0.0013
-2.9	0.0014	0.0014	0.0015	0.0015	0.0016	0.0016	0.0017	0.0018	0.0018	0.0019
-2.8	0.0019	0.0020	0.0021	0.0021	0.0022	0.0023	0.0023	0.0024	0.0025	0.0026
-2.7	0.0026	0.0027	0.0028	0.0029	0.0030	0.0031	0.0032	0.0033	0.0034	0.0035
-2.6	0.0036	0.0037	0.0038	0.0039	0.0040	0.0041	0.0043	0.0044	0.0045	0.0047
-2.5	0.0048	0.0049	0.0051	0.0052	0.0054	0.0055	0.0057	0.0059	0.0060	0.0062
-2.4	0.0064	0.0066	0.0068	0.0069	0.0071	0.0073	0.0075	0.0078	0.0080	0.0082
-2.3	0.0084	0.0087	0.0089	0.0091	0.0094	0.0096	0.0099	0.0102	0.0104	0.0107
-2.2	0.0110	0.0113	0.0116	0.0119	0.0122	0.0125	0.0129	0.0132	0.0136	0.0139
-2.1	0.0143	0.0146	0.0150	0.0154	0.0158	0.0162	0.0166	0.0170	0.0174	0.0179
-2.0	0.0183	0.0188	0.0192	0.0197	0.0202	0.0207	0.0212	0.0217	0.0222	0.0228
-1.9	0.0233	0.0239	0.0244	0.0250	0.0256	0.0262	0.0268	0.0274	0.0281	0.0287
-1.8	0.0294	0.0301	0.0307	0.0314	0.0322	0.0329	0.0336	0.0344	0.0351	0.0359
-1.7	0.0367	0.0375	0.0384	0.0392	0.0401	0.0409	0.0418	0.0427	0.0436	0.0446
-1.6	0.0455	0.0465	0.0475	0.0485	0.0495	0.0505	0.0516	0.0526	0.0537	0.0548
-1.5	0.0559	0.0571	0.0582	0.0594	0.0606	0.0618	0.0630	0.0643	0.0655	0.0668
-1.4	0.0681	0.0694	0.0708	0.0721	0.0735	0.0749	0.0764	0.0778	0.0793	0.0808
-1.3	0.0823	0.0838	0.0853	0.0869	0.0885	0.0901	0.0918	0.0934	0.0951	0.0968
-1.2	0.0985	0.1003	0.1020	0.1038	0.1056	0.1075	0.1093	0.1112	0.1131	0.1151

z	0.09	0.08	0.07	0.06	0.05	0.04	0.03	0.02	0.01	0.00
-1.1	0.1170	0.1190	0.1210	0.1230	0.1251	0.1271	0.1292	0.1314	0.1335	0.1357
-1.0	0.1379	0.1401	0.1423	0.1446	0.1469	0.1492	0.1515	0.1539	0.1562	0.1587
-0.9	0.1611	0.1635	0.1660	0.1685	0.1711	0.1736	0.1762	0.1788	0.1814	0.1841
-0.8	0.1867	0.1894	0.1922	0.1949	0.1977	0.2005	0.2033	0.2061	0.2090	0.2119
-0.7	0.2148	0.2177	0.2206	0.2236	0.2266	0.2296	0.2327	0.2358	0.2389	0.2420
-0.6	0.2451	0.2483	0.2514	0.2546	0.2578	0.2611	0.2643	0.2676	0.2709	0.2743
-0.5	0.2776	0.2810	0.2843	0.2877	0.2912	0.2946	0.2981	0.3015	0.3050	0.3085
-0.4	0.3121	0.3156	0.3192	0.3228	0.3264	0.3300	0.3336	0.3372	0.3409	0.3446
-0.3	0.3483	0.3520	0.3557	0.3594	0.3632	0.3669	0.3707	0.3745	0.3783	0.3821
-0.2	0.3859	0.3897	0.3936	0.3974	0.4013	0.4052	0.4090	0.4129	0.4168	0.4207
-0.1	0.4247	0.4286	0.4325	0.4364	0.4404	0.4443	0.4483	0.4522	0.4562	0.4602
-0.0	0.4641	0.4681	0.4721	0.4761	0.4801	0.4840	0.4880	0.4920	0.4960	0.5000

Table A-2 Positive z Scores

z	0.00	0.01	0.02	0.03	0.04	0.05	0.06	0.07	0.08	0.09
0.0	0.5000	0.5040	0.5080	0.5120	0.5160	0.5199	0.5239	0.5279	0.5319	0.5359
0.1	0.5398	0.5438	0.5478	0.5517	0.5557	0.5596	0.5636	0.5675	0.5714	0.5753
0.2	0.5793	0.5832	0.5871	0.5910	0.5948	0.5987	0.6026	0.6064	0.6103	0.6141
0.3	0.6179	0.6217	0.6255	0.6293	0.6331	0.6368	0.6406	0.6443	0.6480	0.6517
0.4	0.6554	0.6591	0.6628	0.6664	0.6700	0.6736	0.6772	0.6808	0.6844	0.6879
0.5	0.6915	0.6950	0.6985	0.7019	0.7054	0.7088	0.7123	0.7157	0.7190	0.7224
0.6	0.7257	0.7291	0.7324	0.7357	0.7389	0.7422	0.7454	0.7486	0.7517	0.7549
0.7	0.7580	0.7611	0.7642	0.7673	0.7704	0.7734	0.7764	0.7794	0.7823	0.7852
0.8	0.7881	0.7910	0.7939	0.7967	0.7995	0.8023	0.8051	0.8078	0.8106	0.8133
0.9	0.8159	0.8186	0.8212	0.8238	0.8264	0.8289	0.8315	0.8340	0.8365	0.8389
1.0	0.8413	0.8438	0.8461	0.8485	0.8508	0.8531	0.8554	0.8577	0.8599	0.8621
1.1	0.8643	0.8665	0.8686	0.8708	0.8729	0.8749	0.8770	0.8790	0.8810	0.8830
1.2	0.8849	0.8869	0.8888	0.8907	0.8925	0.8944	0.8962	0.8980	0.8997	0.9015
1.3	0.9032	0.9049	0.9066	0.9082	0.9099	0.9115	0.9131	0.9147	0.9162	0.9177
1.4	0.9192	0.9207	0.9222	0.9236	0.9251	0.9265	0.9279	0.9292	0.9306	0.9319
1.5	0.9332	0.9345	0.9357	0.9370	0.9382	0.9394	0.9406	0.9418	0.9429	0.9441

z	0.00	0.01	0.02	0.03	0.04	0.05	0.06	0.07	0.08	0.09
1.6	0.9452	0.9463	0.9474	0.9484	0.9495	0.9505	0.9515	0.9525	0.9535	0.9545
1.7	0.9554	0.9564	0.9573	0.9582	0.9591	0.9599	0.9608	0.9616	0.9625	0.9633
1.8	0.9641	0.9649	0.9656	0.9664	0.9671	0.9678	0.9686	0.9693	0.9699	0.9706
1.9	0.9713	0.9719	0.9726	0.9732	0.9738	0.9744	0.9750	0.9756	0.9761	0.9767
2.0	0.9772	0.9778	0.9783	0.9788	0.9793	0.9798	0.9803	0.9808	0.9812	0.9817
2.1	0.9821	0.9826	0.9830	0.9834	0.9838	0.9842	0.9846	0.9850	0.9854	0.9857
2.2	0.9861	0.9864	0.9868	0.9871	0.9875	0.9878	0.9881	0.9884	0.9887	0.9890
2.3	0.9893	0.9896	0.9898	0.9901	0.9904	0.9906	0.9909	0.9911	0.9913	0.9916
2.4	0.9918	0.9920	0.9922	0.9925	0.9927	0.9929	0.9931	0.9932	0.9934	0.9936
2.5	0.9938	0.9940	0.9941	0.9943	0.9945	0.9946	0.9948	0.9949	0.9951	0.9952
2.6	0.9953	0.9955	0.9956	0.9957	0.9959	0.9960	0.9961	0.9962	0.9963	0.9964
2.7	0.9965	0.9966	0.9967	0.9968	0.9969	0.9970	0.9971	0.9972	0.9973	0.9974
2.8	0.9974	0.9975	0.9976	0.9977	0.9977	0.9978	0.9979	0.9979	0.9980	0.9981
2.9	0.9981	0.9982	0.9982	0.9983	0.9984	0.9984	0.9985	0.9985	0.9986	0.9986
3.0	0.9987	0.9987	0.9987	0.9988	0.9988	0.9989	0.9989	0.9989	0.9990	0.9990
3.1	0.9990	0.9991	0.9991	0.9991	0.9992	0.9992	0.9992	0.9992	0.9993	0.9993
3.2	0.9993	0.9993	0.9994	0.9994	0.9994	0.9994	0.9994	0.9995	0.9995	0.9995
3.3	0.9995	0.9995	0.9995	0.9996	0.9996	0.9996	0.9996	0.9996	0.9996	0.9997
3.4	0.9997	0.9997	0.9997	0.9997	0.9997	0.9997	0.9997	0.9997	0.9997	0.9998

B

t-Distribution

Table B-1 *t*-Table

Degrees of Freedom (d.f.)	Level of confidence, c	0.50	0.80	0.90	0.95	0.98	0.99
	One tail, α	0.25	0.10	0.05	0.025	0.01	0.005
	Two tails, α	0.50	0.20	0.10	0.05	0.02	0.01
1		1.000	3.078	6.314	12.706	31.821	63.657
2		0.816	1.886	2.920	4.303	6.965	9.925
3		0.765	1.638	2.353	3.182	4.541	5.841
4		0.741	1.533	2.132	2.776	3.747	4.604
5		0.727	1.476	2.015	2.571	3.365	4.032
6		0.718	1.440	1.943	2.447	3.143	3.707
7		0.711	1.415	1.895	2.365	2.998	3.499
8		0.706	1.397	1.860	2.306	2.896	3.355
9		0.703	1.383	1.833	2.262	2.821	3.250
10		0.700	1.372	1.812	2.228	2.764	3.169
11		0.697	1.363	1.796	2.201	2.718	3.106
12		0.695	1.356	1.782	2.179	2.681	3.055
13		0.694	1.350	1.771	2.160	2.650	3.012
14		0.692	1.345	1.761	2.145	2.624	2.977
15		0.691	1.341	1.753	2.131	2.602	2.947
16		0.690	1.337	1.746	2.120	2.583	2.921
17		0.689	1.333	1.740	2.110	2.567	2.898
18		0.688	1.330	1.734	2.101	2.552	2.878
19		0.688	1.328	1.729	2.093	2.539	2.861
20		0.687	1.325	1.725	2.086	2.528	2.845

Degrees of Freedom (d.f.)	Level of confidence, c	0.50	0.80	0.90	0.95	0.98	0.99
	One tail, α	0.25	0.10	0.05	0.025	0.01	0.005
	Two tails, α	0.50	0.20	0.10	0.05	0.02	0.01
21		0.686	1.323	1.721	2.080	2.518	2.831
22		0.686	1.321	1.717	2.074	2.508	2.819
23		0.685	1.319	1.714	2.069	2.500	2.807
24		0.685	1.318	1.711	2.064	2.492	2.797
25		0.684	1.316	1.708	2.060	2.485	2.787
26		0.684	1.315	1.706	2.056	2.479	2.779
27		0.684	1.314	1.703	2.052	2.473	2.771
28		0.683	1.313	1.701	2.048	2.467	2.763
29		0.683	1.311	1.699	2.045	2.462	2.756
∞		0.674	1.282	1.645	1.960	2.326	2.576

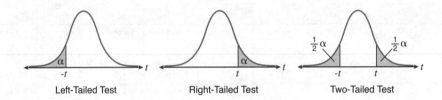

Left-Tailed Test Right-Tailed Test Two-Tailed Test

C

Binomial Probability Distribution (From $n = 2$ to $n = 10$)[1]

These tables give the probability of achieving maximum x number of successes in n number of independent trials with probability of the success of each trial equal to p).

Table C-1 Binomial Probability Distribution

p=		0.01	0.02	0.03	0.04	0.05	0.06	0.07	0.08	0.09	0.1	0.15	0.2	0.25	0.3	0.35	0.4	0.45	0.5
n=2	x=0	0.9801	0.9604	0.9409	0.9216	0.9025	0.8836	0.8649	0.8464	0.8281	0.8100	0.7225	0.6400	0.5625	0.4900	0.4225	0.3600	0.3025	0.2500
	1	0.9999	0.9996	0.9991	0.9984	0.9975	0.9964	0.9951	0.9936	0.9919	0.9900	0.9775	0.9600	0.9375	0.9100	0.8775	0.8400	0.7975	0.7500
	2	1.0000	1.0000	1.0000	1.0000	1.0000	1.0000	1.0000	1.0000	1.0000	1.0000	1.0000	1.0000	1.0000	1.0000	1.0000	1.0000	1.0000	1.0000
n=3	x=0	0.9703	0.9412	0.9127	0.8847	0.8574	0.8306	0.8044	0.7787	0.7536	0.7290	0.6141	0.5120	0.4219	0.3430	0.2746	0.2160	0.1664	0.1250
	1	0.9997	0.9988	0.9974	0.9953	0.9928	0.9896	0.9860	0.9818	0.9772	0.9720	0.9393	0.8960	0.8438	0.7840	0.7183	0.6480	0.5748	0.5000
	2	1.0000	1.0000	1.0000	0.9999	0.9999	0.9998	0.9997	0.9995	0.9993	0.9990	0.9966	0.9920	0.9844	0.9730	0.9571	0.9360	0.9089	0.8750
	3	1.0000	1.0000	1.0000	1.0000	1.0000	1.0000	1.0000	1.0000	1.0000	1.0000	1.0000	1.0000	1.0000	1.0000	1.0000	1.0000	1.0000	1.0000
n=4	x=0	0.9606	0.9224	0.8853	0.8493	0.8145	0.7807	0.7481	0.7164	0.6857	0.6561	0.5220	0.4096	0.3164	0.2401	0.1785	0.1296	0.0915	0.0625
	1	0.9994	0.9977	0.9948	0.9909	0.9860	0.9801	0.9733	0.9656	0.9570	0.9477	0.8905	0.8192	0.7383	0.6517	0.5630	0.4752	0.3910	0.3125
	2	1.0000	1.0000	0.9999	0.9998	0.9995	0.9992	0.9987	0.9981	0.9973	0.9963	0.9880	0.9728	0.9492	0.9163	0.8735	0.8208	0.7585	0.6875
	3	1.0000	1.0000	1.0000	1.0000	1.0000	1.0000	1.0000	1.0000	0.9999	0.9999	0.9995	0.9984	0.9961	0.9919	0.9850	0.9744	0.9590	0.9375
	4	1.0000	1.0000	1.0000	1.0000	1.0000	1.0000	1.0000	1.0000	1.0000	1.0000	1.0000	1.0000	1.0000	1.0000	1.0000	1.0000	1.0000	1.0000
n=5	x=0	0.9510	0.9039	0.8587	0.8154	0.7738	0.7339	0.6957	0.6591	0.6240	0.5905	0.4437	0.3277	0.2373	0.1681	0.1160	0.0778	0.0503	0.0313
	1	0.9990	0.9962	0.9915	0.9852	0.9774	0.9681	0.9575	0.9456	0.9326	0.9185	0.8352	0.7373	0.6328	0.5282	0.4284	0.3370	0.2562	0.1875
	2	1.0000	0.9999	0.9997	0.9994	0.9988	0.9980	0.9969	0.9955	0.9937	0.9914	0.9734	0.9421	0.8965	0.8369	0.7648	0.6826	0.5931	0.5000
	3	1.0000	1.0000	1.0000	1.0000	1.0000	0.9999	0.9999	0.9998	0.9997	0.9995	0.9978	0.9933	0.9844	0.9692	0.9460	0.9130	0.8688	0.8125
	4	1.0000	1.0000	1.0000	1.0000	1.0000	1.0000	1.0000	1.0000	1.0000	1.0000	0.9999	0.9997	0.9990	0.9976	0.9947	0.9898	0.9815	0.9688
	5	1.0000	1.0000	1.0000	1.0000	1.0000	1.0000	1.0000	1.0000	1.0000	1.0000	1.0000	1.0000	1.0000	1.0000	1.0000	1.0000	1.0000	1.0000
n=6	x=0	0.9415	0.8858	0.8330	0.7828	0.7351	0.6899	0.6470	0.6064	0.5679	0.5314	0.3771	0.2621	0.1780	0.1176	0.0754	0.0467	0.0277	0.0156
	1	0.9985	0.9943	0.9875	0.9784	0.9672	0.9541	0.9392	0.9227	0.9048	0.8857	0.7765	0.6554	0.5339	0.4202	0.3191	0.2333	0.1636	0.1094
	2	1.0000	0.9998	0.9995	0.9988	0.9978	0.9962	0.9942	0.9915	0.9882	0.9842	0.9527	0.9011	0.8306	0.7443	0.6471	0.5443	0.4415	0.3438
	3	1.0000	1.0000	1.0000	1.0000	0.9999	0.9998	0.9997	0.9995	0.9992	0.9987	0.9941	0.9830	0.9624	0.9295	0.8826	0.8208	0.7447	0.6563
	4	1.0000	1.0000	1.0000	1.0000	1.0000	1.0000	1.0000	1.0000	0.9999	0.9999	0.9996	0.9984	0.9954	0.9891	0.9777	0.9590	0.9308	0.8906
	5	1.0000	1.0000	1.0000	1.0000	1.0000	1.0000	1.0000	1.0000	1.0000	1.0000	1.0000	0.9999	0.9998	0.9993	0.9982	0.9959	0.9917	0.9844
	6	1.0000	1.0000	1.0000	1.0000	1.0000	1.0000	1.0000	1.0000	1.0000	1.0000	1.0000	1.0000	1.0000	1.0000	1.0000	1.0000	1.0000	1.0000

---

[1] Source: https://mat.iitm.ac.in/home/vetri/public_html/statistics/binomial.pdf.

Table C-1 Binomial Probability Distribution (Contd.)

	p=	0.01	0.02	0.03	0.04	0.05	0.06	0.07	0.08	0.09	0.1	0.15	0.2	0.25	0.3	0.35	0.4	0.45	0.5
n=7	x=0	0.9321	0.8681	0.8080	0.7514	0.6983	0.6485	0.6017	0.5578	0.5168	0.4783	0.3206	0.2097	0.1335	0.0824	0.0490	0.0280	0.0152	0.0078
	1	0.9980	0.9921	0.9829	0.9706	0.9556	0.9382	0.9187	0.8974	0.8745	0.8503	0.7166	0.5767	0.4449	0.3294	0.2338	0.1586	0.1024	0.0625
	2	1.0000	0.9997	0.9991	0.9980	0.9962	0.9937	0.9903	0.9860	0.9807	0.9743	0.9262	0.8520	0.7564	0.6471	0.5323	0.4199	0.3164	0.2266
	3	1.0000	1.0000	1.0000	0.9999	0.9998	0.9996	0.9993	0.9988	0.9982	0.9973	0.9879	0.9667	0.9294	0.8740	0.8002	0.7102	0.6083	0.5000
	4	1.0000	1.0000	1.0000	1.0000	1.0000	1.0000	1.0000	0.9999	0.9999	0.9998	0.9988	0.9953	0.9871	0.9712	0.9444	0.9037	0.8471	0.7734
	5	1.0000	1.0000	1.0000	1.0000	1.0000	1.0000	1.0000	1.0000	1.0000	1.0000	0.9999	0.9996	0.9987	0.9962	0.9910	0.9812	0.9643	0.9375
	6	1.0000	1.0000	1.0000	1.0000	1.0000	1.0000	1.0000	1.0000	1.0000	1.0000	1.0000	1.0000	0.9999	0.9998	0.9994	0.9984	0.9963	0.9922
	7	1.0000	1.0000	1.0000	1.0000	1.0000	1.0000	1.0000	1.0000	1.0000	1.0000	1.0000	1.0000	1.0000	1.0000	1.0000	1.0000	1.0000	1.0000
n=8	x=0	0.9227	0.8508	0.7837	0.7214	0.6634	0.6096	0.5596	0.5132	0.4703	0.4305	0.2725	0.1678	0.1001	0.0576	0.0319	0.0168	0.0084	0.0039
	1	0.9973	0.9897	0.9777	0.9619	0.9428	0.9208	0.8965	0.8702	0.8423	0.8131	0.6572	0.5033	0.3671	0.2553	0.1691	0.1064	0.0632	0.0352
	2	0.9999	0.9996	0.9987	0.9969	0.9942	0.9904	0.9853	0.9789	0.9711	0.9619	0.8948	0.7969	0.6785	0.5518	0.4278	0.3154	0.2201	0.1445
	3	1.0000	1.0000	0.9999	0.9998	0.9996	0.9993	0.9987	0.9978	0.9966	0.9950	0.9786	0.9437	0.8862	0.8059	0.7064	0.5941	0.4770	0.3633
	4	1.0000	1.0000	1.0000	1.0000	1.0000	1.0000	0.9999	0.9999	0.9997	0.9996	0.9971	0.9896	0.9727	0.9420	0.8939	0.8263	0.7396	0.6367
	5	1.0000	1.0000	1.0000	1.0000	1.0000	1.0000	1.0000	1.0000	1.0000	1.0000	0.9998	0.9988	0.9958	0.9887	0.9747	0.9502	0.9115	0.8555
	6	1.0000	1.0000	1.0000	1.0000	1.0000	1.0000	1.0000	1.0000	1.0000	1.0000	1.0000	0.9999	0.9996	0.9987	0.9964	0.9915	0.9819	0.9648
	7	1.0000	1.0000	1.0000	1.0000	1.0000	1.0000	1.0000	1.0000	1.0000	1.0000	1.0000	1.0000	0.9999	0.9998	0.9993	0.9983	0.9961
	8	1.0000	1.0000	1.0000	1.0000	1.0000	1.0000	1.0000	1.0000	1.0000	1.0000	1.0000	1.0000	1.0000	1.0000	1.0000	1.0000	1.0000	1.0000
n=9	x=0	0.9135	0.8337	0.7602	0.6925	0.6302	0.5730	0.5204	0.4722	0.4279	0.3874	0.2316	0.1342	0.0751	0.0404	0.0207	0.0101	0.0046	0.0020
	1	0.9966	0.9869	0.9718	0.9522	0.9288	0.9022	0.8729	0.8417	0.8088	0.7748	0.5995	0.4362	0.3003	0.1960	0.1211	0.0705	0.0385	0.0195
	2	0.9999	0.9994	0.9980	0.9955	0.9916	0.9862	0.9791	0.9702	0.9595	0.9470	0.8591	0.7382	0.6007	0.4628	0.3373	0.2318	0.1495	0.0898
	3	1.0000	1.0000	0.9999	0.9997	0.9994	0.9987	0.9977	0.9963	0.9943	0.9917	0.9661	0.9144	0.8343	0.7297	0.6089	0.4826	0.3614	0.2539
	4	1.0000	1.0000	1.0000	1.0000	1.0000	0.9999	0.9998	0.9997	0.9995	0.9991	0.9944	0.9804	0.9511	0.9012	0.8283	0.7334	0.6214	0.5000
	5	1.0000	1.0000	1.0000	1.0000	1.0000	1.0000	1.0000	1.0000	1.0000	0.9999	0.9994	0.9969	0.9900	0.9747	0.9464	0.9006	0.8342	0.7461
	6	1.0000	1.0000	1.0000	1.0000	1.0000	1.0000	1.0000	1.0000	1.0000	1.0000	1.0000	0.9997	0.9987	0.9957	0.9888	0.9750	0.9502	0.9102
	7	1.0000	1.0000	1.0000	1.0000	1.0000	1.0000	1.0000	1.0000	1.0000	1.0000	1.0000	1.0000	0.9999	0.9996	0.9986	0.9962	0.9909	0.9805
	8	1.0000	1.0000	1.0000	1.0000	1.0000	1.0000	1.0000	1.0000	1.0000	1.0000	1.0000	1.0000	1.0000	1.0000	0.9999	0.9997	0.9992	0.9980
	9	1.0000	1.0000	1.0000	1.0000	1.0000	1.0000	1.0000	1.0000	1.0000	1.0000	1.0000	1.0000	1.0000	1.0000	1.0000	1.0000	1.0000	1.0000
n=10	x=0	0.9044	0.8171	0.7374	0.6648	0.5987	0.5386	0.4840	0.4344	0.3894	0.3487	0.1969	0.1074	0.0563	0.0282	0.0135	0.0060	0.0025	0.0010
	1	0.9957	0.9838	0.9655	0.9418	0.9139	0.8824	0.8483	0.8121	0.7746	0.7361	0.5443	0.3758	0.2440	0.1493	0.0860	0.0464	0.0233	0.0107
	2	0.9999	0.9991	0.9972	0.9938	0.9885	0.9812	0.9717	0.9599	0.9460	0.9298	0.8202	0.6778	0.5256	0.3828	0.2616	0.1673	0.0996	0.0547
	3	1.0000	1.0000	0.9999	0.9996	0.9990	0.9980	0.9964	0.9942	0.9912	0.9872	0.9500	0.8791	0.7759	0.6496	0.5138	0.3823	0.2660	0.1719
	4	1.0000	1.0000	1.0000	1.0000	0.9999	0.9998	0.9997	0.9994	0.9990	0.9984	0.9901	0.9672	0.9219	0.8497	0.7515	0.6331	0.5044	0.3770
	5	1.0000	1.0000	1.0000	1.0000	1.0000	1.0000	1.0000	0.9999	0.9999	0.9986	0.9936	0.9803	0.9527	0.9051	0.8338	0.7384	0.6230
	6	1.0000	1.0000	1.0000	1.0000	1.0000	1.0000	1.0000	1.0000	1.0000	1.0000	0.9999	0.9991	0.9965	0.9894	0.9740	0.9452	0.8980	0.8281
	7	1.0000	1.0000	1.0000	1.0000	1.0000	1.0000	1.0000	1.0000	1.0000	1.0000	1.0000	0.9999	0.9996	0.9984	0.9952	0.9877	0.9726	0.9453
	8	1.0000	1.0000	1.0000	1.0000	1.0000	1.0000	1.0000	1.0000	1.0000	1.0000	1.0000	1.0000	0.9999	0.9995	0.9983	0.9955	0.9893
	9	1.0000	1.0000	1.0000	1.0000	1.0000	1.0000	1.0000	1.0000	1.0000	1.0000	1.0000	1.0000	1.0000	1.0000	0.9999	0.9997	0.9990
	10	1.0000	1.0000	1.0000	1.0000	1.0000	1.0000	1.0000	1.0000	1.0000	1.0000	1.0000	1.0000	1.0000	1.0000	1.0000	1.0000	1.0000	1.0000

Index

A

Activity on Note (AON), 233-235
Affinity Diagram, 302
Agile project management
    defined, 307
    vs. Lean, 307-308
    Lean techniques in, 308-309
    Six Sigma tools in, 310
AHP. *See* Analytic Hierarchy Process (AHP)
Alternative hypothesis, defined, 120
American Society for Quality (ASQ), 184
Analysis. *See also* Analytic Hierarchy Process
  (AHP)
    vs. analytics, 2
    analyze phase, DMAIC tools, 190, 206-209
    comparison matrix, creation and
      normalization, 271
    criteria *vs.* sub-criteria analysis, 273
    definition, 2
    goal *vs.* criteria mind map, 270
Analysis paralysis, 27
Analysis toolset, Microsoft Excel, 247-250
Analytic Hierarchy Process (AHP)
    advantages and disadvantages, 162
    analysis, performance of, 154-159, 269-277
    change requests, prioritization of, 285
    comparison matrix, creation and
      normalization, 271
    criteria *vs.* sub-criteria analysis, 273
    decision hierarchy, development of, 153-154,
      268-269
    decision-making and, 31, 161-162, 265-266,
      281-283
    Eigen (Priority) vector calculation, 272-273

evaluation criteria, 153, 267-268
goal *vs.* criteria mind map, 270
overview of, 152
procedures for use, 152-162
project complexity estimation, 283-284
project evaluation and selection, 267-283
project management approaches, 19-20
project risk assessment, 284-285
Saaty Scale, use of, 154-155
strategic alignment criteria, 273-277
summary mind map, 163, 287
synthesizing and ranking priorities, 159-161,
  279-281
Analytics *vs.* analysis, 2
    applications for project management, 4-8
    defined, 2
    project metrics, value of, 1-2
    value in project management, 4

B

Backward pass, float of activity, 234-235
Bar (GANTT) chart, 213
Bell curve, 9-10
Beta distribution, 14
BETA distributions, 232
Big data, decision-making and, 31
Binomial distributions, 94-95, 232
Black Belts, LSS, 194
Brainstorming
    decision-making factors, 28
    DMAIC tools, 201-202
    Lean Six Sigma tools, 18
    nominal group technique, 203

Cost considerations, AHP evaluation criteria, 267-268
Cost Performance Index (CPI), 258
Cost Variance (CV), 257
Covariance, applications of, 240-245
Critical chain method (CCM), 235-236
Critical Path Method (CPM), 14, 232-235
Critical values, 121, 125
Current state of process, DMAIC tools, 197-198
Customer acceptance documentation, 59-60
Customer relationship management (CRM), 6-8
Cycle time, DMAIC and, 189

D

Dashboards, analytics and, 5, 305
Data
    qualitative, defined, 79
    quantitative, defined, 79
    range, 87
    statistical studies, designing of, 82-83
Data analytics
    data quality, questions for, 34
    defined, 2
Data collection
    experiments, 83
    observations, 83
    surveys, 83
Data-driven decision-making. *See* Decision-making
Data overload
    analysis paralysis, 27
    managing with analytics, 4-5
Davenport, Thomas H., 34
Decision-making. *See also* Analytic Hierarchy Process (AHP); Statistics, applications of
    analytics, value of, 4
    analytics *vs.* analysis, 2
    automation and management of process, 30-31
    data-driven decision-making, 31-33
    data quality and, 34
    decision hierarchy, AHP, 268-269
    decision log, 63

decisive project managers, value of, 28-30
factors for decision-making, 27-28
good decisions, characteristics of, 26
Lean Six Sigma approach, 15-19
nominal group technique, 203
project management decisions, types of, 25-26
statistical approaches, project management, 8-9
summary of process, 34
Defect prevention and detection, 15-19
Define phase, DMAIC, 190, 194-200, 295
Degrees of freedom, defined, 129
Deliverables, project
    closing stage, 59-60
    conceptual stage, 56-57
    defined, 57
    definition stage, 57-58
    evaluation stage, 60
    execution stage, 59
    planning stage, 58
    project life cycle, overview, 55-56
    project management life cycle (PMLC), 60-65
Deming, Edward, 191
Deming cycle, 191-194
Design, development and implementation (DDI), 59. *See also* Systems development life cycle (SDLC)
Design of experiment
    DMAIC tools, 210
    Lean Six Sigma tools, 18
    Project Management Life Cycle (PMLC) tools, 303
Deviation
    for population data, 91
    for sample data, 92-93
Discrete variables, probability distributions and, 87-94
Distribution curve, rejection region, 125
DMAIC cycle (Define, Measure, Analyze, Improve/Implement, Control). *See also* Lean Six Sigma (LSS)
    analyze phase, tools for, 206-209
    define phase, tools for, 190, 194-200
    improve phase, tools for, 210

H

I

J

K

L

Project Management Body of Knowledge Guide
(PMBOK), 4
    Lean Six Sigma tools and, 298-306
    project charter definition, 46
Project management (PM) framework
    defined, 45-46
    process map for, 65
    project, characteristics and constraints, 46-49
    project life cycle, overview of, 55-60
    project management life cycle (PMLC), 60-65
    Project Management Office, role of, 55
    projects, success and failure of, 50-52
    projects *vs.* operations, 52-53
    projects *vs.* programs or portfolios, 53-55
    summary of, 70
    systems development life cycle (SDLC), 67-70
    work breakdown structure (WBS),
        overview of, 66
Project Management Life Cycle (PMLC). *See also*
    Systems development life cycle (SDLC)
    closing stage, 65, 305-306
    executing and controlling stage, 63-65, 303
    initiating stage, 61-62, 298-300
    vs. Lean Six Sigma DMAIC, 294-297
    Lean Six Sigma tools and, 298-306
    monitoring and controlling stage, 304-305
    overview of, 60-61
    planning stage, 62-63, 301-302
    summary mind map, LSS and, 312
Project Management Office, role of, 55
Project Management with Lean Six Sigma
    (PMLSS)
    overview of, 291-292
    PMLC *vs.* DMAIC stages, 294-297
    role of LSS tools in PMLC process, 298-306
Project managers
    analytics applications to project
        management, 4-8
    decisive managers, value of, 28-30
    selection of, Lean Six Sigma tools for, 298-300
    soft competencies, measurement of, 27
Project network diagram, 232-235
Project Office, role of, 55

Projects. *See also* Schedules, project;
    Scope of project
    characteristics and constraints of, 46-49
    complexity, estimations of, 283-284
    project metrics, value of, 1-2
    project plans, 58
    project portfolios, 5, 54-55
    project reports, 59-60
    projects *vs.* operations, 52-53
    success and failure, reasons for, 50-52
    work breakdown structure, overview of, 66
Project selection and prioritization
    analytic hierarchy process (AHP), 19-20,
        267-283
    analytics, applications of, 4-8
    evaluation criteria, determination of, 267-268
    making the final decisions, 281-283
    synthesizing and ranking priorities, 279-281
p-value, defined, 121-122

Q

QFD (Quality Function Deployment), 311
Qualitative data, 27, 79
Quality. *See also* Lean Six Sigma (LSS)
    analytic hierarchy process (AHP) approach,
        19-20
    data quality, questions for, 34
    DMAIC, use of, 184
    integration and testing, systems
        development, 69
    Lean Six Sigma, overview, 15-19
    project execution stage, 59
    project management life cycle (PMLC), 60-65
    QFD (Quality Function Deployment), 311
    quality plan, project planning stage, 58
Quality Function Deployment (QFD), 311
Quantitative data, defined, 79
Quantitative measures, project management, 8-9

R

Random Consistency Index (RI), 161, 272-273
Random variables, probability distributions and, 87-94
Range, data sets, 87
Range, probability, 81
Ranking, Analytic Hierarchy Process and, 159-161
Raw materials costs, 267-268
Rectangular distribution with constant probability, 12-13
Regression analysis
    applications of, 245-251
    Lean Six Sigma tools, 18
    linear regression, process for, 134
    multiple variable predictions, 140-141
    regression line equation, 135-136
    single variable predictions, 136-140
Relative frequency, 231
Relative weight matrix, 156-162
Requirements
    analytics *vs.* analysis, 2
    project failure, reasons for, 51-52
    project planning stage, 58
    systems development life cycle (SDLC) and, 68-69
Requirements traceability matrix (RTM), 58
Resource buffer, 236
Resource requirements
    analytic hierarchy process (AHP) approach, 19-20
    analytics, applications of, 5-16
    cost considerations, 267-268
    project definition stage, 57-58
    project execution stage, 59
    project management life cycle (PMLC), 60-65
    project planning stage, 58
    projects *vs.* operations, 52-53
    work breakdown structure, overview of, 66
Responsibility assignment matrix (RAM), 58
Result, defined, 79
Return on investment (ROI), 5, 267-268
Right-tailed test, 122-125

Risk assessment and management
    AHP and risk assessments, 284-285
    analytic hierarchy process (AHP) approach, 19-20
    analytics *vs.* analysis, 2
    feasibility study and, 67-68
    project charter and, 61-62
    project execution stage, 59
    project management life cycle (PMLC), 60-65
    risk register, 63
    uniform distributions and, 12-13
Roles and responsibilities, project planning, 58
Root cause analysis, 18, 189, 207-208
Rouse, Margaret, 69
Run charts, 18

S

Saaty, Thomas, 19, 152, 154
Saaty Scale, 154-155, 270
Sample, statistics
    correlation coefficient for, 133
    defined, 79
    mean, deviation, variance, and standard deviation calculations, 92-94
Sample space, defined, 80
Scatter diagram, DMAIC tools, 207
Scatter plots, 240-245. *See also* Linear regression
Schedules, project
    analytics, applications of, 7-8
    Budgeted Cost of Work Performed (BCWP), 255
    Budgeted Cost of Work Schedule (BCWS), 255
    critical chain method (CCM), 235-236
    critical path method and, 232-235
    GANTT chart, 213
    linear regression, predictions and, 245-251
    PERT, application of, 237-239
    predictions, EVM and confidence intervals, 251-254
    predictions, EVM applications, 254-258
    project constraints, overview of, 48-49
    project definition stage, 57-58

hypothesis, defined, 118
hypothesis, rejection region, 125
hypothesis, testing of, 119-125
left-, right-, and two-tailed tests, 122-124
level of significance, 121
linear regression, overview of, 134-140
measures of central tendency, 83-87
multiple regression equation, 140-141
normal distribution, 96-98
null hypothesis, 120
Poisson distribution, 95-96
probability, classical or theoretical, 80
probability, conditional, 81-82
probability, empirical or statistical, 80
probability distributions, 87-94
probability range, 81
p-value, 121-122
range, 87
summary mind map of, 101, 120-142
terminology, 78-80
test statistic, defined, 121
t-test, 129-131
Type I and II errors, 120
value of statistics, 78
z-test, 127-129
Status reports, 59
Stockburger, David W., 117
Strategic decisions
AHP, sub-criteria analysis, 273-277
AHP evaluation criteria, 267-268
analytics, applications of, 6-8
applications of analytics, 4-8
Strategy Updates, 306
Subjective information, measurement of, 27
SUCCESS mnemonic, 15
Supply chain management, DMAIC and, 189-194
Surveys
Lean Six Sigma tools, 18
overview of, 83
Project Management Life Cycle (PMLC) tools, 299, 305
SWOT analysis, 30, 196-197
Synthesizing priorities, AHP and, 159-161

Systems development life cycle (SDLC)
design stage, 69
development, integration, and testing stages, 69
evaluation stage, 70
feasibility study, 67-68
implementation, operations, and maintenance stages, 70
overview of, 67
requirements and analysis planning, 68-69

T

Target state, DMAIC tools, 199
Tasks, work breakdown structure, 52, 58, 66
Team members, project planning, 58
Test statistic, defined, 121
The Improvement Guide (1996), 191
Theoretical probability, 80
Theory of Constraints, 302
Three-Point Estimation, 237-239
Training requirements, 5
Transition criteria, 306
Trend analysis, DMAIC tools, 204-205
Triangular distribution, 13-14, 232
Triple constraints of projects, 48-49
t-test, 129-131
Two-tailed test, 122-125
Type I and II errors, defined, 120

U

Uniform distribution, 12-13, 232
Upper specification limit, 200-201

V

Value stream map (VSM)
DMAIC tools, 197-199, 213
Lean Six Sigma tools, 18
overview of, 197-199
use in Planning stage of PMLC, 302
Variables, probability distributions and, 87-94